CALVIN'S
TORMENTORS

Europe during the Time of John Calvin
© Baker Publishing Group

CALVIN'S TORMENTORS

UNDERSTANDING THE CONFLICTS
THAT SHAPED THE REFORMER

GARY W. JENKINS

Baker Academic

a division of Baker Publishing Group
Grand Rapids, Michigan

Published by Baker Academic
a division of Baker Publishing Group
PO Box 6287, Grand Rapids, MI 49516-6287
www.bakeracademic.com

Printed in the United States of America

Library of Congress Cataloging-in-Publication Data
Names: Jenkins, Gary W., 1961– author.
Title: Calvin's tormentors : understanding the conflicts that shaped the reformer / Gary W. Jenkins.
Description: Grand Rapids : Baker Publishing Group, 2018. | Includes bibliographical references and index.
Identifiers: LCCN 2017052473 | ISBN 9780801098338 (pbk. : alk. paper)
Subjects: LCSH: Calvin, Jean, 1509–1564. | Reformation.
Classification: LCC BX9418 .J46 2018 | DDC 284/.2092—dc23
LC record available at https://lccn.loc.gov/2017052473

18   19   20   21   22   23   24   7   6   5   4   3   2   1

For Professors William J. Tighe and Gary R. Hafer,
in gratitude for decades of friendship.

"Vos autem hortor ut ita virtutem locetis, sine qua
amicitia esse non potest, ut ea excepta nihil amicitia
praestabilius putetis." —Cicero, *Laelius de Amicitia*

"Par ce que c'estoit luy; par ce que c'estoit moy. . . . Nous nous
cherchions avant que de nous estre veus." —Montaigne, "De l'amitié"

Contents

Illustrations

John Calvin

Preface

I owe a debt to John Calvin. Having been reared in the austere rigorism of Methodism, I found myself, my first semester in college, reading Calvin on the threefold office of Christ. Pretty heady stuff for a young Methodist. More reading followed—the *Institutes*, the commentaries (especially Galatians)—and by the time I was a junior I had started attending a Presbyterian church, much to the chagrin of my parents. (Ironically, my mother, who greeted my Calvinian ways with a distinct horror, came from a line of French Huguenots, whose ancestor, Marin Duval, born in Nantes, came to Maryland in 1650.) Some months back over lunch a colleague asked me, in light of my childhood, "So how did you get here? How is it you aren't a fundamentalist any longer?" When I gave him the quick bio, he responded, "Calvin probably saved you from modern American enthusiasm." His words got me thinking. My debt to Calvin is not just that he kept me from snake handlers, but rather that he started me down the trail of questions that in one sense has never ended. And while I am sure the Genevan Reformer would not be amused by where the trail has led me (he would probably think me more an idolater than Sadoleto and the Sorbonnists), how is it that I think as I do (I am an Orthodox Christian)? And have I betrayed some secret covenant or pact that should have kept me happily Presbyterian forever? I began this book as a sequel to another author's efforts on Calvin's friends, but it quickly turned into something else—namely, a study on how controversy shaped Calvin. The young French émigré who sat shaking before the thunderous anathemas of Farel in 1536 became the de facto force in the life of Geneva in 1555, facing down the native-born opposition while seeking to implement his vision of a church truly reformed; ultimately he would emerge as the tacit leader, even if in exile, of the French Reformed church, a position reflected in many of the controversies here discussed. Along the way he would employ his excellent intellect not just to prepare a learned ministry for France but also to take on numerous interlocutors whom he believed threatened what God had clearly called him to do. Thus, one of the questions that arises concerns how Calvin's notion of his vocation shaped his approach to the controversies that beset him.

Each of these chapters presents individuals who in one way or another opposed Calvin's agenda, and for Calvin, who certainly believed himself a participant in the words of Christ, "He who rejects you, rejects me," these contradictions were an assault on the very work of God. He was God's man, God's ambassador, God's prophet: not a prophet in the sense that he had come to herald the dawn or broach some new understanding, but a prophet to call a wayward people besotted by superstition, ignorance, and idolatry back to the pure faith, both in doctrine and morals. This calling was the source of his ministry. Every conflict seemingly brought greater assurance to Calvin of his calling, steeling him in his purpose for the next one that emerged.

That Geneva became the fulcrum of so much controversy arises from its geographical and historical place in Europe. At the beginning of the sixteenth century, Geneva was part of Savoy; just before Calvin's arrival, it became a protectorate of Berne. Lastly, it became part of the Swiss Confederation, a denouement that came about partly because of the affinity of religion among the cities of Geneva, Berne, Basle, and Zurich, one that Calvin helped effect. More than this, Geneva also lay along one of the key routes between Italy and the Low Countries, and thus became the frequent stop of Italians heading north, and Flemings, Rhinelanders, and others heading south. Consequently, radicalism from Italy flowed through Geneva. But controversy was not primarily an accident of geography, for Calvin's notoriety seemed to invite disputes; it was with Calvin that Servetus, for instance, began a correspondence, not with Bullinger, or Haller, or Musculus.

Controversy, as now so then, invites invective. The sixteenth century was long suited in the art of insult, and the characters in this book were no different. Calvin, given both his zealous personality and his sharp intellect, became an easy target for abuse. And while he was the object of tremendous opprobrium—among other things he would be called a brothel keeper—he could give as good as he got; Calvin labeled the author of this insult a shape-shifting werewolf (meaning one who could never seem to get his theological confession right). This type of writing certainly spiced up the polemical literature, whether theological or political, and makes for interesting reading. The late Robert K. Webb once told me that to be a historian was to be bored out of your mind. I think the highest compliment I can give a student applying for graduate school is that she can be bored to tears and still keep reading.

Happily, I was not often bored in this endeavor, but there were lots of trails that need not have been followed and that made the journey longer than it should have been. All the same, this book only scratches the surface of what were doubtless aggravating, exasperating, and infuriating episodes in the lives of all involved.

The commonplaces of sixteenth-century polemics aside, the amount of material is daunting, not just from Calvin's *Opera*, which would take years to comprehend were one to read it all in the original Latin and French (I have been years at this and certainly have not accomplished it yet), but also the even more ponderous *Opera* of his tormentors, almost all of whom were productive scholars in their own right. Thankfully, as the footnotes will show, most of them have not lacked later scholars to investigate their lives, whose acumen has been no end of help in writing this book. I owe them more than footnotes, and they are the giants on whose shoulders I have stood. I hope I have seen, through their scholarship, if not more, at least clearly. Of the writing of books on Calvin there is no end, and I hope this one will open up some new avenues of inquiry. There is no list of abbreviations, for while some authors' or editors' works could have used them—for example, Herminjard—the only one that was necessary was for the *Calvini Opera* (CO), and its publication details can be found in a corresponding footnote. Unless otherwise noted or conveyed in the citation, all translations are my own.

March 30, 2017, Feast of St. John Climacus

Acknowledgments

So often after I have given a paper proposal for a conference, with the paper still needing to be written over the summer, I have ended up with a completely different paper from what I had planned. This truth I know is not lost on many of my colleagues in the Sixteenth Century Studies Conference who frequently start their papers with "I've changed my title." While I started this book with the working title *Enemies of Calvin*, a title in some respects still usable, the title I have ended up with, suggested to me by the novelist G. W. Hawkes (who, in chorus with the rest of the Faculty Irregulars, has been cheering me on for the past few years), turned my thoughts ever so slightly but enough to take me down a very different path from the way I had first conceived this book. Frequently people asked me how I winnowed down my choices, for there are certainly some who could have been added. But finally time and space constrain everything; the opponents I have chosen best fit the purpose of the book, which is how controversy shaped Calvin's life and, to a large degree, his thought. In this trek down many trails, I have picked up many debts. The foremost of them is to my wife, Carol, who has been more than patient with me as I have buried myself in my office or in libraries trying to get this done. The same can be said of my daughter, Kristen, who has missed our weekly movie dates on many occasions so Dad could sit and read. They are two of the foundational pieces of my life without whom I could not have done this. I thank also the faithful of St. Paul's Orthodox Church, Emmaus, Pennsylvania, and Father Andrew Stephen Damick, as they have been persistent in their encouragement.

I owe a true debt to Emmalee Moffitt of the History Department at Eastern University. Emmie formatted the chapters per Baker Publishing Group's request, pointed out lots of errors on my part, and excellently performed every demand I placed on her. I also owe thanks to the estate of Charles van Gorden, which has endowed the chair I hold at Eastern University, and by whose munificence I am able to travel for research. I am also the beneficiary of a grant from the Agora Institute for Civic Virtue and the Common Good, which allowed me to spend two months at the University of Oxford in 2015 for research. I am thus indebted to the librarians of the Bodleian Library, Oxford, for all their courtesies, both in the Duke Humfrey reading room and in the Weston reading room. The same obtains of the Taylor Institute and especially of Christine Ferdinand and the staff of Magdalen College Library for sitting with me several raw days in the old library as I pored over books there. All of this would have been much more difficult without the grand hospitality of the Oxford Study Abroad program and its director (a scholar in his own right), Robert L. Schuettinger, and with him his staff, in particular Adam Brown and Tim Moore, who looked after me in Oxford, put me up in grand digs on numerous occasions, and were always magnificent company on Friday evenings: you gentlemen have no idea how grateful I am for all your kindnesses. I need also thank the librarians of Warner Memorial Library, Eastern University, and Trexler Library, Muhlenberg College.

I need to thank my editors and friends at Baker Academic, David Nelson and Brandy Scritchfield, for their tireless help and patience, and especially to Brian Bolger, whose editorial work has saved me from myriad errors. Thanks as well to my friend Steve Ayres, sales manager at Baker, as he has nurtured this project over many years: my deepest gratitude, Steve. I need to give particular thanks to Professor Jon Balserak of Bristol University for his comments on several chapters and his pointing me down some straight paths; and the same must be said for Dr. Jordan Ballor of the Acton Institute as regards the chapter on Bolsec, Professor Ted Van Raalte of the Canadian Reformed Theological Seminary for his thoughts on Calvin and Farel, and Professor Richard Muller of Calvin Seminary on the question of Calvin and his relationship with the *Augustana*. I must thank Professors Torrance Kirby of McGill University, Kathleen Comerford of Georgia Southern University, and Brennan Pursell of Desales University for their encouragement of my efforts and for their letters to Baker Publishing Group in support of my proposal. I need to pay a debt of homage to Dr. David Sytsma and the Junius Institute for hosting and continually updating the Post-Reformation Digital Library, a resource par excellence, without which this work could not have been completed. In every case, whatever virtue this work possesses redounds to these fine scholars, and all its vices are mine alone to bear. Penultimately I wish to thank my colleagues in the History Department, Professors Tyler Flynn, Michael Lee, and Chris Butynskyi, for their constant encouragement and good cheer.

This same holds true for Professors Fred Putnam, R. J. Snell, Steve McGuire, Michael Dondzila, and Dean Jonathan Yonan of the Templeton Honors College, scholars each in the mold of what the Renaissance desired. Last I wish to thank Professor William J. Tighe of Muhlenberg, who has never stopped encouraging me in my efforts, told me I needed to do a chapter on Joachim Westphal (and I am glad he did), read every chapter (and a few more than once), has been tireless in conversation, and could certainly have written this book so much better than I have.

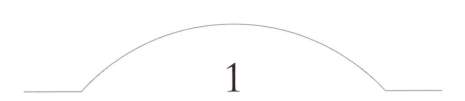

1

Louis du Tillet and Calvin the Nicodemite

The Fitful Separation from the Whore of Babylon's Church

Calvin had not always been a candidate for the caricature he later obtained, not always the proper prophet or icon of the virulent, violent, capricious, and wrathful God so often conjured when his name is mentioned, nor the definitive traducer of the false religion of Rome. The course of Calvin's theology, like the course of his life, followed its undulant age. Although Calvin was clearly a child of his times, not every child of that age was a Calvin, and indeed, as this chapter will show, not even Calvin began as a Calvin; and in all justice, the frail French émigré who died in Geneva, far from home in what the French then still considered Germany, bears only a resemblance to the shade so often conjured from the nethermost polemical hell.

Treatment, therefore, of Louis du Tillet as the first of Calvin's tormentors proves apt, for it shows Calvin at a crucial period in his spiritual and intellectual formation, long before the great and bold tracts against Servetus, Castellio, Westphal, and Baudouin, inter alios, and his confrontations with the Enfants de Genève (the Genevan patriots). We have in this early period a Calvin who is more the Erasmian, more a Reformer, more a *moyenneur* (a word he coined for those who stood in the middle, neither fully embracing Protestantism, nor at all repudiating Catholicism). This is not to claim that Calvin was an Erasmian, not at least in any formal way, though materially, for a time, he was. Beginning this study with Louis du Tillet and his family also shows a young Calvin whose hopes for the future of reform could be stated with milder assertions and less invective, when lines had not yet been so precisely drawn, and when there were still those in both camps who thought something could be salvaged of a united Christendom. All this changed on all sides by the early 1540s, but by then Calvin and du Tillet, at first close and dear friends, had already parted company.

While this chapter focuses on Louis du Tillet, it does so in the context of the wider du Tillet family. Louis was the fourth son of Elie du Tillet, who had been ennobled by Charles VIII in 1484 and held an estate in l'Angoumois, below Poitiers and to the west of Limoges. Elie had succeeded handsomely as an accountant, first in the province, but then as vice president of the Chambre des Comptes in Paris. Consequently Louis's older brothers were each already men of notable accomplishment when in 1533 he met Calvin. Jean, the second son, who is often known as the *Greffier*, was the clerk of the Parlement of Paris, where he recorded laws, certified that the laws as published were correct in their wording, and represented the Parlement to the king; he also functioned as a royal archivist and historian whose contributions to the discipline of history are immense. The *Greffier* was joined in his historical endeavors by the third brother, also named Jean, who immersed himself as well in antiquarian and humanist studies of the past.[1] The second Jean, bishop first of Saint-Bieuc (1553), and then of Meaux (1562), had received from Francis I full access to the vast royal archives, which he put to great use in uncovering the past.[2] It was he who first published the *Liber Carolini*, Charles the Great's (Charlemagne) response to the seventh ecumenical council, and the very edition that Calvin would use when brandishing the work against the Catholic use of images, statuary, and icons. The oldest brother, Séraphim, had also been the clerk of the Parlement of Paris before being replaced (apparently by legal proceedings) by his brother.[3]

At some point in Calvin's time as a student at Paris he had befriended Louis du Tillet. In late 1533, owing to the reaction of the university against Nicholas Cop's convocation sermon—a homily animated by Lutheran ideas and linked by the authorities to the young Calvin—Calvin took refuge at the du Tillet estate.[4] The du Tillet home bestowed on Calvin more benefits than mere asylum, for Louis, the priest of Claix, a village outside Angoulême, and also a canon of the cathedral of Angoulême, enjoyed the large library of his two brothers,

1. Donald R. Kelley, *Foundations of Modern Historical Scholarship: Language, Law and History in the French Renaissance* (New York: Columbia University Press, 1970), 215–38.

2. Alexandre Crottet, *Chronique protestante de France, ou documents historiques sur les églises réformées de ce royaume* (Paris: n.p., 1846), 95.

3. Elizabeth A. R. Brown, ed., *Jean du Tillet and the French Wars of Religion: Five Tracts, 1562–1569*, Medieval and Renaissance Texts and Studies 108 (Binghamton, NY: Center for Medieval and Early Renaissance Studies, 1994).

4. Bernard Cottret, *Calvin: A Biography*, trans. M. Wallace McDonald (Grand Rapids: Eerdmans, 2000), 76.

a library that numbered several thousand volumes on history and theology, along with a great many manuscripts. Here Calvin spent hour upon hour in study, producing his first theological treatise, a tract against the Anabaptist doctrine of soul sleep, titled *Psychopannychia*. Calvin also used the library as he began work on the first edition of his *Institutes*. He saw his time there as fulfilling a duty, with his studies as repayment for du Tillet's hospitality: "The humanity of my patron is so great that I understand it to be bestowed for the benefit of learning, not me."[5] But his studies were not Calvin's only activity in l'Angoumois, for he also taught Louis Greek, and so adept did Louis become that he was given the title "the Greek of Claix." Calvin also took two trips, the first to Nérac in the southwest, where he sought out Jacques Lefèvre d'Étaples, the great humanist and leader of reform in Paris, who had taken refuge with Marguerite of Navarre. Marguerite, the sister of King Francis I, patronized both humanism and a group of humanist and evangelical Reformers known as the circle of Meaux. Francis I himself had a deep interest in humanism and could easily turn a blind eye to the Reformers' dalliances in evangelicalism, though this is not to say he countenanced Lutheranism, albeit there was some of that within the circle as well. The circle came under scrutiny, and the University of Paris was none too happy with their activities. Lefèvre, while no Lutheran, certainly appeared to the conservatives of the university to skirt orthodoxy, and thus he sought refuge out of the reach of the Sorbonne. His reputation drew Calvin. The other trip was to Noyon in April and May of 1534 to resign his benefices, cures, and livings.[6] While in Angoumois, Calvin and du Tillet met with notable clergy from the area, doubtless to discuss theology, humanism, and the state of the church. Participants included Anthony Chaillou, the prior of Bouteville (later called the pope of the Lutherans); the abbot of Bassac; and also two brothers, the *Sieur* of Torsac and the young Pierre de la Place, who would later be a historian of the Reformed church but was only fourteen or fifteen at this point.[7] Otherwise, Calvin was tireless in his scholarly endeavors: Florimond de Raemond remarks that Calvin threw himself into his studies, neither stopping to eat during the day nor going to bed at night.[8]

5. Quoted in Alexandre Ganoczy, *The Young Calvin*, trans. David Foxgrover and Wade Provo (Edinburgh: T&T Clark, 1988), 83–84.
6. Crottet, *Chronique*, 99.
7. Florimond de Raemond, *L'Histoire de la Naissance, Progrez, et Decadence de l'Heresie de Ce Siecle* (Paris, 1610), 884. Most of what we know about Calvin and his time at Claix/ Angoumois is from Florimond, one of the great antiquarians and historians of his day, and an ardent Catholic apologist. Cf. Barbara Sher Tinsley, *History and Polemics in the French Reformation: Florimond de Raemond, Defender of the Church* (Selinsgrove, PA: Susquehanna University Press, 1992).
8. De Raemond, *L'Histoire*, 884.

But the halcyon days, no doubt an ideal that always remained with Calvin, formally ended on October 17, 1534, finished off by the Affair of the Placards. On that night, broadsheets denouncing the Mass as an abominable abuse, written by Antoine Marcourt and printed in Neûchatel, were posted throughout France, and particularly in Paris, Orleans, and Blois. One even found its way to the royal bedchamber in Amboise.[9] Francis I, who had until that time showed some restraint in dealing with the "evangelicals," now turned on them with a fury. Calvin and du Tillet, on du Tillet's franc, thought it best to leave France. Traveling under pseudonyms, du Tillet as Haulmont (a village on his family's estate) and Calvin as d'Espeville (one of his first benefices near Noyon), the pair made for Strasbourg, where they met the city's Protestant leaders, Martin Bucer and Wolfgang Capito. From there they traveled to Basle, arriving in January of 1535, where Calvin further worked on his *Psychopannychia* and continued work on the *Institutes*, finding a publisher for the work, which came out in 1536. In Basle Calvin also may possibly have met the thundering Reformer Guillaume Farel.[10] Though a meeting in Basle seems improbable, Farel certainly somehow had the measure of Calvin before their confrontation in Geneva in August 1536. Farel had been part of the circle of Meaux, but like a number of others of the group, he decided to quit France instead of conforming. Indeed, Farel had been an easy target, for though a gifted speaker, he was not a clerk, and in 1525 was forbidden to preach. Farel, never forgiving the members of the circle of Meaux who had acquiesced in the demands of the hard line taken in Paris, headed to the French-speaking regions of western Switzerland, first to Basle, where his antihumanism and insults directed at Erasmus soon had him drummed out of the city. Then he went to the Pays de Vaud, where he operated as an ecclesiastical agent of Berne, a city that had converted to Protestantism in 1528.[11] Pierre Caroli, another member of the circle and a doctor of theology from Paris, whom we shall meet in a subsequent chapter, also left France. Farel was a man of little flexibility, who saw clearly what other people ought to do. He certainly had little time for those who took less than a clear stand on the questions of the day and thought that most of his former colleagues who had stayed behind

9. See Frans Pieter van Stam, "The Group of Meaux as First Target of Farel and Calvin's Anti-Nicodemism," *Bibliothèque d'Humanisme et Renaissance* 68 (2006): 253–75, who, following Atance (cf. note 38 in van Stam), sees the rhetoric of the placards arising from the Sorbonne to push the group of Meaux into a corner.

10. T. H. L. Parker, *John Calvin* (Hunts, UK: Lion, 1975), 75.

11. Van Stam, "Group of Meaux," 260. Jason Zuidema and Theodore Van Raalte also give 1525 as the date of Farel's expulsion but give 1524 as the date for his activities in Basle; Zuidema and Van Raalte, *Early French Reform: The Theology and Spirituality of Guillaume Farel* (Farnham, UK: Ashgate, 2011), 9–11.

and outwardly conformed, even if they thought Rome in desperate need of reform and sought to bring this reform about, were endangering not only their own souls but also the souls of those who looked to them. Farel saw in their lives no real awareness that being in communion with idolaters posed a real danger not only to their own souls but also to the souls of their spiritual wards. Such clerics would be termed Nicodemites (the term first appears in 1544), those whose error was believing in evangelical doctrines (i.e., Protestantism) but attending Mass for conformity's or safety's sake (so named for Nicodemus in John's Gospel, who sought out Jesus under the cover of darkness for fear of the Jews).

Calvin and du Tillet remained in Basle about a year, with Calvin seeing the *Institutes* through the presses. But in spring of 1536, the first edition of the *Institutes* having come out in March, Calvin and du Tillet set off again, this time to Ferrara, where the duchess of the city, Renée of France, the daughter of Louis XII and sister-in-law to Francis I (who was married to Renée's sister, Claude), had married Ercole di Este, Duke of Ferrara. Much like her sister-in-law, Marguerite of Navarre, Renée sympathized with French humanists and Reformers and harbored many of them at her court (French subjects constituted her personal retinue). Almost nothing is known about Calvin's time there. He did meet the duchess, with whom he subsequently carried on a lasting, though erratic, correspondence. He also made the acquaintance of Johannes Sinapius, the duchess's physician, whom Calvin would recommend to one Françoise de Boussiron de Grand-Ry for marriage (Françoise also served at Renée's court).[12] Perhaps while in Ferrara, but perhaps during his time at Basle, Calvin sent two letters back to France. The letters are lost, though Calvin kept copies that he subsequently published as a single tract in the spring of 1537, his *Epistolae duae*. The letters were aimed at an erstwhile friend from school and a fellow traveler of the Meaux circle—namely, Nicholas Duchemin and Gerard Roussel, respectively.[13] Calvin had been at Orléans with Duchemin, having lived in one of his houses, though Duchemin had since decamped to work at the episcopal court of Orléans. Roussel had actually become the bishop of Oloron, in the very southwest of France toward Navarre. What the original content of each letter was can only be surmised, as clearly later events and reappraisals are reflected in Calvin's published versions, most notably the disputation in Lausanne in

---

12. Erik Alexander de Boer and Frans Pieter van Stam, eds., *Ioannis Calvini Epistolae Scripta Didactica et Polemica*, vol. 4, *Epistolae Duae (1537), Deux Discours (Oc. 1536)* (Geneva: Librairie Droz, 2009), xvi–xviii.

13. De Boer and van Stam, *Epistolae Duae*, xx–xxvi. For a broader framework, see van Stam, "Group of Meaux," 253–75; and Cottret, *Calvin*, 101–4.

October 1536, as Calvin incorporated much of what was said there by Farel into his treatises. Clearly the letters covered the question of Nicodemism, though how virulent they were and whether they rose to the level of his 1537 *Epistolae duae* must be questioned; the reason why will be held off until the conclusion of this chapter.

Calvin and du Tillet's time in Ferrara came to an abrupt end when all the evangelical French at Renée's court had been compromised to the unforgiving duke. One of their company, Leon Jehanent, during the veneration of the cross on Good Friday, had left church without performing the expected devotion; brought under suspicion, he was arrested and questioned, then others were questioned, and apparently Calvin and du Tillet, having stayed there probably no more than six weeks, left.[14] Calvin went back to France to put his affairs in order, and du Tillet ended up in Geneva with Farel. Calvin's father had died in 1531, and although Calvin had renounced his own benefices and livings in April of 1534,[15] he still needed to make arrangements for the affairs of his family. Once that had been done he took his brother, Antoine, and sister, Marie, and intended to go to Basle via Strasbourg.

Here Calvin's story takes its fateful turn. French and imperial armies were between Paris and Strasbourg, and so Calvin decided to take a circuitous route to Strasbourg via Geneva. Perhaps a desire to see his friend du Tillet produced the detour, though Calvin, oddly, planned to stay only one night. Upon learning that his friend had arrived, du Tillet went to Farel to tell him that Calvin was in Geneva. Farel immediately went to the inn where Calvin was and demanded, in no uncertain terms, that he stay in Geneva and help him with the reformation of the city. Calvin protested that he was a scholar seeking the quiet of study and contemplation. Farel, imperious and menacing, invoked divine imprecations on Calvin were he to pursue a life of study and thus abandon God's work in Geneva. Calvin stayed. What would prove a momentous event the Genevan authorities met by innocent indifference, Calvin being registered in the city records simply as "ille Gallus."[16]

For the next eighteen months, Calvin, Farel, and du Tillet sought the reform of Geneva. The peculiarities of Calvin's relationship with Geneva will be treated specifically in the chapter on Calvin and the Genevan patriots, but a few points are called for here. Geneva had thrown off its temporal and spiritual lords in 1535—namely, the Duke of Savoy and his governor of the

14. De Boer and van Stam, *Epistolae Duae*, xiii–xiv.
15. Ganoczy, *Young Calvin*, 86.
16. William G. Naphy, *Calvin and the Consolidation of the Genevan Reformation* (Manchester: Manchester University Press, 1994), 53.

city, its bishop. In order to do this, the leadership of Geneva had to obtain the aid of Berne, and this assistance came with the understanding that Geneva would adopt Protestantism. The ministers that Geneva thus acquired, chiefly now Farel and Calvin, had no room for half measures and insisted that the city reform its ecclesiastical life completely in line with their ardent vision of the church. Part of this reform was that Communion should be observed weekly at every church in the city and its environs (though this was an ideal rather than an adamant demand) and that the company of pastors were to guard the table—that is, exercise the power of excommunication on those deemed unfit to receive the sacrament.[17] The government of the city completely opposed this arrangement, for having thrown off their bishop they were not about to turn such power over to a group of foreigners. Recognizing the link between frequent eucharistic celebrations and the power of church discipline, the magistrates allowed Communion only quarterly, and the struggle thus centered on the book of church order.[18]

Matters came to a head on April 19, 1538—Easter Sunday. Although the Reformers had never obtained from the government the ability to celebrate Communion every week, it was to be celebrated that Easter. At this point Farel and Calvin decided to raise the pressure on the town council and make a statement regarding what they perceived to be their prerogatives as ministers. They simply did not have Communion at all anywhere in the city, effectively for that Easter excommunicating the whole city. Enraged, the council dismissed Calvin and Farel. But even before this happened, earlier in 1538 or in late 1537, du Tillet had already departed from Geneva, leaving but a note that he was returning home.[19] He went via Strasbourg.

Calvin took up a correspondence with du Tillet that spanned the rest of 1538.[20] The letters present a number of insights into Calvin's early thought. Unlike most of Calvin's letters, these were written in French and were of such a seemingly private nature that they lay untouched in Paris till the 1840s and were only formally published in 1850.[21] Thus the letters themselves give us an entirely private side of Calvin, unlike the very public squabbles that dominated

17. John T. McNeill, *The History and Character of Calvinism* (Oxford: Oxford University Press, 1954), 139.

18. Cottret, *Calvin*, 128–29.

19. Ganoczy, *Young Calvin*, 119.

20. Martin Bucer also corresponded with du Tillet over the latter half of 1538 and at the beginning of 1539. See Jacques V. Pollet, *Martin Bucer*, vol. 2, *Etudes sur la correspondance avec de nombreux textes inédits* (Paris: Presses universitaires de France, 1962), 528–33.

21. Alexandre Crottet, *Correspondance Française de Calvin avec Louis du Tillet, chanione d'Angoulême et curè de Claix sur les questions de l'Église et du ministère évangélique* (Genève: Cherbuliez, 1850).

so much of his life.[22] What is more, they offer us an insight into a formative turn in his life, a turn that prompted du Tillet's actions. No firm date stands out for du Tillet's departure. Alexandre Crottet in his introduction to the correspondence gives no date; Bruce Gordon gives early 1538;[23] and Machiel A. van den Berg in *Friends of Calvin* gives August 1537, but with no explanation, though clearly such an early date would give room for another letter other than the short note that du Tillet would have left, for Calvin implies he has two letters from different quarters.[24] The first letter from du Tillet to Calvin in Geneva, the one somewhat explaining his actions, can be pieced together from Calvin's response, sent in January 1538 from Geneva.[25] Du Tillet had been preparing to leave for some months, and perhaps the break was thought out as early as spring of 1537 with the publication of Calvin's *Epistolae duae*, since Calvin's anti-Nicodemism seems the basis of du Tillet's misgivings. Du Tillet still attended all the debates and meetings, showing little sign of his growing unrest. It seems most likely that du Tillet left at the beginning of 1538, leaving only a note, prompting Calvin to ask whether he had been rude or a bore, and that perhaps such behavior on his part was what had alienated du Tillet, for he could not bring himself to believe that Louis had left for the reasons given.

Calvin, in grief, claimed that joy had left his life and wondered whether an offending imprudence on his part had brought about this unhappy state.[26] But more than this, he was baffled, for he asserted that he was as he had always been; we can only suppose that du Tillet, as will be seen, had asserted that Calvin had changed. Bewilderment also arose, Calvin wrote, because du Tillet's resolve and steadfastness, his constancy and strength, characteristics that could only show an unshakeable commitment to reform, had always elicited great admiration from him.[27] Indeed, it seems Calvin thought that du Tillet was only going home, and not returning to the communion of Rome, at least formally. Obviously du Tillet had met with Bucer and Capito (Calvin

22. The letters are treated briefly in both Cottret, *Calvin*, 138–39; and Bruce Gordon, *Calvin* (New Haven: Yale University Press, 2009), 92–94; a good read on the correspondence is Olivia Carpi-Mailly, "Jean Calvin et Louis du Tillet: entre foi et amitié, un échange révélateur," in *Calvin et ses contemporains: Actes du colloque de Paris 1995*, ed. Olivier Millet, Cahiers d'Humanisme et Renaissance 53 (Geneva: Librairie Droz, 1998), 7–19. See also George H. Tavard, "Calvin and the Nicodemites," in *Calvin and Roman Catholicism: Critique and Engagement, Then and Now*, ed. Randall C. Zachman (Grand Rapids: Baker Academic, 2008), 62–72.

23. Gordon, *Calvin*, 92.

24. Crottet, *Correspondance*, 24; Machiel A. van den Berg, *Friends of Calvin* (Grand Rapids: Eerdmans, 2009).

25. Crottet, *Correspondance*, 24–28.

26. Crottet, *Correspondance*, 24–25.

27. Crottet, *Correspondance*, 24–25.

mentions du Tillet's advisers in Strasbourg), who had a very different view on Nicodemism, not that they counseled it, but they still took a softer line than either Calvin or Farel.[28]

And this comes to the main point for Calvin: he did not question du Tillet's faith as to its substance, but he worried to no end about du Tillet's association with Rome and even his seeming softening on Rome's decadence. For Calvin, Rome was worse than Israel in the days of Jeroboam and was more like Israel under Ahab, having obtained a long tradition of corruption. Rome cannot be the church, for the church is the pillar and ground of the truth (something that du Tillet must have referenced in the first letter), and since Rome obviously lacks the truth, how can they be the church? Du Tillet had asserted in the first letter that since the name of God was still among the Catholics, the blessing of God should not be thought so quickly lost. To this, Calvin maintained that ignorance so dominated them that they were incapable of doing God's will.[29] Calvin ended his letter by praying for du Tillet's health and for God to save him from his scruples. This was the longest of Calvin's letters.[30]

Du Tillet's response, sent from Paris in March 1538, fleshed out what had been implicit in his first letter. While he lamented Calvin's ennui, his own conscience had been suffering worse. For two years he had watched Calvin (thus going back at least to their time together in Ferrara), and he never believed that Calvin had a calling from God to do what he was doing. To du Tillet, his time with Calvin had brought him to the place where in order to follow Christ, to take up the cross, to embrace the bitterness (*amertume*) that results in sweetness (*douceur*), he had but one option.[31] He had come to the conviction that a false persuasion had dominated his life to such a degree that he did not want to ask questions. But enormous questions raged all around him: for instance, the just do not live by faith alone, and over this issue two sides had emerged. Who has the disposition of fear and humility to admit that one could be wrong? Should we not live in fear that we might be believing things not taught to us by God?[32] This fear should plague every individual, for what single person has seen at all times and in all places that which ought rightly to be held, especially since the angel of Satan can transform himself into an angel of light? This is not, du Tillet maintained, a pardon for those who do not want to listen to Christ, for those who have no desire to reform their lives. Du Tillet assured Calvin that he had no love of abuses, but rather

28. Crottet, *Correspondance*, 25.
29. Crottet, *Correspondance*, 26–27.
30. Crottet, *Correspondance*, 28.
31. Crottet, *Correspondance*, 30.
32. Crottet, *Correspondance*, 32–33.

wished to aid those seeking to fix them. In the end, it was not his scruples that were the problem, but Calvin's, for du Tillet stood astonished that Calvin would condemn those seeking to reform the church (e.g., the Meaux circle). Ironically, du Tillet wrote, "What good I find in you I find in them as well, but do you praise them for it? You do not." Du Tillet then gave a cutting retort: "Am I not able to give them this title 'the churches of God' because I don't hold you for a schismatic, certainly I don't want to dissimulate."[33] Du Tillet did not think Calvin ungifted, but these same gifts he saw also in others and asked whether they were not from God as well.

Further, du Tillet rejected the claim that the Catholics were worse than the ancient Jews, or at least in the same condition as the Jews in the days of Jeroboam, let alone in the days of Ahab. He then came to what was the heart of the matter for him: neither Calvin nor he had ever had baptism except at the hands of the ministers of God, and that was where he was now going in answer to the scruples made above, to where he knew the ministers of God were. "Because where there is a true ministry of God, there necessarily also is the true Church of God."[34] It should be noted that to this point du Tillet had persistently used the plural, churches (*Eglises*), but here he now used the singular, the definitive. Again, he admitted that abuses existed, even idolatry, but at the same time the Word was preached and sacraments administered. It would be a great error, du Tillet continued, if he did not see that the Spirit indeed was at work there. In a rejoinder to Calvin, du Tillet noted that in Rome many heard the Shepherd's voice, even though many did not, just as there are wise and foolish virgins called to the last feast.[35]

As for the pillar and ground of the truth, what, asked du Tillet, does Calvin do with all those called "church" by Christ in the Apocalypse? What of the Galatians or the Corinthians? Did not the first churches arise out of the synagogues, so that God made the synagogues his very churches? How could Rome be worse than the Jews at the time of Christ who actually rejected and murdered him? Yet Christ observed the scruples of Judaism in the face of such hypocrisy and immorality.[36] Rome has a ministry especially appointed by Christ, whom the Jews rejected. Du Tillet cited Calvin at least tacitly for Donatism. What Ahab and Jeroboam did was so utterly against anything that God had commanded that it was bad in and of itself, for it sought to supplant true religion and manifestly contradicted the Word of God. But many of those things in the church that Calvin now thought of as abuses God had used to

33. Crottet, *Correspondance*, 33–34.
34. Crottet, *Correspondance*, 35.
35. Crottet, *Correspondance*, 37.
36. Crottet, *Correspondance*, 39–40.

call people to repentance, for what constituted a good might be abused, but an abuse does not destroy the use.[37]

Calvin finished his second letter, the shortest of the exchange, dated July 1538, only when he had arrived in Strasbourg. In brief, Calvin told du Tillet that he was no longer in Geneva, and while the letter did not explain why, it seems that Calvin assumed du Tillet knew. Calvin simply asserted that he had retired from Geneva and was waiting on the Lord's will for direction. He did give some news about the Swiss churches, and commented on his own trouble discerning what God wanted of him.[38] Du Tillet focused on this bewilderment in his reply of September 1538. He began by writing that Calvin seemed to suffer from people who care more for earthly things than for things of God. Obviously du Tillet, who as the letter made clear was formally going back to Rome, had at the same time no desire to treat Calvin as if he were a pestilence, for he wrote that all of Calvin's troubles would eventuate in his knowing what God's calling for him entailed.[39] Saying this, he revisited the question of knowledge brought up in the first letter, that all too often people think they know God's will and quickly convince themselves of it. He focused on Calvin's situation, pointing out that he had been called to his life as a Protestant only five years ago, and yet he acted in an imperious manner, condemning people even if they also condemned the things that Calvin himself censured.[40] Du Tillet pointed out that he was writing this not to impugn Calvin or to enter into controversy but to give him an occasion for self-examination. For du Tillet, the Lord often throws people into a thousand perplexities in order for them to rectify their lives, and, in his view, Calvin needed to rectify his self-assured attitude about his calling to be a minister of God.[41] In du Tillet's mind, how had Calvin not assumed the status of an oracle? To this du Tillet reasserted something already noted in his first letter, that the Lord does not bestow all his gifts on one person but spreads them among all. Further, only with fear and moderation can we hear God, for prejudices weigh everyone down, and without fear and humility no one will ever be rid of them.[42] Du Tillet closed by telling Calvin that he had put some money aside for him, perhaps hoping that Calvin would return to Paris.

In Calvin's last letter, dated October 1538, he admitted the constant need to examine oneself but maintained that ultimately the problems at Geneva said

37. Crottet, *Correspondance*, 42–43.
38. Crottet, *Correspondance*, 49–51.
39. Crottet, *Correspondance*, 52.
40. Crottet, *Correspondance*, 53.
41. Crottet, *Correspondance*, 53–54.
42. Crottet, *Correspondance*, 55.

more about the Genevans than about him, for he was faultless in the matter, nor would he hold the calamity as chastisement.[43] Further, he had given du Tillet's interrogation of his calling some thought and took his friend to task for questioning it. He had talked to some people whom they both knew, probably meaning Capito and Bucer, though possibly also Farel, inquiring about their thoughts on his vocation. The note this sounds at first seems an answer to du Tillet's criticism that Calvin had not been called by the church, but in the end, it turned into something else. Even if du Tillet did not accept their mutual acquaintances as confirmation of Calvin's call to the ministry, it was immaterial, for he, like Jonah before him, had a prophetic calling to take the gospel to the nations and thus had little need of external confirmation for his office.[44] Calvin's claim of a charisma directly from God may well have been taken from Farel, who was never ordained, and whose lack of ordination was completely known by both Berne and Johannes Oecolampadius, Farel's first Protestant sponsor, when the Bernese sent him out to preach.[45] Further, Calvin wrote that du Tillet obscured matters by calling darkness light (Geneva's motto, once having thrown off the prince bishop, was *post tenebras lux* [after the darkness, light]) and ascribing the abuses of Rome to the work of God, for those things were never goods.[46] He closed, thanking him for the offer of money, but stating that others were taking care of his needs.

Du Tillet in his third letter, sent from Paris in December 1538, denied attacking Calvin, but rather, du Tillet asserted, he had written out of concern for Calvin's soul. He wrote because he doubted Calvin's calling to the ministry, for what minister would condemn that which is not condemnable, even if in need of reform?[47] Further, du Tillet maintained that he wrote because Calvin had fallen, and this gave du Tillet an occasion to help him, since he also wrote to warn him that great-hearted people are beset by great problems and distractions, and that Calvin should examine himself in God's sight with fear and trembling.[48] And this forms the basis for the largest part of the last letter of this exchange. Du Tillet noted that Calvin had asserted his calling by God based on his own say-so, his own opinions. But how had God in the person of his Son established the ministry of the church but by calling and

43. Crottet, *Correspondance*, 59.
44. Crottet, *Correspondance*, 60.
45. Zuidema and Van Raalte, *Early French Reform*, 26; and see 47n68. For a discussion of this topic and its very wide implications, see Jon Balserak, *John Calvin as Sixteenth-Century Prophet* (Oxford: Oxford University Press, 2014). Professor Balserak notes Calvin's letter to du Tillet, 95.
46. Crottet, *Correspondance*, 60.
47. Crottet, *Correspondance*, 62.
48. Crottet, *Correspondance*, 63.

setting apart the apostles and then Paul, who then confirmed this calling through the laying on of hands? This calling was done with signs and outward forms, and du Tillet cited Paul about the ministry given to Timothy by the laying on of the hands of his fellow priests, and then by the imposition of Paul's own hands.[49] Du Tillet closed, again reprimanding Calvin for his lack of humility and for having asserted that the incident in Geneva had nothing to teach him and that he had been justified in his actions since the Genevans were such recalcitrant people.[50]

Louis du Tillet faded from Calvin's life, though years later, in his preface to the Psalms, Calvin recalled him as someone who had turned back to Rome. And in the church of Rome Louis du Tillet remained, living the remainder of his life in the shadow of his brothers, both of whom, Jean the *Greffier* and Jean the bishop, played such important roles in the great affairs of France. Both became completely devoted to the cause of Catholic France, and their services were duly rewarded. But the incident of younger brother Louis with Calvin seems to have left some impact. Jean the *Greffier* had actually come to worry about his brother in 1538 and went looking for him to bring him home. He apparently came to Geneva just as Calvin was being expelled, saw the Reformer again briefly in Basle, and then once more in Strasbourg.[51] That Louis had "come to his senses" on his own perhaps made things easier for Jean.

Eventually Jean would distinguish himself in the service of France, and particularly during the Wars of Religion. His original duties were unremarkable, however important, but at the beginning of the 1560s he came to the attention of the powerful family of Guise, chiefly Charles of Guise, the cardinal bishop of Lorraine, and brother of Henry of Guise, the duke. That his work in the royal archives had vast importance for how to think about the power of the monarchy and the role of history in governance was not lost on the cardinal, and he summoned the *Greffier*.[52] The Guise family was interested because, with the death of Henry II in 1559, their niece Mary, the daughter of their sister Mary of Scotland, had come to the throne as Francis II's queen, and they saw in the *Greffier* a powerful polemicist with the resources of his studies at their disposal. The Guise's time at court was short-lived, but their influence in France was not, and both the *Greffier* and the bishop became loyal supporters not only of the Guises but also of their ardent devotion to

49. Crottet, *Correspondance*, 67–69.
50. Crottet, *Correspondance*, 77–78.
51. Crottet, *Correspondance*, 49.
52. For the significance of Jean du Tillet on the discipline of history, see Kelley, *Foundations*, 215–38.

the Catholic faith.[53] Ironically, as the two of them rose in prominence outside the royal house proper, Louis's second brief time in prominence came to a close. From 1552 to 1560, Louis, perhaps at the instigation of one or both brothers, served as one of many chaplains to Catherine de Medici, Henry II's widow, then dowager-queen of France.[54]

Had Calvin been a Nicodemite? The obvious answer is yes, for he could not have lived almost a year at the estate of du Tillet, his host the curè of Claix, without attending Mass. We cannot explain his audience with Lefèvre either, nor his attendance at the court of Renée of France in Ferrara, without assuming that he went to Mass, since coincident with the time of his arrival the whole of Renée's French retinue was under scrutiny. But it seems that from their time together in Ferrara du Tillet had noticed a change beginning in Calvin that must have reached its denouement sometime in late 1536 (the Lausanne Disputation) or 1537 (the publication of the *Epistolae*, which used material from the Disputation to bolster the content of the earlier letters), which prompted du Tillet to the conclusion that he and Calvin had fundamentally different views of faith and the church. The correspondence reveals du Tillet's essential understanding of the church as an objective reality existing irrespective of its adherents' faith, and he thus placed a great deal of weight on its externals as those things that guaranteed its indefectibility. This stands in stark contrast to Calvin's appeal to his charismatic calling. As Alexander Ganoczy notes, "Du Tillet in fact remained committed to the idea of apostolic succession and the hierarchical constitution of the church, and he could not understand how his friend had received this extraordinary vocation to a prophetic mission."[55] Calvin, to the contrary, had come to profess that the church is found among the faithful—those professing the right faith—and inextricably within the context of the purely preached Word, right administration of the sacraments, and due direction of church discipline.

Calvin's letters to Roussel and Duchemin seem the beginning of Calvin's more precise attitudes, for were the letters sent from Ferrara, this would have been the two years marked by du Tillet's March 1538 letter, though sentiments reached their peak in his strident publication in 1537 of the *Epistolae duae*. Doubtless the catalyst of this change was the year spent with Farel, from

---

53. During the Wars of Religion, Jean du Tillet the *Greffier* wrote multiple tracts against the Huguenots and in favor of the Guises and their particular view of the French royal position. See Brown, *Jean du Tillet and the Wars of Religion*.

54. Hector de la Ferrière et al., eds., *Lettres de Catherine de Médici* (Paris: Imprimerie nationale, 1880–1943), 10:530, lists Loys du Tillet, frère de Jean du Tillet, évêque de Brieuc et Meaux, as one of Catherine's chaplains from 1552 till 1560.

55. Ganoczy, *Young Calvin*, 119.

whose austere gaze Calvin had hid du Tillet's first letter. The *Epistolae duae* is replete with lines and thoughts drawn directly from Farel's anti-Nicodemite harangue at the October 1536 disputation in Lausanne, and little more is needed to see that it was Farel who weighed most heavily in Calvin's formulation of his stricter stance. Calvin's correspondence with du Tillet does show that at least for friendship's sake Calvin was willing to admit that faith might be found in Rome, but this opinion was more testimony of the embers of friendship, embers that had died by the time Calvin coldly referred to du Tillet in the preface to his commentary on the Psalms as that "someone who now disgracefully defected back to the Papists."[56]

---

56. *Ioannis Calvini, Opera Quae Supersunt Omnia* (hereafter CO), 31:25, in Corpus Reformatorum (Saale, 1834–): "Unus homo, qui nunc turpi defectione iterum ad papistas rediit, statim fecit ut innotescerem." Calvin uses "vilenement" for "turpi" in the French, 26.

2

Pierre Caroli and Calvin

Arianism, Sabellianism, and the Heretical Farellistae

Both Calvin and Luther hesitated over such words as "hypostasis." Luther actually expressed himself boldly on the matter: "What if my soul hates the word *homoousion*, and I do not wish to use it, I will not be a heretic."[1] He also expressed his wariness of the word "Trinity"; not that he denied what it taught but that it was an extrabiblical theologoumenon and it would be better to refer to God as "God" than as "Trinity," and to rely on Scripture.[2] Calvin's first edition of the *Institutes* contained none of the fourth-century vocabulary, including the word "Trinity"; or, as Wilhelm Gass put it, Calvin avoided all "stickling for words."[3] Calvin's initial hesitancy to employ such terms also arose from his denial of the church's power to create binding definitions of faith. Essentially, as he saw the Protestant theological canon, creeds, like the writings of the fathers, were pious advice for confirming the teachings of Holy Scripture. One has only to look at Calvin's comments on

1. Martin Luther, *Against Latomus*, 1521, in *Werke* (Weimar: Hermann Bohlaus Nachfolger, 1883–2009), 32:24: "Quod si odit anima mea vocem homoousion, et nolim ea uti, non ero haereticus. quis enim me cogit uti, modo rem teneam quae in concilio scriptuas definita est?"

2. See the old but still informative article by Adam Stump, "Luther's Relation to the Dogmatic Tradition," *Lutheran Quarterly* 31 (1901): 186–96; originally published in Reinhold Seeberg, *Lehrbuch der Dogmengeschichte* (Erlangen and Leipzig: Deichert, 1895), 2:283–93.

3. Wilhelm Gass, "Geschichte der protestantischen Dogmatik," 1:105 (written in 1854). Quoted in B. B. Warfield, "Calvin's Doctrine of the Trinity," in *Augustine and Calvin* (Philadelphia: P&R, 1950), 197. Calvin does mention the words, but, as will be seen, only to reference what the ancients taught.

Monica's request to her son, Augustine, that he should remember her at the altar to see what stock he put in even so exalted and revered a father. Calvin's slighting Nicene language played no small part in his confrontations with the theological and ecclesiastical vagabond Pierre Caroli, a doctor of the Sorbonne. Calvin's mode of expression survived the polemical jousts with Caroli, but its use had a cost when Calvin faced those who bearded him by his own theological prolegomena.

The Caroli incidents (there were more than one) present some rather confused trinitarianism on all sides, and it has only been in the last few decades that Caroli's own voice in the whole affair has emerged. This chapter's purpose is not merely to rehash the trinitarian fight but to show that Caroli, as he wavered between Catholicism and Protestantism, actually steeled Calvin for his later posture with respect to Servetus, the rest of the antitrinitarians, and his other theological interlocutors. This stiffening of Calvin's theological and judicial spine was not, moreover, merely a result of the 1537 controversy but arose from events and controversies that spanned the years from 1537 to 1545, Caroli present in them all. We thus see that Calvin himself goes through a transformation, not that he becomes more anti-Catholic, as this stance fills his earliest controversies and writings (e.g., his treatise on Nicodemism), but that how he addressed theological differences curves to the embittered. In this, Caroli and his multiple lapses and relapses between Catholicism and Protestantism play a crucial, pivotal role, his place at the epicenter of the storms of the early 1540s providing illumination into Calvin's postures in later conflicts.

Caroli was born in Rozay-en-Brie in the diocese of Meaux, sometime around 1480, and studied at the Collège of Bourgogne, obtaining his MA in 1505.[4] By 1510 he was a *hospes* (literally "paying guest") at the Sorbonne (the theology faculty of the university), made *socius* (fellow) in 1512, and in 1518 he served as the faculty's prior. He passed his doctoral acts in 1520, under Guillaume Duchesne, "one of the most rigid traditionalists in the Faculty of Theology."[5] At some point before 1512 he was ordained, for then begin the records of his ineffectual attempts at obtaining clerical benefices. His fortunes turned in 1521 when he went back to his native diocese of Meaux and became part of the famous circle around Guillaume Briçonnet, bishop of Meaux, along with

4. For the outlines of Caroli's biography, see James K. Farge, *Biographical Register of Paris Doctors of Theology, 1500–1536* (Toronto: Pontifical Institute of Medieval Studies, 1980), 65–71; Frans Pieter van Stam, "Le livre de Pierre Caroli de 1545 et son conflit avec Calvin," in *Calvin et ses contemporains: Actes du colloque de Paris 1995*, ed. Olivier Millet, Cahiers d'humanisme et Renaissance 53 (Geneva: Librairie Droz, 1998), 21–41; and Alexandre Ganoczy, *The Young Calvin*, trans. David Foxgrover and Wade Provo (Edinburgh: T&T Clark, 1988).

5. Farge, *Register*, 66.

Jacques Lefèvre d'Étaples, Gérard Roussel, François Vatable, Jean Lecomte de la Croix, and Guillaume Farel.[6] Briçonnet appointed him priest of Germigny-l'Évèque in the diocese of Meaux that year, and thus he fell under Briçonnet's direct reforming oversight.[7] Bishop Briçonnet, along with Lefèvre especially but also others, sought moderate reforms within the diocese that sprang from their humanist tendencies. Leaning heavily on the text of Scripture, and influenced by both Erasmus and the thought of the church fathers, Lefèvre emerged as the force behind the group. He and the circle of Meaux informed the whole of Caroli's later life, both as a Catholic and Reformed, and provide a key to his peregrinations, which began in Paris with the reaction of the Faculty of Theology to the content of Caroli's preaching, content he had drawn from his associations with Meaux.[8]

The Sorbonne's first actions against him appear in a denunciation on June 6, 1523, for preaching heresy. Although the Faculty of Theology addressed the matter of Caroli's doctrines more than one hundred times between 1523 and 1533, the records detail Caroli's heresies only in broad terms, citing him for his views on the Virgin and the saints, relics, prayers for the dead, and the canon of the Mass. In 1523 Noël Béda, erstwhile principal of the Collège de Montaigu, Calvin's first college at Paris (though Béda was gone when Calvin arrived), and regarded as the most prominent traditionalist in the university's faculty of theology, directly oversaw Caroli's case. Béda had written extensively against Erasmus and Lefèvre, and consequently was mercilessly pilloried by Paris's students favorable to humanism, and also by Rabelais, who satirized him in *Gargantua and Pantagruel* as the author of *De optimate triparum* (*Concerning the Excellence of Tripe, or, of the Stomach*).[9] Caroli quickly made a full recantation of his errors, but by July 1524 his case was reopened by the theology faculty, with Caroli's criticisms of the faculty only complicating his predicament. When the faculty found against him and expelled him from the university, Caroli refused to recant, and he appealed to the Parlement of Paris. When in defiance he began preaching at the Collège de Cambray,

6. Michel Veissière, "Lefèvre d'Etaples et Guillaume Briçonnet," in *Jacques Lefèvre d'Etaples (1450?–1536), Actes du colloque d'Etaples les 7 et 8 novembre 1992*, ed. Jean-François Pernot (Paris: Honoré Champion Éditeur, 1995), 121; and Farge, *Register*, 66.

7. Francis M. Hinigman, *La Diffusion de la Réforme en France: 1520–1565* (Geneva: Labor et Fides, 1992), 31.

8. Max Engammare, "Pierre Caroli, véritable disciple de Lefèvre d'Etaples?," in Pernot, *Jacques Lefèvre d'Etaples*, 55–79.

9. James K. Farge, "Noël Beda and the Defense of the Tradition," in *Biblical Humanism and Scholasticism in the Age of Erasmus*, ed. Erika Rummel (Leiden: Brill, 2008), 141; François Rabelais, *Gargantua and Pantagruel*, trans. J. M. Cohen (New York: Penguin, 1955), 188. Pantagruel found the book in the library of the convent of St. Victor.

the faculty proceeded against him as a lapsed heretic. Facing ruin and death, Caroli remonstrated yet again, suspending his lectures (he put a notice on the door to the lecture hall: "Pierre Caroli, wishing to submit to the orders of the most sacred Faculty, is suspending his classes. He will again take up these lectures—DV—at this verse where he had to stop: 'They have pierced my hands and my feet.'"[10]), but the faculty refused to hear him, since the case was now remanded to the Parlement of Paris, the faculty having passed their judgments about Caroli to the Parlement on November 7, 1525. Yet Caroli remained largely unscathed, for he had powerful allies—namely, Marguerite of Navarre, the king's sister, who provided him benefices in Alençon and Bayeux; and the bishop of Paris François Poncher, who allowed Caroli to preach in his diocese throughout the proceedings.[11] James K. Farge asserts that Poncher did this to stick his finger in the eye of the theology faculty for trying to regulate preaching in Paris.[12] But Caroli also survived because, despite his status as a doctor and regent of the faculty, he seems not to have been the prey the faculty hunted, for they wanted the leaders at Meaux.

The defeat of the French at Pavia and the capture of Francis I in February 1525 crippled Marguerite's ability to protect the Meaux circle. From prison Francis I placed the regency of France in the hands of his mother, Louise of Savoy, who acceded to the requests of the Parlement of Paris and Pope Clement VII that heresy tribunals be established and that the power of investigation be given to the Parlement. Louise of Savoy's support for the tribunals enfeebled Marguerite of Navarre's protection of the members of the Meaux circle, many of whom fled to Strasbourg.[13] Caroli, however, seemingly felt no need for flight. Why remains obscure, but he had royal patronage beyond the kindnesses of Marguerite of Navarre. Between 1527 and 1533, in the nine references to Caroli seeking readmission to the faculty, not just Marguerite but both Francis I and Guillaume Petit, the king's confessor (also a Parisian doctor), are listed as interested in the case and no doubt tipped the scales of justice in his favor. How it was that Caroli had gained such patronage is unclear, but it is also the case that Caroli in 1525 still maintained some measure of the faith as professed by the traditionalists on the Faculty of Theology—at the Lausanne Disputation in 1536. Caroli, then holding forth for the Protestants of Geneva and Berne, found himself taken to task by one of the Catholic priests, Jean

10. Farge, *Register*, 67.
11. For Marguerite of Navarre, see the near-magisterial study by Jonathan A. Reid, *King's Sister—Queen of Dissent: Marguerite of Navarre (1492–1549) and Her Evangelical Network*, 2 vols. (Leiden: Brill, 2009). For Caroli, the circle of Meaux, and Marguerite, see 73–75.
12. Farge, *Register*, 68.
13. Bruce Gordon, *Calvin* (New Haven: Yale University Press, 2009), 15.

Michaud, who maintained that he had heard Caroli preaching on the Psalms in Paris in 1525, and at that time Caroli certainly held none of the heresies that he professed eleven years later at the disputation. Caroli confessed that in 1525 he had been still in error, and dependent on the thought of traditional commentaries and authors, but now he was enlightened by Scripture.[14]

Caroli spent these years as minister in Alençon not only preaching but also working with Simon du Bois on the French New Testament, and Farge believes he was the translator of the Psalter, which included Luther's preface.[15] But whatever his life entailed at Alençon, this all ended with the *Affaire des Placards* in October 1534. By January 1535 his name was foremost on a list of people to be arrested, and as sixteen people had been burned at the stake between the Affaire and January, Caroli fled. He appeared first in Geneva, where he took up with his old colleague from Meaux Guillaume Farel (see chap. 6). Caroli there confronted one of his old students, the Dominican priest and Sorbonne doctor Guy Furby, who had been imprisoned by the Genevans when Furby preached against Geneva's new Protestant benefactors, the Bernese. Caroli took part in an interrogation of Furby, who broke into tears upon seeing Caroli, whom he had thought a defender of traditional Catholicism.[16] Shortly afterward Caroli turned up in Basle, where he met Erasmus and entered the university to study Hebrew under Sebastian Münster. He served as a minister in Neuchâtel under Antoine Marcourt in 1536, and from there he attended and participated in the disputation at Lausanne in October of that year.[17]

Berne had organized the disputation following their putative coup in Geneva as a way to champion the Reformation in Lausanne and the Pays de Vaud, for Berne itself had joined the cause of the Reformation following disputations—first at Baden in 1526, and then more importantly in Berne, 1528—like the one they planned for Lausanne.[18] Caroli acquitted himself well at the disputation, holding forth on several of the articles, and in particular on justification by faith and not works (for "it is impossible to be justified without living faith which produces in time and place its fruits, which the dead faith does not effect"[19]); the spiritual

14. In Arthur Piaget, *Les Actes de la Dispute de Lausanne, 1536: Publiés intégralement d'après le manuscrit de Berne* (Neuchâtel: Secrétariat de l'Université, 1928), 128–29.

15. Farge, *Register*, 68.

16. Jeanne de Jussie, *The Short Chronicle*, ed. and trans. Carrie F. Klaus (Chicago: University of Chicago Press, 2006), 96.

17. For the disputation and Caroli's part in it, see Piaget, *Actes*.

18. See Irena Backus, *The Disputation of Baden, 1526 and Berne, 1528: Neutralizing the Early Church*, Studies in Reformed Theology and History 1, no. 1 (Princeton: Princeton University Press, 1993).

19. Piaget, *Actes*, 98: "Et n'est possible d'estre justifié sans foy vive qui produict en temps et lieu son fruict, ce que ne faict la foy morte estant sans fruict."

eating of Christ in the Eucharist (*mangé par foy*); and the need to read Scripture in light of Scripture.[20] The outcome of the debate was never in doubt, as Berne saw this as the way to convince the people of the region to accept the Reformation (previously only 15 of the 124 parishes in the Pays de Vaud had shown any sign of evangelical inclination).[21] Caroli was hardly the most auspicious champion of Protestantism at the disputation, for Farel and Viret together assumed that role, joined by Antoine Marcourt and the newly arrived Calvin, who also spoke on the question of the Eucharist. Though playing but an ancillary role, Caroli had nonetheless made a favorable impression on the magistrates of Berne, and the council appointed him the chief pastor at Lausanne, an appointment that set him on course for a conflict with Geneva, as one of their close associates—namely, Pierre Viret—had been in Lausanne since the beginning of the year.[22] But Caroli's undoing was not wholly the accomplishment of Geneva's ministers, for according to their correspondence not only did Caroli himself show a surprising lack of tact, he also had taken up prayers for the dead. Viret's fellow minister Christopher Fabri, in a letter to Farel from Thonon (across the lake from Lausanne), cast Caroli as self-aggrandizing and self-serving, referring to him as Diotrephes, a person mentioned in 3 John as someone who ought to be avoided since "he seeks preeminence."[23] The clash of personalities seems most germane to the conflict, for the matter of prayers for the dead, according to Max Engammare, seems merely "le prétexte du conflit."[24] Engammare points out that the prayers offered were not strictly speaking heretical; they were offered for the speedy coming of Christ and that those who died in Christ might soon have their resurrection. Called to account, Caroli responded by accusing Farel, Viret, and Calvin of Arianism, in that they were spreading the heresy of Servetus.[25] The basis of this accusation was the absence of not only the language of the fourth century but indeed of the very word "Trinity" in the works of Farel and Calvin, and in particular the 1536 edition of the *Institutes*.

20. Piaget, *Actes*, 128–30, 330; and see Engammare, "Pierre Caroli," 63.
21. Gordon, *Calvin*, 66.
22. Viret had accompanied Farel to Geneva, but in early 1536 was in Neuchâtel. Geneva had requested he come, and thus he ultimately ended up in Lausanne. See Aimé Louis Herminjard, *Correspondance des réformateurs dans les pays de langue française, recueillie et publiée avec d'autres lettres relatives à la réforme et des notes historiques et biographiques* (Geneva: H. Georg, 1866–97), 3:392–96.
23. Herminjard, *Correspondance*, 4:176: "hic Diotrephes omnino partes tuetur, magnisque insignit titulis et laudibus."
24. Engammare, "Caroli," 66.
25. Servetus had riled the Rhineland and the western Swiss cities with his 1531 *De Trinitatis erroribus*.

When Calvin countered that the confession of Geneva maintained the doctrine of the Trinity, Caroli responded that the Genevans, or the Farellistae—or Farellisticoi, as he sometimes called them—should affirm the Nicene and Athanasian Symbols, for the Genevan confession of 1536 never used the term "Trinity," and when it noted any creed, which it did in article 6, it was only the Apostles' Creed.[26] Calvin replied that the church has not the power to bind people's consciences. Alexander Ganoczy ironically notes that while apparently the church catholic has not this power, the church Genevan did.[27] Calvin and Farel hastened to Berne with extended written confessions of their orthodoxy. Calvin wrote the Bernese pastor Kaspar Megander (a near friend to Heinrich Bullinger in Zurich) that Caroli would not calm down, and that the Sorbonne doctor held the Genevans suspect until they would subscribe to the Athanasian Symbol. Calvin maintained that he made no practice of approving anything except it be rightly judged by the Word of God. He then added, "I recognized here the madness of a wild beast [*Hic beluae rabiem agnosco*]."[28] Calvin also labeled Caroli a buffoon, immoral, and without reason. Bruce Gordon calls the letter "an effective piece of character assassination."[29] Calvin pleaded for a synod before Easter of that year, but it only took place on May 14 in Lausanne. The synod exonerated Calvin, Farel, and Viret, whereas Caroli, refusing to admit their integrity, fled Bernese territory. Calvin's victory was hardly final, as rumors still swirled, and in August 1537 Calvin and Farel again had to assert their orthodoxy, this time affirming their explicit belief in the Trinity and in the Nicene understanding of the use of the word "person."[30]

But how did Calvin come to his idiomatic theology of the Trinity, standing athwart of what Caroli saw as the received tradition and teaching of the Christian tradition? John T. Slotemaker, seeking to rehabilitate the early Calvin, asserts that he stood in the mainstream of Western scholastic thought.[31] Slotemaker is correct in his reading of the late scholastics and the division among them concerning the eternal origins of the persons of the Trinity (i.e., relational models versus originist models). It may be relevant that Calvin was a student of John Major, but the significance of this has been gainsaid by many, including Bernard Cottret, who sees themes from Major present in Calvin,

---

26. CO 22 (*Confession de la Foy*): 85–96.
27. Ganoczy, *Young Calvin*, 114.
28. CO 10:86.
29. Gordon, *Calvin*, 73.
30. *Confessio de Trinitate propter Calumnias P. Caroli*, 1537, in CO 5:703–10.
31. John T. Slotemaker, "John Calvin's Trinitarian Theology in the 1536 *Institutes*: The Distinction of Person as a Key to His Theological Sources," in *Philosophy and Theology in the Middle Ages: A Tribute to Stephen F. Brown*, ed. Kent Emery Jr. et al. (Leiden: Brill, 2011).

but also in others who were never associated with the Collège de Montaigu.[32] More telling is Slotemaker's assertion that somehow Augustine stood for a relational model of the Trinity. This is not to say that this theme is not found in Augustine, but it is difficult to say this model ruled supreme in his thought (e.g., comparing his sermons to *De Trinitate*, and especially the end of *De Trinitate*).[33] Even more significantly, Slotemaker asserts that the Greeks held to a relational notion of the divine persons as regards origin and even says that Gregory of Nazianzus used "God" as equivalent of essence and that it was the absolute term for him. However, we read in the third theological oration (Oration 29.12) that Gregory explicitly denied this, asserting that it was the doctrine of the Arians; Gregory's position was that "God" is a relative term and "Unbegotten" the absolute term (God is God of everyone and everything, but the Unbegotten is begotten of no one).[34] Further, Slotemaker's dismissal of Paul Helm's obvious observation that Calvin slighted classical terminology falls very short.[35] Calvin did note the terms *essentia* and *substantia*, and the Greek *hypostasis*, but only in noting that this was how the "veteris orthodoxi" spoke. Calvin himself does not use the terms either in 1536 or in the first confession of Geneva, but does in the confession that he and Farel gave to the city of Berne in response to Caroli's first invective in 1537. Most importantly, Calvin does not appeal to any of these terms to answer Caroli, and he writes as if they never existed. Richard Muller points out that Calvin really only took up the scholastics after 1536, and then largely in an as-needed way when preparing sermons or commentaries.[36]

Caroli's flight, first to the French embassy in Soleure, eventually landed him in Lyons, where he implored the Inquisitor General, Cardinal Tournon, to bring him back to the Catholic fold. Tournon obtained the necessary dispensations (as an apostate priest and lapsed heretic, Caroli needed absolution by the pope) along with a restoration of his privileges as doctor and priest and all his benefices. But by the end of 1537 Caroli again fled France, because in the presence of the royal chancellor, Guillaume Poyet, he apparently preached justification *sola fide*. From France he sought refuge under Jacopo Sadoleto

32. Bernard Cottret, *Calvin: A Biography*, trans. M. Wallace McDonald (Grand Rapids: Eerdmans, 2000), 60.

33. See Lewis Ayres, *Nicaea and Its Legacy: An Approach to Fourth-Century Trinitarian Theology* (Oxford: Oxford University Press, 2004).

34. Gregory of Nazianzus, *The Five Theological Orations of Gregory of Nazianzus*, ed. Arthur James Mason (Cambridge: Cambridge University Press, 1899), 90–91.

35. Slotemaker, "Trinitarian Theology," 800–801n72.

36. Richard Muller, "Scholasticism in Calvin: Relation and Disjunction," in *Calvinus Sincerioris Religionis Vindex / Calvin as Protector of the Purer Religion*, ed. Wilhelm H. Neuser and Brian G. Armstrong (Kirksville, MO: Sixteenth Century Essays and Studies, 1993), 252, 264.

in Carpentras, who, according to Farge, refused to grant it to him. But Farel implied otherwise, actually accusing Caroli of being the inspiration not only for Sadoleto's letter to the Genevans that year but also for a letter attempting to woo Antoine Marcourt back to Rome.[37] Caroli probably found little aid or comfort in Carpentras, for by July of 1539 he was again among the Swiss in Neuchâtel, where he was reconciled with Viret and Farel.[38] He would also later be reconciled with Calvin, who was then in Strasbourg, though Calvin showed every intention of not trusting Caroli in the least. Before Calvin finally consented to reconciliation, Caroli was arrested by the magistrates of Berne for having skipped out in 1537.

Calvin's caution proved justified, for by 1540 Caroli had gone back to the communion of Rome, never to look back. He took up residence near Metz, where he remained for at least the next five years. He spent a great deal of time writing and preaching against the Reformers, and according to the Reformed sources, caused them no end of problems. The Council of Neuchâtel claimed that it was Caroli who thwarted Reformed attempts to preach in Metz. It was also in Metz that Caroli composed his account of the theological differences with the Farellistae. Up until 1971 it had been thought that Calvin's treatise against Caroli was the only extant source for this pamphlet war. But when Caroli's treatise was unearthed, it showed, as Frans Pieter van Stam has stated, a polished and rhetorically effective piece of theology.[39] More than that, the treatise makes sense of seeming contradictions in Caroli, explaining why he could accuse the Reformers of Arianism at one time and Sabellianism at another. In 1543 Caroli wrote a letter, sent to the emperor, the king of France, the regent of the Low Countries, and the pope, stating his willingness to debate Farel on the matter of the Trinity before a faculty of theology approved by the Holy See, for they alone possessed the competency to judge: thus the acceptable places would be Paris, Louvain, Salamanca, Padua, Toulouse, before the council at Trent, or in Rome, but not in Metz.[40] Little in the letter tells us of the complexities of Caroli's thought, though these are contained in the 1545 *Refutatio*.[41]

37. Herminjard, *Correspondance*, 6:85–86.

38. CO 11: cols. 3–10.

39. Van Stam, "Le livre de Pierre Caroli," 24.

40. Van Stam, "Le livre de Pierre Caroli," 35; Farge, *Register*, 70. For Viret's letter on the matter, see Herminjard, *Correspondance*, 8:434–36. For Caroli's letter, see Herminjard, *Correspondance*, 8:403–5. For the whole correspondence of the Reformers, see Herminjard, *Correspondance*, 8:349–52, 369–75 (Farel's first letter to Caroli in Metz), 403–7, 416–18, 421–41 (Farel's second letter to Caroli, 421–34).

41. Pierre Caroli, *Refutatio blasphemiae Farellistarum in Sacrosanctam Trinitatem* (Paris: V. Goltherot, 1545). The first part is largely biographical, with the theological observations

Caroli's initial criticisms of Calvin, Farel, and Viret may seem merely a game of brinkmanship, using their reticence about patristic language as a way to deflect criticisms of his personal character and the quibbles over prayers for the dead. Indeed, one may wonder whether Caroli would have brought the matter up had he not been called to account for other concerns. Be that as it may, Caroli's criticisms hit a nerve. The efficient cause of Caroli's 1545 publication was the expansion sought by the Schmalkaldic League in its attempts to entice Metz into their confederation. The city of Metz, in Lorraine, standing on the border of the empire and France, constantly found itself in the middle of the wars of the emperor Charles V and Francis I of France. For Metz to become a Protestant city, Reformers needed to come and bolster Metz's Protestant community; though the Schmalkaldic League was a Lutheran enterprise, Farel was seen as the appropriate minister for the situation. Caroli wrote that he had already spent three years at the monastery of St. Paul in Verdun working in opposition to the Protestant heresies, when "behold, it was announced that Farel was coming to Metz."[42] First and foremost Caroli attacked Farel, Calvin, and Viret for having neglected the proper vocabulary of the Catholic faith, and then for having eschewed the creeds—like Arius, they had disregarded the language of consubstantiation.[43] Caroli asked whether Calvin and Farel would denounce Paul of Samosata, Arius, and Sabellius while denouncing the ancient creeds.[44] Calvin could have replied that the faith lay in things and not in words (a comment made by Gregory of Nazianzus when justifying the use of the Latin word *persona* as a cognomen for the Greek word *hypostasis*), but instead he attempted to reinvent the wheel, and here Calvin showed himself quite out of step with the church fathers. Calvin embraced what must have seemed to Caroli initially as tritheism, but which later he would identify as Sabellianism, specifically in Calvin's identifying Christ with Jehovah of the Old Testament.[45] This scandalized Caroli, and for an orthodox reason: Calvin viewed the term "Jehovah" as a statement about the aseity of God, and here, about the aseity of the Son, the crux of Calvin's *autothean* doctrine, that essentially Christ was fully God for he was God in his own right, God in se, just as much as the Father was, and most importantly, for the same reason that the Father was.[46] Christ, just as the Father, was naturally unbegotten, but at

---

beginning on page 10 (the work is not paginated, and pages are here counted from where the text begins).

42. Caroli, *Refutatio*, 3.

43. Caroli, *Refutatio*, 26–27.

44. Caroli, *Refutatio*, 32.

45. *Confessio de Trinitate propter Calumnias P. Caroli*, 1537, in CO 5:708–9.

46. It should be noted that the church fathers identified Christ with the LORD (Jehovah) of the Old Testament: Athanasius wrote that Moses worshiped Christ in the burning bush

the same time still coming from the Father, for he is fully monarch as is the Father, something that Calvin added to the 1539 edition of the *Institutes*. For Caroli, this made hash of the eternal generation of the Son; eternal generation now became nothing other than a manner or dispensation of the Word's existence, a theology he claimed came from Servetus, though with its roots in the pre-Nicene heretic Paul of Samosata.[47] For Caroli, Farel (he repeatedly addressed Farel in the *Refutatio*, as Farel was slated to oversee the church in Metz) and Calvin had crossed a line on their road to Arianism by slighting the fathers and falling in with Servetus:

> Servetus, whose doctrine you recently introduced when he restored the impious error of Samosata, denied that the word is to be understood as "person" in the place where it is written "In the beginning was the word." He asserted the great authority of Scripture, and demanded that this be placed before the decrees of the church; this same which you are accustomed to assert. Then cleverly he disputed that the passage ought to be understood simply. . . . While the word in common human language does not signify person, [Servetus] denied that it should signify "person" when used in John's Gospel, and with him you did not discern the divine way of speaking.[48]

Further, Caroli charged Farel and Calvin with denying the concrete reality of the persons (*hypostasis, hoc est, substantia individua et intellegens*).[49] Caroli based this charge on the Genevan's confession not asserting the concrete distinction of persons within the Trinity but simply confessing "In una dei essentia patrem cum verbo et spiritu suo agnoscimus." For Caroli, this had made the essence indistinguishable as persons, but only as adjectives: "In respect to these particular concerns, do you distinguish the Word from the Father either merely rationally, or as regards to their very properties? If solely by the contrivance of thought, I indict you as Sabellians; since these intellections would be mere naked adjectives without substance, which you publicly refuse to deny; if the properties themselves are distinguished, it is unavoidable that the Father would be a one thing, the Son another."[50] As touching Calvin's doctrine of the Son as *autothean*, this just brought more confusion, for the aseity of God belonged to the Father alone as the source of divinity. Further, to predicate self-existence to the Son resulted in two principles in

---

(*Contra Arianos* 11.38) and Irenaeus that he who enslaved Israel at Sinai set them free in the gospel (*Adversus Haereses* 4.17).

47. Caroli, *Refutatio*, 30–31.
48. Caroli, *Refutatio*, 33.
49. Caroli, *Refutatio*, 36.
50. Caroli, *Refutatio*, 36–37.

the Godhead, and thus a denial of the monarch for a dyarchy, or else it would make aseity the cause of divinity in the Son, as opposed to the Father as its cause. Thus Father, Son, and Spirit are but aspects or modalities of the one existent deity. Caroli emphasized this point in his *Refutatio* by noting that if the Word does not have substantial existence from the substance of the Father, then from what do either have their existence? Is the Word existent from something around the Father, or is the cause of divinity something predicated of them both (aseity? self-existence?)? For Caroli the substance of God must be plainly confessed as individuate without partition in the divine persons: the Son substantially generated from the substance of the Father, and not a verbal predicate, which is what he was accusing the Genevans of implying, if not asserting, but a subsistent hypostasis.[51] Despite the beauty of the modern English translation of an ancient hymn, the Son is not "of the Father's love begotten." This is a poor rendering of Aurelius Prudentius's original Latin, which does not have this connotation, as it reads, *Corde natus ex parentis*, "born from the heart of the Father" (*parens, parentis*, besides being indifferently "parent," can also be either "father" or "mother"). The Son or Word is not the mere product of an attribute.

Calvin's and his fellow Genevan Reformers' language plagued them, and when in 1543 Caroli offered the challenge of a disputation, a number of ministers thought this must be done.[52] The situation with Metz was urgent, as Charles V, now in league with Francis I, was at last ready to act against the Schmalkaldic League. Francis I had already moved against the Waldensians in Savoy/Piedmont, an action that Johann Sleiden (1506–56) declared was the prelude to the Council of Trent. The Leaguers themselves, putatively Lutheran, were ready to incorporate Metz even when the chief minister would be Guillaume Farel, but Caroli now stood in the way. And despite a Protestant military presence in the lancers of Count Wilhelm von Furstenberg, the whole enterprise collapsed as the town council, pressured from both Charles V and Francis I, rejected Leaguer overtures and thus the ministry of Farel. The Swiss blamed the failure on Caroli. But the affair testified to more than simply the

---

51. "If the Word is subsistent, is it distributable to many or is it only to an individual? If you would have said severally distributable, then concerning those pluralities, as touches the Word, I will ask you separately: would it thus extend to infinity (which implies a contradiction), or will its condition be indivisible? Therefore (the first being impossible) the Word of God remains set, an indivisible substance, and this the Greeks designate hypostasis, by the Latins truly named subsistence, this which the philosophers call in creatures a particular and a prime substance" (Caroli, *Refutatio*, 37). This is a point missed in Brannon Ellis's *Calvin, Classical Trinitarianism, and the Aseity of the Son* (Oxford: Oxford University Press, 2012); see chap. 3, "The Autothean Controversies: Calvin's Complex Solidarity with Classical Trinitarianism," 64–102.

52. Van Stam, "Le livre de Pierre Caroli," 35.

persuasive power of one Parisian doctor. In concert with Charles V, Pope Paul III had asserted that the forthcoming council in Trent would be for the suppression of heresy. For some years prior, Charles V and his brother, Ferdinand of Austria, had sought religious reconciliation via a series of colloquies, a program championed in Rome by the so-called Erasmian party, which included cardinals Contarini, Pole, and Morone. But with the abysmal failure of the Colloquy of Regensburg in 1541 (attended by Calvin)—at which agreement was tentatively reached on justification but which came to no resolution on the questions of papal power or the Mass, among others—both Charles V and Ferdinand despaired of this approach. This stemmed both from the failure in Regensberg and the death of its foremost champion, Contarini, which set the Erasmian party in eclipse. Even some of those who sympathized with Contarini—chiefly here Cardinal Giovanni Morone—had never fully backed the colloquy approach, believing a council the better alternative.[53] Further, both Paris with its index and Louvain with its declaration of faith had enacted stringent norms for the faith. Martin Bucer gave voice to the tightening of the noose around the Protestant neck, reacting to Charles V's implementation of the Louvain declarations on the Low Countries, calling it "our new Koran."[54]

The early 1540s also marked a turning in the mind of Calvin. He certainly was no more cantankerous than before 1540, as his letter to Megander makes clear that he lacked no invective prior to 1540. But as can be seen from his interactions with Roussell and Duchemin, and especially in his letters with Louis du Tillet, his longtime friend who decamped from Geneva without a word early in 1538 to return to France and to Rome (he would later become the chaplain to Marie de Medici), Calvin was ready to debate, ready to use his vast powers as an orator and gifts of rhetoric to address questions with an end for persuasion. With Caroli, this attitude starts to break down. By 1544, Calvin could not endure the slightest variances in doctrine within the company of pastors, dismissing Castellio from his post for disagreeing with his own idiomatic interpretation of the *descensus* clause (see chap. 5) and declining from Calvin's interpretation that the Song of Songs was an allegory about Christ and the church.

In a letter to Martin Bucer in 1550, Farel wrote that Caroli had died— "Carolus perditus"—and that same year the Sorbonne removed Caroli's name for having an outstanding debt,[55] yet his criticisms of Calvin's trinitarianism lived on. At the Colloquy of Poissy, the Parisian doctor Claude de Sainctes

53. Adam Patrick Robinson, *The Career of Cardinal Giovanni Morone (1509–1580): Between Council and Inquisition* (Farnham, UK: Ashgate, 2012), 53–56.

54. Van Stam, "Le livre de Pierre Caroli," 37.

55. Van Stam, "Le livre de Pierre Caroli," 41; Farge, *Register*, 71.

revived them with his attack on the Reformed declaration of faith at Poissy, in particular its sixth article on the Trinity, even though the article embraced the terms slighted by Calvin—namely, "Trinity" and "person"—and did not address the Son as Jehovah. But de Sainctes focused on what it means that the Father is Father to the Word, and whether he is Father by dint of creation or eternally so, and whether the Son draws his essence and nature from the Father. He quotes from Caroli's *Refutatio*, and his own subsequent tome on Calvin makes heavy weather against Calvin and Beza on these points.[56] Beza in 1570 published a florilegium in response that showed the complete coincidence of Genevan and Reformed doctrine with that of the church fathers, particularly drawing on Athanasius and Basil the Great.

Caroli's wanderings admit no easy explanation: to Farge, Caroli lacked the conviction and stomach to be a martyr and thus could not commit to any creed.[57] Engammare, on the other hand, sees his creed well enough and says it was not that of either the Sorbonne or Geneva but that of Erasmus, and most of all, of Jacques Lefèvre d'Étaples; Caroli and Lefèvre held not to what Engammare sees as the three extremes—of the Sorbonne, the French evangelicals, and Geneva ("réforme fondamentale d'influence allemande"),[58] but to a land between them all, Lefèvre with humility and wisdom, Caroli with arrogance and hesitation. In this regard, Caroli seemingly could have no home other than the one he appears to have made as a foil to Geneva, which seems far more than the Sorbonne to have been his bête noir. Whatever Caroli's motives in attacking Calvin, his invective and polemic altered both the Reformer himself and how the Reformed did theology. Calvin wrote in his *Defense of Farel* that Caroli's attacks were only to stir trouble and asked what need there was for Caroli to raise such questions, since unanimity abounded among the Protestants and everyone agreed on the doctrine of the Trinity. Eventually, however, Servetus and his sequel, along with de Sainctes at Poissy, would stamp QED to Caroli's assertions.

---

56. Irena Backus, *Historical Method and Confessional Identity in the Era of the Reformation: 1378–1615*, Studies in Medieval and Reformation Traditions (Leiden: Brill, 2003), 180–83.
57. Farge, *Register*, 70.
58. Engammare, "Caroli," 78–79.

3

Sadoleto

The Erasmian from Rome

Jacopo Sadoleto's life reflects the seeming friction between humanism and dogmatic theology, the use or abuse of humanism in defense of one's theology, and how humanism shaped the minds, methods, and manners of its practitioners across theological lines. While Calvin held humanism in common with almost all of his interlocutors, it may easily and vigorously be argued that with none of them was humanism more integral a part of life than with Jacopo Sadoleto. Born into the *familia* of the powerful d'Este dukes of Ferrara, Jacopo Sadoleto,[1] as his father before him and his brother after him, seemed destined for a life as a legal clerk in the employ of the duke. His father, Giovanni, was Ferrara's ambassador to both Naples and France, and also after 1488 a teacher of law in Ferrara. For all this, the "Sadoleto family was prosperous rather than rich, bourgeois rather than noble."[2] Jacopo was born

---

1. Richard M. Douglas, *Jacopo Sadoleto, 1477–1547: Humanist and Reformer* (Cambridge, MA: Harvard University Press, 1959), provides most of the biographical information for this chapter, but see also John F. D'Amico, *Renaissance Humanism in Papal Rome* (Baltimore: Johns Hopkins University Press, 1983); Kenneth Gouwens, "Recognition and Remembrance: Jacopo Sadoleto's Letters to Curial Friends, 1527–1529," in *Remembering the Renaissance: Humanist Narratives of the Sack of Rome* (Leiden: Brill, 1998), 103–42; and P. G. Bietenholz and Thomas B. Deutscher, eds., *Contemporaries of Erasmus: A Biographical Register of the Renaissance and Reformation* (Toronto: University of Toronto Press, 2003; reproduction of original three volumes published between 1985 and 1987).

2. Michael J. Walsh, *The Cardinals: Thirteen Centuries of the Men behind the Papal Throne* (Grand Rapids: Eerdmans, 2011), 78.

in Modena in 1477, and his father had already established what his life would be. His brother indeed made a remarkable name for himself in law: counselor of justice in Florence, later envoy of Modena to Rome, and ultimately made Knight of the Spur and Count Palatine by Pope Leo X.[3]

Jacopo followed his father into legal studies in Ferrara, where his family had moved from Modena in 1488. In 1498 he made the formative acquaintance of Pietro Bembo, who, like Sadoleto, was then studying law. Not unlike a great many others in the Renaissance (e.g., Petrarch, Laelius Socinus, and even Calvin), they both desired to pursue the life of humane letters, the *studia humanitatis*, and together, against both their fathers' wishes, left off the study of law and initiated machinations to go to Rome. While Bembo barely settled into his studies in Ferrara before decamping, he spent years trying to secure a position in the curia.[4] Sadoleto, conversely, found employment in what must have seemed an idyllic situation, joining himself to the household of Oliviero Caraffa, erstwhile archbishop of Naples (by a special arrangement Caraffa held the right to appoint the succeeding archbishops) and cardinal priest of Santi Marcellino e Pietro.[5] Caraffa was a powerful member of the curia when Sadoleto became his client, as the archbishop was head of the Sacred College, a fitting climax to a career that had seen him made cardinal in 1467, serve as an envoy multiple times on behalf of the papacy (unremarkable considering his ties to King Ferdinand I of Aragon, who had seen to Caraffa's appointment as archbishop of Naples), and also commanded the papal fleet that sacked Smyrna in 1472.[6] Caraffa hired Sadoleto to be his amanuensis, for while Caraffa had a legal education, he sought, as did many of the cardinals, the eloquence of the humanists. Caraffa devoted himself to the study of the fathers, and he introduced them to his young ward. It can be easily enough surmised that the powerful cardinal saw an ecclesiastical career for his talented secretary.

Despite all the advantages connected to Cardinal Caraffa, Sadoleto's life in Rome proved less than gratifying. He certainly moved in the circles of the humanists, frequenting the several villas and semi-organized *collegia*, or academies, known as *horti*, since meetings were held in the gardens of the villas. Sadoleto was particularly attached to the *hortus* of Angelo Colocci. While Colocci dedicated his villa in particular to humane studies, in a 1529 letter to his frequent host, Sadoleto recalls that all the arts and sciences were discussed there. The most well-known of the *horti* was Johannes Goritz's.

3. Douglas, *Sadoleto*, 4.
4. Carol Kidwell, *Pietro Bembo: Lover, Linguist, Cardinal* (Montreal: McGill-Queens University Press, 2004), 114–19.
5. Douglas, *Sadoleto*, 7–8.
6. Walsh, *Cardinals*, 142–46.

Born in Luxembourg around 1450, Goritz Latinized his name to Coricius. Whereas Colocci's *hortus* left no legacy, Coricius transferred the popular Rhenish cult of St. Anne to Rome and dedicated his *hortus* to her.[7] Every year on the feast of St. Anne, the members of the *hortus* would gather in the church of St. Agostino in which Coricius had commissioned statues of St. Anne, the Blessed Virgin, and the Christ child, and there affix poems written to St. Anne or to Coricius, to the patronal statue. These were all gathered into a book by Blosio Palladio in 1524, titled *Coryciana*.[8] Sadoleto spent his leisure writing poetry, but he thought so little of it that he kept only a few poems, with only three examples extant: his *De Cajo curtio*, *Curtio Lacu*, and the most well-known of his works, *Carmen de statua Laocoontis*, which has interested even contemporary scholars.[9] The Laocoön was a statue from the ancient world depicting the death of Laocoön (a Trojan priest) and his sons by serpents sent by Poseidon. The statue was known in antiquity, as Pliny the Elder mentions it (*Naturalis historiae* 36.37), and it is through Laocoön's mouth that Virgil warned the Trojans in the *Aeneid* (2.49) that "timeo Danaos et dona ferentes" (I fear Greeks bearing gifts). In 1506 a farmer tilling ground in the old palace of Titus unearthed the sculpture, offering an occasion for Sadoleto to pen his poem. So well was Sadoleto's *Carmen* received that he obtained his first benefice at San Lorenzo in Damaso, conferred on him by Cardinal Caraffa, who himself had seen to the restoration of a statue of "Pasquino."[10] Pope Julius II liked the poem so much that he rewarded Sadoleto with a manuscript of Plato.[11]

Rome also brought Sadoleto into contact with numerous other humanists, chief among them Baldassare Castiglione, who took Sadoleto's friend Pietro Bembo as one of the models for his *Book of the Courtier*. Sadoleto seems to have been in love with a well-known courtesan in Rome, the beauty Lucrezia Cugnatis, also called Imperia. The Bolognese poet and Vatican librarian Beroaldo on three different occasions identified Sadoleto as a suitor for her. We know little more than what Beroaldo states, and as Sadoleto was not in orders at the time, there is little need to make anything of this other than infatuation.[12]

7. Kidwell, *Bembo*, 171.

8. D'Amico, *Renaissance Humanism*, 109.

9. Marian H. Lo, "Outscreaming the Laocoön: Sensation, Special Effects, and the Moving Image," *Oxford Art Journal* 34, no. 3 (2011): 393–414.

10. Douglas, *Sadoleto*, 10.

11. E. T. Campagnac and K. Forbes, introduction to *Sadoleto on Education: A Translation of the "De Pueris recte Instituendis,"* ed. and trans. E. T. Campagnac and K. Forbes (Oxford: Oxford University Press, 1916), xiii.

12. Douglas, *Sadoleto*, 10.

Yet however much the curia's demands for rhetoricians made Rome a humanist paradise, Sadoleto's life proved hectic, and this only increased in the decade following Caraffa's death in 1511. That year also saw the death of both his father and Imperia, and though attaching himself to the household of the Genoese émigré Federigo Fregoso, he left Rome for Genoa upon the accession of Leo X. In 1512, however, Leo X recalled Sadoleto, along with Pietro Bembo, to Rome to be his secretaries. Leo X's court hardly resembled a humanist *hortus*, for Leo X preferred the hunt to books, and instead of lively after-dinner debates over Platonism, Leo X found amusement in the Dominican jester Fra Mariano Fetti.[13] Leo X charged Sadoleto, as had Caraffa, with crafting his correspondence, and Sadoleto's hand appears in numerous documents, some mundane, such as the numerous grants of indulgences, but others of real significance, including letters touching Leo X's part in the Luther controversy.[14] Leo X prized Sadoleto and Bembo, and while their lives consisted to a great extent of curial bureaucratic drudgery, and while they also had little influence at the papal court, they both accrued benefices, and Sadoleto to such an extent that in 1518 he was able to purchase a villa on the Quirinal Hill, just inside the old city walls. Though the property was filled with ruins, Sadoleto was able to set up his own garden and start a vineyard. The biggest benefice came in April 1517, when Leo X bestowed on him the bishopric of Carpentras, the erstwhile abode of Petrarch. Sadoleto, as was the form, balked, but eventually accepted the post, even though he would for years be an absentee bishop.[15]

The year 1518 would begin peacefully enough, but by August Sadoleto was involved in the Luther affair, instructing Cajetan in Augsburg on August 23 to take Luther into custody and bring him to Rome, and to ask the emperor for assistance if needed. On the same day, Sadoleto penned a letter to Frederick the Wise asking for help, but when Frederick balked, Leo X through Sadoleto wrote to Cajetan again, giving him legatine authority to try the case in Augsburg.[16] In 1518 Sadoleto emerged as one of Leo X's chief advocates for a proposed Crusade against the Turk. After a procession in which Leo X walked barefoot as a penance, Sadoleto held forth on the great danger of the Turk. He

13. Fra Mariano was also a patron of the arts in his own right; see Cynthia Stollhans, "Fra Mariano, Peruzzi and Polidoro da Caravaggio: A New Look at Religious Landscapes in Renaissance Rome," *Sixteenth Century Journal* 23, no. 3 (Autumn 1992): 506–25.

14. For Sadoleto's correspondence as papal secretary, see Vincenzo Costanzi, ed., *Jacopi Sadoleti S. R. E. Cardinalis, Epistolae Leonis X., Clementis VII., Pauli III. Nomine scriptae. Accessit Antonii Florebelli, De vita ejusdem Sadoleti commentarius et Epistolarum liber* (Rome: G. Salomonius, 1759).

15. Douglas, *Sadoleto*, 22.

16. Douglas, *Sadoleto*, 25.

proved inadequate as a homilist to the extent that few could hear him, but he preached loudly enough that the Venetian ambassador took offense (Venice feared a Crusade would endanger its interests in the East). The substance of his sermon touched on the need for the unity of Christendom in the face of the Turkish menace.[17] Sadoleto would later pen a long *oratio* to the French on the war with the Turk.[18] The death of Emperor Maximilian at the start of 1519 accelerated the Luther affair and put added pressure on Sadoleto as papal secretary, especially as Bembo had grown ill and listless, leaving Rome in April 1519 to return to Venice. Sadoleto had yet to go to Carpentras, which doubtless posed a real enticement, for when Bembo returned to Rome later in 1519, he found an anxious Sadoleto.[19]

Sadoleto's growing desire to get out of Rome can be seen in his series of letters to his friend and fellow humanist Christophe Longueil at the end of 1519 and the beginning of 1520, complaining of the pace of life and expressing the hope to find leisure in Carpentras (*trans alpes*). There he could devote himself to serious study and writing something of his own, as opposed to being a cipher for Leo X.[20] But in 1521 with Leo X's death, Sadoleto, instead of going to Carpentras, went first to Modena and then back to Rome. His meanderings seem related to Pope Adrian VI's ambivalence about humanism. Though certainly an admirer of Erasmus—Adrian VI had obtained a post for him at Louvain—the new pontiff, as portrayed by Girolamo Negri, was at best lukewarm to the Renaissance mind: "[Sadoleto] is well . . . secluded from the public and indifferent to preferment especially in view of the fact that the Pope, while reading a certain elegant work in Latin the other day happened to remark, 'This is the work of a poet' as though he were ridiculing eloquence. And again, when he was shown the Laocoön in the Belvedere as a wonderful and excellent thing, he said, 'Those are the idols of the ancients.'"[21]

Unsurprisingly, Sadoleto left Rome in April 1523, finally coming to Carpentras in May, but he was there only a brief time, for with Adrian VI's death, yet another Medici—Giulio, the cousin of Leo X—was elected Clement VII on November 18, 1523. Clement VII's pontificate eventuated in disaster, as his series of alliances and his dealings with England all ended calamitously.

17. Walsh, *Cardinals*, 79; Douglas, *Sadoleto*, 23–24.

18. Jacopo Sadoleto, *De Bello susipiendocontra Turcas ad Ludonicum Christianissimum Galliarum Regem*, in *Opera quae extant omnia: ad eloquentiam, philosophiam, ac theologiam pertinentia* (Moguntiae: Rhodius, 1607), 695–737 (the *oratio* actually runs fifty-four pages—it is mispaginated in this work).

19. Douglas, *Sadoleto*, 23.

20. Jacopo Sadoleto, *Epistolae quotquot extant proprio nomine scriptae, etc.*, Pars Prima (Rome: G. Salomonius, 1760), 41–49, 52–76.

21. Letter of March 17, quoted in Douglas, *Sadoleto*, 32.

Sadoleto for his part strongly counseled Clement VII to take a neutral position in the Habsburg-Valois wars, but to no avail. Clement VII entered
into league with Francis I in December 1524, only to see the French army
crushed at Pavia on February 24, 1525, after only a few hours of fighting,
with Charles V capturing Francis I.[22] Clement VII now had to scramble for
new allies, and a hesitant Sadoleto oversaw correspondence to Machiavelli
in Florence and Francesco Guiccardini in the Romagna. Sadoleto also had
a correspondence with Lorenzo Campeggio in the Holy Roman Empire,
who wrote Sadoleto that the pope's alliance with Francis I had emboldened
the Lutherans, leading them to think that the emperor would be willing to
meet with them on new terms. Campeggio, seemingly obtuse to the religious
questions, argued for a political solution to the Luther controversy, which
Sadoleto found untenable.[23]

In May of 1526 everything that Sadoleto had stood for, and for which he
had argued in his private entreaties to the pope, came to frustration when
Clement VII, to stem the emperor's power, entered into the League of Cognac
with Francis I and the northern Italian city-states. Both Sadoleto and Castiglione prophesied doom for Rome, and Sadoleto protested that not Charles V
but Suleiman the Magnificent was the real threat to peace. The league hardly
survived its constitution, for Francis I had no motivation to enter Italy again.
With the league faring poorly, the imperial ambassador to Rome Don Hugue
de Mancado, in collusion with the powerful family of Colonna, led an assault
on Rome on September 20, 1526, that met no resistance from the populace
but left Sadoleto and Clement VII hiding in Castel Sant'Angelo, with the
Vatican—Sadoleto's apartment included—ransacked by the brigands.[24] The
episode showed Clement VII his tenuous hold on the city and indeed that his
intrigues with the league could hardly end happily. He made peace with the
Colonna and recalled the papal troops from Romagna, which allowed him by
October 1526 to regain control of the city, but as Mendell Creighton noted,
ultimately his "only policy was to lean on those bruised reeds, the Kings of
France and England."[25] This proved not enough, as Clement VII's actions
irritated Charles V, to whom Clement VII maintained that he was only pro-
tecting himself and therefore had joined the league. The news that the Turks
had crushed the Hungarian army at Mohács on August 29, 1526, however,

22. James D. Tracy, *Emperor Charles V, Impresario of War: Campaign Strategy, International Finance, and Domestic Politics* (Cambridge: Cambridge University Press, 2002), 44–45.
    23. Douglas, *Sadoleto*, 42–43.
    24. Walsh, *Cardinals*, 80.
    25. Mandell Creighton, *A History of the Papacy during the Period of the Reformation*
(London: Longmans, Green, 1894), 5:280.

demonstrated the truth of Sadoleto's and Castiglione's unheeded laments about the wars among the Christians. Even with peace restored to Rome through the intervention of Guiccardini with papal troops from the Romagna, nothing could prevent the advance of the twin armies of Charles V, his Spanish force led by Duke Charles III, Constable de Bourbon; and the German Landsknechts (mercenaries) under Georg von Frundsberg. With Clement VII's ally the Duke of Urbino already outwitted and Giovanni de Medici, the lone league commander of note, having been killed in battle, the league's only attempt at an offensive against the emperor ground to a halt, its hapless forces withering before the imperial armies.[26] But the imperial armies themselves were under duress, with pay in arrears and near revolt in March of 1527. Von Frundsberg, overwrought by the riot, died of a stroke. Clement VII had made terms, agreeing to pay but 60,000 ducats to Charles V (originally the imperial general Lannoy had asked for 200,000), but, even so, it was money Clement did not have. The Duke of Bourbon, taking advice from the Duke of Ferrara, made first for Florence to try to collect monies there, but here the league armies gathered, and Bourbon thought better of an attempt to take the walled city and instead turned south. When demands came to Rome for 300,000 ducats for the imperial coffers, Clement VII decided to put his money into Rome's defenses.

Rightly fearing an impending calamity, Sadoleto decamped from Rome by April 17, 1527. He arrived in Carpentras on May 3. On May 5, Charles of Bourbon and the imperial troops arrived outside Rome, and on May 6, under cover of fog, stormed the city. The sack lasted for three days, though both the Spaniards and the Germans invented ways to prolong it on a more systematic level.[27] Upon hearing of the enormity, Sadoleto penned laments about its cause, affixing his blame to the appropriate malefactors: the policies of the pope's councillors, the wiles of *fortuna*, the evil of the Lutheran Landsknechts, and the decadence of the curia. With regard to the last one, the papal court, the cause effected divine justice. Further, while it may seem that by his absence Sadoleto had abandoned the pope, in reality, as he wrote to Bembo, it was actually God who had brought him to a safe haven, "a place itself free from every terror and tumult." But even this did not slake his sorrow, which conquered any medicine. He was so distraught, so overcome

26. Judith Hook, *The Sack of Rome, 1527* (New York: Macmillan, 1972), 107–8.
27. Luigi Guicciardini, *The Sack of Rome*, ed. and trans. James H. McGregor (New York: Italica, 1993), 106–16. This is the only substantial contemporary source for the campaign leading up to the sack, and the sack itself. Luigi Guicciardini was the brother of the well-known humanist Francesco Guicciardini.

with anguish, that he declared, "I am not able to strive for quietude, as I have forgotten humane letters."[28]

He remembered them soon enough. Carpentras became a new *hortus* for him, the garden of a life spent composing treatises and commentaries and crafting epistles. Sadoleto's correspondence mirrors the worlds of both humanism and the church: besides Erasmus and Bembo, he corresponded with members of the Sacred College, including Gonzaga, Negri, Contarini, Pole, Farnese, Cajetan, and Fregoso; but he also wrote to Bonifacio Amerbach in Basle, Guillaume Bude in Paris, Andrea Alciato in Bourges (and later in Avignon), and even King Sigismund of Poland. His letters often took hortatory turns. In one letter to Erasmus, he urged the prince of humanists to hold the course for Christendom's survival. After setting out the dire world, in which the church is assaulted on all sides by the machines of war and wickedness, and asserting that only the grace of God can sustain her, he concluded: "Indeed to this God and Lord, if we will try to recall this grace as we ought, both we ourselves shall find the blessed life, and our labor will be neither useless nor unfruitful to others."[29] He had already published a commentary on Psalm 50 (51), the *Miserere mei*, in 1525.[30] The work garnered high praise from Erasmus, who lauded Sadoleto's lucidity, clarity, and joining of candid diction with the heights of piety; such a book, Erasmus said, gave him hope for the future of Rome (*confido futurum*).[31] To this Sadoleto would add a defense of philosophy, *De Laudibus Philosophiae*;[32] a treatise on education, *De liberis recte instituendis liber*;[33] and a commentary on Paul's Epistle to the Romans.[34] Arguably his treatise on education most clearly gives the measure of Sadoleto's soul and mind. Translated into both English and French, it championed the study of Plato, poured contempt on the scholastics, and saw philosophy as the pinnacle of life, for in it was the love and cultivated appreciation of wisdom. This love of liberal learning marked his letters, and in particular one he wrote to his friend Nicolaus Teupulaus after just four years as papal secretary, lamenting that his work kept him from those things that actually gave life meaning and without which life had no value—that is, those studies that were ends in themselves, having value apart from whatever utility may be drawn from them, namely, humane studies.[35] He also penned a treatise,

28. Sadoleto, *Epistolae quotquot . . . Pars Prima*, 209.
29. Sadoleto, *Epistolae quotquot . . . Pars Prima*, 338.
30. Sadoleto, *Interpretation in Psalmum Miserere Mei Deus*, in *Opera* (1607), 859–90.
31. Sadoleto, *Epistolae quotquot . . . Pars Prima*, 136–37.
32. Jacopo Sadoleto, *De Laudibus Philosophiae* (Basileae: Bryling[erus]), 1541.
33. Jacopo Sadoleto, *De liberis recte instituendis liber* (Lyons: Gryphius, 1535).
34. Jacopo Sadoleto, *In Pauli Epistolam ad Romanos Commentarii* (Lyons: Gryphius, 1535).
35. Sadoleto, *Epistolae quotquot . . . Pars Prima*, 21–26.

Ad Senatum Populumque Germaniae, tracing how Germany received its faith from Rome, beckoning the wayward Germans back to the fold of Rome and away from the heresies of Luther.[36] Despite his defense of the Catholic faith, Sadoleto's scriptural work was not met with enthusiasm in Rome; indeed, his commentaries on the Psalms were proscribed by Tammaso Badia, Master of the Sacred Palace. In response, in 1534, Sadoleto sent his cousin's son, Paulo Sadoleto, to Rome to intercede for him. Sadoleto wisely directed his young cousin, armed with a clarification, to Contarini, and through him was able to obtain approval for his books.[37]

In December 1536 Pope Paul III, having recalled Sadoleto to Rome to take part in a commission, made him a cardinal. Now with Contarini, Reginald Pole, Gian Pietro Caraffa, and his erstwhile nemesis Badia, inter alios, Sadoleto joined the commission, headed by the former Venetian diplomat Contarini, formed to address the pressing matter of reform.[38] The members of the commission may be thought largely Erasmian in their sentiments: advocates for reform but hardly clerics who wanted to give in to Protestant demands. Sadoleto would preach the opening sermon to the commission, prophetically addressing the papal court, declaring that it was up to Paul III to act for the church's benefit and that the clergy were held in bad odor by the laity and were in need of reform. The current ills of the church Sadoleto placed at the feet of past popes.[39] In 1537 the commission produced the *Consilium de emendanda ecclesia*, which called for sweeping reforms. Sadoleto wrote his own report, but whether in dissent or clarification is not clear. Richard M. Douglas intimates that he sought some new ways beyond the constant cycle of reform, reform, reform; Gleason thinks it largely an elaboration of ways forward.[40] Sadoleto's own proclivities as they touched reform can be gauged by a 1537 letter to Duke George of Saxony. Sadoleto stated his agreement with Erasmus that, had cooler heads prevailed at the beginning of the Luther affair, the church would have never suffered schism, or at least would have been unified shortly after the whole storm broke. His letter also details his hopes for reform involving the whole church, though certainly centered on Paul III, "vir natura bonus" (a man good by his very nature).[41]

36. Sadoleto, *Ad Principes Populosque Germania exhortatio*, in *Opera*, 738–73.
37. Douglas, *Sadoleto*, 88–89.
38. Elizabeth Gleason, *Gasparo Contarini: Venice, Rome, and Reform* (Berkeley: University of California Press, 1993), 140–49.
39. Gleason, *Contarini*, 142.
40. Douglas, *Sadoleto*, 106; Gleason, *Contarini*, 143.
41. Sadoleto, *Epistolae Pars Secunda*, 500–506.

Sadoleto's conciliatory approach sheds light on his June 1537 letter to Philip Melanchthon. In it Sadoleto praised the humanist and educator, commending him for his talents and virtues, lauding the genius and eloquence of his writing,[42] and noting that he valued talented scholars, even if they dissented from him in important ways, for the contrary opinions were the dispositions of the arrogant and the haughty; thus, Sadoleto concluded, Melanchthon had no little part of his love.[43] He signed it, "Farewell my most learned Melanchthon, and hold us your most beloved friend."[44] Melanchthon's favorable impression led him to copy the letter to two friends, but he never responded, initially it seems from not knowing exactly what to make of the letter. Later, when he read the *Consilium de emendenda ecclesia*, he recoiled on learning that Sadoleto, along with Jerome Aleander, had signed a letter that prohibited Erasmus's *Colloquies*.[45] But Melanchthon's slight proved of no real moment when compared with reactions by the controversialists in the empire. Johann Cochlaeus, Johann Eck, and Johannes Fabri of Vienna all saw the letter as a poor precedent, and one that tried to distinguish the humanist Melanchthon from the heretic Melanchthon. Whatever the letter was, it showed the divergence within the church of Rome about how best to approach Protestants. Cardinal Giovanni Morone thought colloquies of little help, since the Protestants were far better at parsing Scripture than the Catholics in general, but this did not mean he was against conciliation. He thought a general council was called for to embolden the faithful of the Roman flock for evangelization. Nonetheless, Morone wrote Sadoleto that the intransigence of such as Cochlaeus had done little to help the situation in the empire.[46] Contarini and Pole, as well as Bembo, all backed the colloquy system, which in 1537 still had both Charles V's and Ferdinand of Austria's support. Sadoleto's letter to Melanchthon was but the first, however, of several epistles that disappointed the more rigorous party in the empire. In October 1537 Sadoleto wrote the dean of Passau, Rupert von Mosham, a letter that irritated Eck more than the one to Melanchthon. In 1538 Sadoleto published his treatise to the German people and princes, in which he asserted that the church had been corrupt and that the grievances of the Reformers, but not their remedies, were legitimate.[47]

---

42. Carlos Gottlieb Bretschneider, ed., *Philippi Melanthonis Opera quae supersunt omnia*, Corpus Reformatorum (Halle: C. A. Schwetschke, 1836), 3:380.

43. Bretschneider, *Melanthonis*, 3:381–82.

44. Bretschneider, *Melanthonis*, 3:382–83.

45. Douglas, *Sadoleto*, 120.

46. For the life and work of Giovanni Cardinal Morone, see Adam Patrick Robinson, *The Career of Cardinal Giovanni Morone (1509–1580): Between Council and Inquisition* (Farnham, UK: Ashgate, 2012).

47. Bietenholz and Deutscher, *Contemporaries of Erasmus*, 185.

Also in 1538 he wrote to Johann Sturm in Strasbourg a letter that got placed on the index in 1559.[48]

This background frames what is perhaps Sadoleto's most famous letter, that written to the people of Geneva in March 1539 and published that year in Lyons. As already noted, Guillaume Farel believed Pierre Caroli was behind Sadoleto's actions, and for some years the former bishop of Geneva, Pierre de La Baume, was also thought to have had a hand in the letter.[49] But given the recent events in Geneva of which Sadoleto had no doubt learned from Caroli (that Calvin and Farel had made themselves odious to the magistrates), and recalling Sadoleto's willingness to appeal for conciliation based on the notion of a purified church that rested its life in the embrace of the past and its traditions, there is nothing in or about the letter that indicates it not to have been wholly from Sadoleto, who himself claimed inspiration for it from the Holy Spirit. Indeed, it models what one would expect from such a humanist cleric. Sadoleto began the epistle noting Geneva's virtues, the qualities it had as a republic, and how love had characterized its life, at least until recently.[50] He then noted how of late, seduced by self-aggrandizing and seditious individuals, Geneva had against its character turned aside from the truth. This elicited an appeal that they should return to moderate ways and to their true Mother, who lamented their loss.[51] Sadoleto then took quick measure of the Reformers, characterizing them as novel interlopers, proclaiming newly learned interpretations of Holy Scripture that were in fact but fraud and malice masquerading as knowledge. Sadoleto actually here quite cleverly turned the Reformers' claims back against them: what the Reformers said the Scriptures taught were the actual novelties; what was clear and obvious the church had always held, and Sadoleto was now ready to declare it to the Genevans anew.[52] Sadoleto even went after the Reformers on the question of justification by faith alone, asserting that they had not invented this doctrine, that the Catholic Church had not buried it, that it was part of the deposit of faith, and that the version preached by the Reformers in fact mutilated the truth of faith. Faith, he asserted, has a far wider meaning than that given it by the Reformers, for it comprehends love, without which we cannot see God, in that love consummates the Christian's life. "And so this is why without the Holy Spirit nothing of ours is either pleasing or acceptable to God, and

48. Douglas, *Sadoleto*, 133–35.
49. See Wulfert de Greef, *The Writings of John Calvin: An Introductory Guide* (Louisville: Westminster John Knox, 2008), 137–38.
50. CO 5:369.
51. CO 5:370–71.
52. CO 5:371–72.

thus nothing can be pleasing or acceptable without love. Therefore when we say that by faith alone in God and Jesus Christ we can be saved, in this very faith we understand that love ought to obtain the highest rank, which is the principle and most powerful cause of our salvation."[53]

Sadoleto also broached themes of humility before the claims of the past, a concern he had raised with the treatise to the Germans. For Sadoleto, the turning aside to false worship could only lead to ruin; the humility of repentance was the one great remedy, looking to those traditions fixed by one's most wise and holy ancestors.[54] Sadoleto also played the Catholic humanist in lampooning the Reformers on the Eucharist, citing them for limiting God's power through the use of philosophy as opposed to holding faithfully to what the church had taught everywhere for the past fifteen hundred years, while these charlatans, however, had been about for less than the past twenty-five.[55] Sadoleto moved to his conclusion with a wonderfully depicted scenario of a Catholic and a Protestant before the throne of God pleading their case on the day of judgment. The Catholic confessed his contempt for wicked prelates, but asserted his love of the faith that the fathers through his ancestors had left him. The Protestant asserted that he stood justified based on his own understanding of what Scripture teaches regardless of what may be learned from the fathers and the church, and that he separated from it because it did not recognize the speaker's prophetic voice (whether Sadoleto overstated his case will not be considered here).[56] In the main, Sadoleto used all his humanistic resources in penning the letter, and it certainly falls within the purview of his life as a humanist.

Calvin, then living in Strasbourg, was asked by the magistrates of Berne (who had been forwarded the letter with a cry for help from Geneva) to write the response, which had not been left to any of the ministers in Geneva, and those in Berne seemed unequal to the task.[57] In brief, after finally consenting, Calvin penned his response in August 1538, and he would have none of Sadoleto's arguments. Calvin's reply cut to the chase rather quickly. After paying due respect to Sadoleto's reputation and learning, the text moved to matters pertaining to authority—tradition or the Bible; bishops and Rome, or the plain text of Scripture; a proper self-regard for our misery through self-indictment,

---

53. CO 5:375: "Quamobrem sicuti sine spiritu sancto nihil nostrum neque gratum, neque acceptum Deo est, ita neque esse sine caritate potest. Quum ergo dicimus fide sola in Deum et Iesum Christum salvos nos esse posse, in hac ipsa fide caritatem vel in primis comprehendendam esse ducimus, quae princeps et potissima nostrae salutis est causa."

54. CO 5:376.

55. CO 5:378.

56. CO 5:379–81.

57. De Greef, *Writings of Calvin*, 138.

which led to thoughts on justification—and ended with thoughts on the purity of faith. Sadoleto had blamed the multiplication of sects on the Protestants, but Calvin retorted at the end of his reply that this was ever the way of Satan, and that it was the Reformers who had borne the burden of answering the sects while Rome was too busy stewing in apathy, Calvin no doubt harkening back to his earlier assertion that Rome had been weakened by its sumptuous laziness. Calvin's reply reveals the energy of a much younger, even more enthusiastic, writer. Sadoleto's missive seems penned at leisure as the cardinal sat in his study, written as it were by a learned uncle to a nephew newly sent off to school, led astray by an unseemly young suitors. Calvin responded as the head of the new masters, to indict the moribund and corrupt establishment of the youth's school. He certainly paid initial deference to Sadoleto, but this was a commonplace as well, for the bulk of the letter, which was well more than twice the length of Sadoleto's,[58] abounded with rote Protestant criticisms of the old faith. Calvin defended his ministry, as he had with du Tillet, as a direct call by God; asserted that Sadoleto should be held suspect because of his office as a cardinal; claimed that the Reformers did not leave Rome because they were hungry (frustrated from lack of preferments); called Sadoleto's letter unbecoming "lest I would say illiberal [*ne dicam illiberale*]"; and then ran through the doctrines of *sola fide*, the Eucharist, auricular confession, the place of the saints, and finally the authority of the church, and with it, the corruption of Rome.[59] As Calvin ended the letter, he affected Sadoleto's putative Protestant before the bar of God pleading his case that neither envy, sedition, nor ambition had brought the Reformers to their choices, but the defense of the honor of God and the protection of scattered sheep (or troops); they thus embraced being cast out of "the church." He also added the plaint of one who is taught by the Reformer.[60] Calvin's reply had as well called forth the humanist and writer in him. While doubtless he would not shrink from owning the doctrines he maintained in the text, ultimately the letter was written not for Sadoleto but for Geneva, even though he doubtless enjoyed bombarding Sadoleto with what he had in his arsenal.

Ironically, the controversialists within the Catholic Church did not share Calvin's sentiments that Sadoleto was the church's champion, for they pressed Rome to do something about Sadoleto, complaining that his efforts in regard to Sturm, Melanchthon, the Germans, and the Genevans (though they had started their recriminations before the letter to Geneva) were counterproductive.

---

58. Sadoleto's letter runs just over fifteen columns in the CO (5:369–84), whereas Calvin's runs almost thirty-two (5:385–416).

59. CO 5:386, 388–89, 391, 396–402.

60. CO 5:407–13.

Cardinal Contarini, ever the diplomat, had already responded to Cochlaeus in December 1538: "I praise, most learned Cochlaeus, your zeal in guarding the doctrine of the Catholic Church: which is not in this or that corner of the world, but spread everywhere," but nonetheless, "I am quite certain that it is better to act with our adversaries so that nothing we write exasperates them, although presently, nothing offered them, however pious, however beyond reproach, does not irritate them bitterly."[61] For all the criticism, Sadoleto's approach in 1539 testifies that his and Contarini's approach held the high ground in the Catholic Church at that moment.

The final eight years of Sadoleto's life he spent trying to stay in his retreat of Carpentras. He worked hard at reforming his diocese, which had over forty parishes, and also had some forty-five priories of the Order of St. Ruf, an eleventh-century order of canons whose mother house was in Valence, some sixty miles north of Carpentras. Sadoleto lacked a schoolmaster for his cathedral school until he was able to employ, in the fall of 1535, Lorentius Volusenus, a Scot from Aberdeen. Volusenus had passed through Carpentras on his way to Italy from Paris when he showed up at Sadoleto's door. A conversation begun in the evening between the young scholar and famous humanist resumed in the morning, and Sadoleto offered him the job, which he took. Still, Volusenus's pay had to be subsidized by Charles de Guise, cardinal of Lorraine.[62] He left the job in 1537. In later years Sadoleto was so pressed for a schoolmaster that he took in Claude Baudel, onetime rector and master at Nîmes, and a known Protestant who corresponded with both Calvin and Bucer. Baudel had shown himself an accomplished scholar, having published on education and the pursuit of learning, and having written commentaries on Cicero as well. He had been at Nîmes in order to reform the university curriculum, and for a brief time was rector, but the faculty fights drove him to the smaller confines of Carpentras. He wrote Calvin that he needed the job and was not playing the Nicodemite but had stood his ground for the faith in Carpentras.[63] After hiring Baudel in the spring of 1544, the consuls released him in 1545 because of lack of means to pay him, and eventually, after returning briefly to Nîmes, he went to Geneva, where he would be ordained.[64]

For all his efforts, Sadoleto's irenic disposition bore little fruit. In 1542 Francis I moved against the Waldensians, and Sadoleto—who had many Waldensians residing in his diocese—hoped for moderation. Yet all of his

61. Fr. Dittrich, ed., *Regesten und Briefe des Cardinals Gasparo Contarini, 1483–1542* (Braunsberg: Huye, 1881), 297.
62. Douglas, *Sadoleto*, 65.
63. CO 20:373–75.
64. Douglas, *Sadoleto*, 184–85.

actions his young cousin Paulo Sadoleto, now his bishop in waiting, fought. Paulo was quick to seek repression in his future diocese and helped set up the ecclesiastical apparatus for what amounted to a martial Inquisition by Francis I in his new provinces. Paulo was a willing accomplice in the suppression of the Waldensians and as diocesan administrator argued against his cousin's conciliatory approaches. Martin du Bellay and Marguerite of Navarre both counseled moderation to Francis I, but du Bellay died in 1542, and matters moved swiftly, especially as the Waldensians themselves had begun acting violently, even attacking abbeys. Francis I's ax fell in 1545 with eleven Waldensian villages destroyed, the chief targets those of Cabrierès and Mérindol.[65]

Sadoleto, however, was not in Carpentras when this occurred. Since early 1542 he had been traveling in the service of Paul III. He had been in Italy when Paul III made him his legate to the court of Francis I to try to broker peace between Francis I and Charles V, a move that angered the emperor, as he was not the one who had broken the truce. Consequently, Sadoleto was recalled from Francis I's court. He unhappily returned to Rome at his own expense, where his counsel to the pope to meet with the emperor roused consternation in the curia, and thus by 1543 he had returned to Carpentras, where he had to battle with the papal vice legate in Avignon, Alessandro Campeggio. Sadoleto sought release from his episcopal duties, and his letters to Alessandro Farnese, the papal chancellor at this time, reflect his anxiety.

Ordered to return to Rome for the start of the Council of Trent, Sadoleto left Carpentras in March 1545, arriving in Rome in April, with the action against the Waldensians executed in that same month. Two matters dominated his years in Rome, and both pertain to the acts of the Council of Trent. The first is his objection to Trent's accepting Jerome's *Vulgata*. The conservatives of the council, along with the Dominicans and Franciscans, wanted no amendments or corrections made to the Latin text, or at best only ones done quietly. For Sadoleto the humanist, the *Vulgata*'s pitiful Latin demanded correction.[66] The other matter was the transfer of the council to Bologna, which he, along with several other cardinals, obstinately opposed. His chief ally in this was Morone, whose work in the council spanned its entirety. For both, it was a matter of imperial support and the need to keep all of Europe involved in the council.

65. Marc Venard, "Jacques Sadolet, évêque de Carpentras, et les Vaudois," *Bolletino della società di studi valdesi* 143 (1978): 44–49; and also Gabriel Audisio, *The Waldensian Dissent: Persecution and Survival, c. 1170–c. 1570*, trans. Claire Davison (Cambridge: Cambridge University Press, 1999), 190–94.

66. Douglas, *Sadoleto*, 209–10.

Over the last several months of his life, as Douglas notes, Sadoleto was in failing health.[67] He died on October 18, 1547, with his main eulogy delivered by Gian Pietro Caraffa, the nephew of his first employer, Oliviero Caraffa. Gian Pietro Caraffa—one of the founders and the first general of the Theatines (the order's name derived from Caraffa's first dioces of Chieti or the Latinized Theate), a canon lawyer, a theologian, and one of the original members of the Oratory of Divine Love—was the emerging leader of a strident Catholicism, one with little patience for conciliatory views such as Sadoleto's, Contarini's, and Morone's. He would, as Pope Paul IV, actually begin proceedings against Morone, and only the pontiff's death brought Morone out of prison.[68] That Caraffa delivered his eulogy speaks to the shift in Rome and across Europe in how Catholicism perceived and related to Protestantism, as a growing reaction emerged—embodied in Caraffa, the Jesuits, and monarchs such as Philip II of Spain—in the wake of the failure of Erasmian reforms, a reaction that mirrored Calvin's own more precise attitudes that emerged in the 1540s.

The Reformers never showed any love for Sadoleto. Luther thought him a lackey, Sleidan found him complicit in the massacre of the Waldensians, Melanchthon formally ignored his letter, and Calvin held him a calumniator at the least, one piping the Genevans to perdition. Sadoleto's life displays all the vagaries that awaited souls who sought the humanist *vita contemplativa*. He certainly was not Erasmus in his humanism or his theology, but his underlying belief, dating back to his first sermon in 1518, was the need for a united Christendom against the real threat to Christian civilization—namely, the Turk. He held no love for heresy, and none of his letters would ever show an openness to it, but his moderation never won him any friends on either side. Unlike Castellio, who wore his Protestantism lightly, Sadoleto maintained that there was no contradiction between his humanism and his Catholic faith. He was buried in his titular church, St. Peter in Chains in Rome, but in 1646 his body was exhumed, and he was interred in his cathedral in Carpentras. The church is still there, but it is no longer a cathedral.

67. Douglas, *Sadoleto*, 212.
68. Robinson, *Morone*, 87–110.

4

Michael Servetus

The Primus Adversarius

The polymath Michel de Villaneuve had a secret: living for twenty-one years in sixteenth-century Lyons, a time and town of Renaissance humanists, this virtuoso had lived a lie, indeed a double life. He might well have pulled it off had ego not gotten the better of discretion, for a vain and fateful correspondence betrayed him. From 1532 till 1553, he worked in Lyons as an editor of Bibles, a geographer, a publisher of medical treatises, and a controversialist. He even spent some years studying medicine in Paris, where his flamboyance brought ill will from his teachers, and his marginal views on judicial astrology skirted the orthodoxy of the university. But enormities written by Michel de Villaneuve's alter ego, his true self, haunted and surpassed even the notoriety of this Renaissance persona, for Michel de Villaneuve was Miguel Serveto, or Michael Servetus, a heretic decidedly odious to the Protestant Rhineland, where he first expressed his antitrinitarianism and for which views the Catholic authorities, the Inquisition, actively hunted him.

Servetus is arguably the best known of Calvin's tormentors, as many of Calvin's subsequent detractors used Servetus to launch their polemics, whether they agreed with Servetus's peculiar antitrinitarian theology or not. Thus, he stands as the *protoadversarius*, setting the stage for so many others. And while Servetus may have a claim to be Calvin's singular bête noir, he managed to make himself execrable to a great many people, both Protestant and Catholic. Jerome Aleander, Luther's antagonist at Worms and Erasmus's erstwhile roommate at the Aldine Press in Venice, in 1532 described the appearance of

Servetus's theology in *De Trinitatis erroribus* as a portent of the apocalypse, and declared that such a monster was a greater enormity than the Lutheran or Zwinglian heretics. Aleander even asserted that the Protestants' reactions to Servetus's theology were a measure of the sincerity of their faith.[1] The controversialist Johann Cochlaeus hastened, perhaps with some schadenfreude, to point out to Cardinal Quintana (Servetus's first ecclesiastical boss) that Germany was not alone in being plagued with heresy, for Spain now also had an infection.[2] The Inquisition in both Sargossa and Toulouse, as early as 1532, was on the watch for Servetus and making inquiries after his whereabouts; the inquisitors of Sargossa even sent Servetus's brother to the empire to try to coax him back to Spain. But ultimately Servetus fell into Geneva's hands, and thus the infamy surrounding his death has redounded to that city, and particularly, if not altogether fairly, to Calvin.

Servetus, as with many who followed in his theological train, was an autodidact. Apart from his academic medical training in Paris in the late 1530s, his formal education seems to have been brief, broad, and incomplete: his liberal arts education ended before he turned twenty.[3] We have no evidence that he took any degrees. His system, if system it can be called, sprang not from within or through a tradition, nor from the dialectic of the debates among the Protestants, but largely from his own keen but highly idiosyncratic imagination. He complained in 1532 that he alone had correctly apprehended God's truth: "I do not in all points agree, nor disagree, with either the one party or the other. All seem to me to have some truth and some error, and every one perceives the other's error and no one sees his own."[4] He would confess toward the end of his life that as "a young man, scarcely twenty, I was moved by a certain divine impulse to treat of this cause [the Trinity], having been taught of no man."[5]

Born September 29, 1511, his parents named him for St. Michael the archangel, whose feast day it was, and he would later, when Servetus was too dangerous a name to keep, take the name of the nearby town of Villaneuve as his toponym. Beginning his studies in Saragossa in 1524, Servetus was distinguished by his precociousness, and he soon became the secretary to Juan de Quintana, one of Charles V's chaplains. Servetus accompanied Quintana in Charles's entourage, and it may have been at the chaplain's instigation

1. Roland Bainton, *Hunted Heretic: The Life and Death of Michael Servetus, 1511–1553* (Gloucester, MA: Peter Smith, 1978), 69–70.

2. Bainton, *Hunted Heretic*, 68.

3. George Hunston Williams, *The Radical Reformation* (Kirksville, MO: Sixteenth Century Essays and Studies, 2000), 52–53.

4. Earl Morse Wilbur, trans., *Two Treatises of Servetus on the Trinity* (Cambridge, MA: Harvard University Press, 1921), 264.

5. Quoted in Bainton, *Hunted Heretic*, 73–74.

Michael Servetus

that, in 1528, he entered the University of Toulouse to study law.[6] There he encountered the world of humanism, but his study of the classics, seemingly a primer to both eloquence and the art of living well, actually turned him

6. Earl Morse Wilbur, *A History of Unitarianism and Its Antecedents* (Boston: Beacon, 1972), 52–53.

to other pursuits, specifically, theological ones. At some point in his studies, possibly in Spain, he picked up Hebrew. Also while at Toulouse, he consorted with students who met to study the Bible. Neither humanism nor the study of Scripture was dissonant with the study of law, as legal studies in France, very much part of the wider world of humanism, leaned on the study of both language and history.[7] Calvin's own life demonstrates this, as his first published work was his commentary on Seneca's *De clementia*.

Whatever Servetus picked up in Toulouse, it did not set him at odds with Quintana, for he accompanied him to Charles V's coronation in 1530 in Bologna. From there Servetus traveled to the Rhineland, where he formally parted company with Quintana and the Catholic faith.[8] The course of Servetus's travels that year remains obscure, but by July he was in Basle, the guest and interlocutor of the Reformer Johannes Oecolampadius, who remained his host for ten months.[9] Already by 1530 Servetus questioned the Nicene doctrine of the Trinity and made his opinions known to Oecolampadius, who in turn breathed them to the other Swiss Reformers. Several letters testify to the Reformer's attempts to instruct Servetus in the faith, thereby illuminating Servetus's early thought. One thing stands out from both Servetus's interaction with Oecolampadius and his later writings: he was not a unitarian in the sense in which the word is understood today, nor in its eighteenth-century Deist guise. While certainly not a trinitarian, he had come to reject the doctrine for reasons other than those of later Deists. First, deism existed in a post-Aristotelian universe of physical as opposed to teleological causality, and thus with at least a tenuously closed universe. The Deists needed their deity to create the universe in the first place, but then, having established its laws, the Deist god must not interfere, for such interference would have admitted mistakes in both the order of creation and in its governing laws. Servetus had no such god. He saw his God as that of the biblical record, the God of the writings of Ignatius of Antioch, Irenaeus of Lyons, and especially Tertullian.[10] A second difference between Servetus and unitarianism, coincident with Servetus's belief in revealed religion, is that for Servetus, Jesus, though a man, was also the Son of God, a manifestation of the eternal Word of God, even though not the eternal Son of God. For him, Jesus was divine and to be worshiped, though not as the Father.

7. Donald R. Kelley, *Foundations of Modern Historical Scholarship: Language, Law and History in the French Renaissance* (New York: Columbia University Press, 1970), see especially chap. 3, "The Science of Philology: Guillaume Budé Begins the Restoration of Roman Law," 53–85.
8. Bainton, *Hunted Heretic*, 21.
9. Williams, *Radical Reformation*, 308.
10. Bainton, *Hunted Heretic*, 42, 45.

In 1530 Servetus's nascent views were clear enough to Oecolampadius: Servetus had strayed in his judgments, giving too much weight to the wrong authors: "You grant to Tertullian more esteem than to all the Church. You deny the one Person in two natures. In denying the eternality of the Son you necessarily deny the Father is also eternal."[11] Like Calvin and the Genevans years later, Oecolampadius communicated his concerns about Servetus to his coreligionists, charging that he was contumacious and dogged in his errors, more interested in debate than in the truth. By 1553, the year of Servetus's confrontation with Calvin, all the participants in Servetus's early confrontations had died, with the exception of Bullinger, who related the history to Calvin. Bullinger referred to Servetus as "Perdetus."[12]

Basle had through the 1520s been a congenial place for dissent. After the city turned Protestant, Catholics remained largely unmolested and still attended Mass; however, after a revolution in 1529, the Mass came to an end, and the city began the prosecution of Anabaptists. Servetus's views would not be long countenanced, and seeing the handwriting on the wall, he took leave and headed in May 1531 for Strasbourg. In Strasbourg Servetus produced his first work on the Trinity, his *De Trinitatis erroribus* of 1531.[13] This text, a turgid read from an autodidact not yet twenty, set the basic contours of Servetus's thought for the rest of his life. Servetus made a clear distinction between the Word of God, which is the eternal reason or logic (logic comes from the Greek *Logos*) or manifestation of God's wisdom, and his Son, the man Jesus, who became the Son at the incarnation. This essentially adoptionist stance drew charges that he was following the ancient heretic Paul of Samosata.[14] Servetus certainly knew the ancient church writers, and probably did pick things out of the antitrinitarians, but he may also have garnered some of his thought on the unity of the deity from the Jews and Moors of his native Spain.[15] His later refinements, especially as regards his anthropology, soteriology, and cosmology, sprang still from his core beliefs but were filtered through the Neoplatonism he acquired in Lyons, doubtless from the humanism that had been fermenting there for years. Alongside Servetus's theology on the unity of the internal life of God, another axiom emerges: Christ first and foremost was known as a man. The man Christ could not be God in the same way that the Father is, yet Servetus admitted that Christ was divine in some way. Humans too are called

11. Williams, *Radical Reformation*, 308; Wilbur, *Unitarianism*, 56–58.

12. Bainton, *Hunted Heretic*, 53.

13. Michael Servetus, *De Trinitatis erroribus libri septem* (Basle, 1531).

14. Bainton, *Hunted Heretic*, 43.

15. Roland Bainton has suggested this. In *Hunted Heretic*, see especially chap. 1, "Dog of a Marrano," 3–20.

to be god, but how humans are, and how Christ is, differed markedly. Christ as God the Father's natural Son (though not natural in the Athanasian sense of sharing the same nature) perfectly expressed the logic and reason (*logos*) of the Father, the logic by which the Father created the world.[16] The man Jesus as the Son is a personification of the Word, and with this, the Word's existence terminated in the Son (Servetus would later alter this). Since through the Word as mediator God created all things, the Word was distinct from the Father, but still divine. Servetus asserted that this teaching was present in the Old Testament in the distinctions between Jehovah and Elohim, to him substantially different entities. Based on his reading of Tertullian, Servetus claimed that the Son was a distinct person only in the incarnation, and that prior to this, as the Word, there was no real separate existence from the Father, except as a manifestation of the Father.[17] Regardless, Servetus's basic understandings about the Word of God that existed from eternity ending with the coming of the "human" Jesus, who was unlike other humans in that he possessed a celestial flesh that kept him from human failings and possessed a divinity in nature analogous only to the divine Father, were all present by 1532.[18]

Bucer could not long tolerate Servetus, who after trying to clarify his ideas with the 1532 publication of *Two Dialogues on the Trinity*, realized that he would find no willing auditors in Strasbourg. And though the city had been slow to implement imperial decrees against Anabaptists, and also had not completely forbidden the Mass (celebrated in those monasteries that still existed), with Bucer's public but unthreatening denunciation of his work, Servetus had not only to go into exile but also to go into hiding. He landed in Lyons, France's second city, which had a thriving merchant class and cloth industry, a royal court, and an active and growing printing community. Humanism thrived there in the person of Symphorien Champier, to whom Servetus attached himself.[19] Other humanist lights such as François Rabelais found the presses sufficiently removed from the Sorbonne that they could print their texts in relative peace. Servetus sought more obscurity than simply distance from Paris or Strasbourg and Basle, for with his arrival in Lyons he assumed the identity of Michael de Villaneuve, the identity he would maintain for the next twenty-one years.

The printers Gaspar and Melchior Trechsel hired Servetus, who proved a talented employee. He twice edited Ptolemy's *Geographia* for them, the first edition published in 1535, a second in 1541. He also edited the Dominican

16. Servetus, *De Trinitatis*, 73–75.
17. Servetus, *De Trinitatis*, 93–94.
18. Wilbur, *Unitarianism*, 62.
19. Williams, *Radical Reformation*, 924.

and Hebraist Fra Xanthes Pagninus's Bible, published in 1542.[20] Yet even in such seemingly mundane acts as editing texts, Servetus produced controversy. With respect to the biblical text, he asserted that the Old Testament prophets spoke not of the future but of their own times, albeit in exalted language (e.g., the servant of the Lord in Isaiah was not a prophecy of Christ but an allusion to Cyrus); he removed the headings from the Pagninus edition of the Song of Songs, headings that presented it as a mystical love ballad between Christ and the soul. For Servetus, the *Canticle Canticorum* was just Semitic love poetry. His edition of Ptolemy's *Geographia* likewise was to cause him problems later, for he included in his preface a statement by Leonard Fries by way of Pirckheimer that Palestine was not a land flowing with milk and honey but rather a desert.[21]

Furthermore, Servetus's erudition was not confined to his linguistic skills, for in Lyons he took up the study of medicine; the Neoplatonist Symphorien Champier was also a medical doctor, and Servetus became his pupil. Indeed, Servetus's first publications in Lyons in 1536 defended Champier from the attacks of the Lutheran doctor Leonard Fuchs.[22] Servetus also would publish on the medicinal use of syrups, a book largely treating digestion. It may have been Champier who pressed Servetus to further his studies in medicine in Paris. His two years at Paris give us a glimpse into why and how the final tragedy of his life played out. Once in Paris in 1536, though apparently not a *magister*, Servetus was allowed to lecture on geography. He also took part in the dissecting of cadavers. It seems that in Paris he discovered the nature of the pulmonary artery of the heart.[23] Even though not understanding it fully (he still held to Galen's theory that blood came from the liver and was consumed by the body for nourishment), he did anticipate William Harvey's later discoveries about the nature of the pulmonary artery and how blood circulates through the heart.[24] He also incorporated astrology into his lectures. Astrology assumed an uneasy place in the sixteenth-century mind. Philosophers and theologians disagreed about both its usefulness and licitness: Pico della Mirandola unequivocally denounced it, while his teacher and friend

20. Pagninus, or Pagnini, was the first translator to use verse divisions in his entire Bible, something that had been previously done with the Psalms. His edition had come out in Paris in 1528. See Paul F. Grendler, "Italian Biblical Humanism and the Papacy, 1515–1535," in *A Companion to Biblical Humanism and Scholasticism in the Age of Erasmus*, ed. Erika Rummel (Leiden: Brill, 2008), 238–47.

21. Bainton, *Hunted Heretic*, 95–96.

22. Bainton, *Hunted Heretic*, 102.

23. Williams, *Radical Reformation*, 501.

24. William Harvey first described the process of blood circulation in his *Exercitatio anatomica de motu cordis et sanguinis in animalibus* (Frankfurt: William Fitzerius, 1628).

Marsilius Ficino asserted that the stars in their courses affected the body but had no hold over the soul; Philip Melanchthon would not travel to England, for the stars portended shipwreck, while his failure to deliver lectures because of omens nettled Luther.[25] No one disagreed that the stars, sun, and moon affected seasons, weather, tides, animal activities, and so on, especially in a world still dominated by Aristotle's cosmology that linked all causes. While the church denounced Plato's doctrine that the stars were intelligences, it professed that God still worked through angelic powers and other secondary causes. Nonetheless, the church roundly denounced judicial astrology—the telling of fortunes and the predicting of future events—on the grounds that such beliefs subjected the soul to the greater created order. Astrology enjoyed a good reception in Renaissance Europe, but it was a two-edged sword, and knaves abounded.[26] Thus, when Servetus began commenting on astrology in his classes, he skirted peril.

The medical faculty, which had little use for astrology and fell to the reactionary side of the debate, became alarmed when it learned that Servetus, or Villaneuve as they knew him, was promoting astrology in his lectures. Servetus in response published an *Apologia*, though really only admitting to the most benign forms of the art. Nonetheless, the dean of the medical faculty, Thagault, took action to suppress the book. Servetus paid the printer extra to get the book published before the Paris court could suppress it, but suppress it they did. And even though Servetus cleared himself before the Parlement of Paris of all charges of teaching judicial astrology, he was nonetheless reprimanded for the haughty way he had addressed his teachers on the matter; without naming names, he had called some of his mentors apes and dunces for neglecting astrology, and had been verbally abusive to Dean Thagault when the latter asked him not to bring out his *Apologia*.[27] Servetus's certitude had almost gotten the better of him, and his abuse of his teachers speaks to a certain intellectual hubris, if not narcissism. One needs no recourse to the stars to see what this foretold.

Servetus did not finish his degree at Paris, but returned to Lyons, becoming the personal physician of Pierre Parmier, the archbishop of Vienne, who had attended his geography lectures in Paris.[28] There he continued his edito-

25. See Sachiko Kusukawa, ed., *Philip Melanchthon: Orations on Philosophy and Education* (Cambridge: Cambridge University Press, 1999), 113–25.
26. Roland Bainton points out the numerous predictions that goaded the 1525 Peasants' War in *Hunted Heretic*, 113.
27. Michael Servetus, *Discussion Aplogétique pour l'Astrologie,* trans. and ed. Jean Dupèbe (Geneva: Librairie Droz, 2004), 23–29.
28. Bainton, *Hunted Heretic*, 129.

rial work, but also began the work that defined and determined his life, the *Christianismi restitutio*. At least a portion of this he sent to Calvin around 1546, for around 1545 the two took up correspondence via a Protestant printer in Lyons.[29] Though Servetus affected de Villaneuve, and Calvin used an old pseudonym, Charles d'Espeville, each knew who the other was. But Servetus became combative, marking up and returning a copy of Calvin's *Institutes* that the Genevan had sent him as a way to inform Servetus of his views and avoid further overly long letters. Servetus's letters turned insulting: to the Genevan minister Abel Poupin he wrote that the Genevans worshiped as their god a three-headed Cerberus (Pluto's dog that guarded the gate to Hades).[30] Calvin wearied of the fruitless correspondence. In 1546 he wrote to Farel, "Servetus lately wrote to me, and added to his letter a long volume of his delusions, arrogantly boasting that I will soon see marvels and hitherto unheard of things. Were I to allow him, he would come here. But I have no wish to make a promise; for were he to come, and were my authority to prevail, I shall never allow him to leave alive."[31] As ominous as this letter sounds, Calvin's biographer T. H. L. Parker feels it could just as easily have been a warning for Servetus to stay away.[32] At the least, Calvin knew in 1546 who Michael de Villeneuve was, yet seemed in no hurry to turn him over to the inquisitors.

Servetus published his *Christianismi restitutio* in 1553, so named perhaps to contrast with Calvin's *Institutio*,[33] but numerous writers, including Erasmus, used the term as equivalent to reform and renewal. Divided into seven books, the total text runs over seven hundred pages and is broken into numerous subsections. Servetus's thought treats numerous concerns: the Trinity, baptism, the Lord's Supper, the Holy Spirit, and the composition of human nature. This sets the context for his first thoughts on the pulmonary artery. Servetus believed that the oxygenation of the blood was actually the vivifying effects of the Holy Spirit, the preliminary steps in making humans divine, in that humans were already bound to God by dint of creation and life itself.[34]

29. Bernard Cottret, *Calvin: A Biography*, trans. M. Wallace McDonald (Grand Rapids: Eerdmans, 2000), 216–18.

30. This letter was brought up at Servetus's trial (CO 8, app. 2, *Actes du Procès de Michel Servet*, 751).

31. CO 12:283: "Servetus nuper ad me scripsit ac literis adiunxit longum volumen suorum deliriorum cum thrasonica iactantia, me stupenda et hactenus inaudita visurum. Si mihi placeat, huc se venturum recipit. Sed nolo fidem meam interponere. Nam si venerit, modo valeat mea autoritas, vivum exire nunquam patiar."

32. T. H. L. Parker, *John Calvin* (Hunts, UK: Lion, 1975), 140.

33. Philip Schaff, *A History of the Christian Church*, vol. 8, *The Swiss Reformation* (New York: Charles Scribner & Sons, 1892), 733.

34. Michael Servetus, *Christianismi restitutio: totius ecclesiae apostolicae est ad sua limina vocatio, in integrum restitua cognitione Dei, fidei Christi, iustificationis nostrae, regenerastionis*

This peculiar doctrine of the Holy Spirit, who brought inspiration through respiration, also marked a change in how Servetus viewed pagan thought. *De Trinitatis erroribus*, whose Christology was determined strongly by Servetus's reading of Tertullian, had showed also Tertullian's phobia of anything smacking of pagan thought: "What hath Jerusalem to do with Athens," as Tertullian famously said. Servetus had said the same, though with less élan: "The doctrine of our teacher, which obviously cannot deceive, is that the blind cannot lead the blind. If the book descended from heaven, would you believe that it contained anything superfluous or not pertinent to learning? I find all knowledge and philosophy in the Bible, do you not clearly see, as Paul says here, that the wisdom of the Greeks is base and mundane."[35] The *Christianismi restitutio*, however, finds a completely different Servetus, one clearly influenced by Neoplatonism, undoubtedly mediated to him by Symphorien Champier at the least. In Servetus's mature thought, the source of all is still the Father, who manifested the Word, as the Good manifested Light in Plato and the Neoplatonists. In Platonic thought, Light mediated existence from the Good to temporal reality. Servetus borrows this whole cloth and reads it into both his Christology and his cosmology:

> Matter is labeled *tohou* and *bohu*, formless and empty, since it had not yet been made to participate in light. By this we know that form arises from light. Material forms and existence alone do not come from light, but souls and spirits do as well, since light is the life of men and the life of spirits. Light excels in beauty all heavenly and earthly things. The very form of Light comprehends everything, for it brings illumination. Light alone, both earthly and heavenly, both spiritual and material, illumines and transforms, and from her comes every form and beautification of the world.[36]

Servetus saw the world as an emanation of God, and his language was taken by his critics as pantheism. It is true that the church fathers looked at the Word's relationship to the cosmos in similar terms, but for them the Word mediated to humans the true God, not some secondhand deity, which was the argument of Arius. Maximus the Confessor could write, "Grace irradiates nature with a supra-natural light, and by the transcendence of its glory raises nature above its natural limits."[37] For the church fathers, Christ as mediator is

---

baptismi, et caenae domini manducatinis. Restituto denique nobis regno caelesti, Babylonis impiae captivitate soluta, et Antichristo cum suis pen itus destructo (Lyons: n.p., 1553), 177–85.

35. Servetus, *De trinitatis*, 78v–79r.

36. Servetus, *Christianismi restitutio*, 151.

37. Quoted in *The Philokalia*, trans. G. E. H. Palmer, Philip Sherrard, and Kallistos Ware (London: Faber and Faber, 1981), 2:182.

a mediator in his one, divine person, by which he mediates deity to humanity and humanity to deity via his single hypostasis—that is, the person of the Word. There is no man Jesus and Christ God.[38] But for Servetus, in both his early and later writings, the simplicity of the earliest church, and certainly Holy Scripture, knew no such distinctions of substances and hypostases, persons and natures. These scholastic accretions weighed down the true glory of Christ (a recurring theme in later antitrinitarianism).

Another key to Servetus's mind is that he thought of his day and age as characterized by the reign of the antichrist, which he marked as beginning with the Council of Nicaea (AD 325) and the church's betrayal of the true Son of God by Pope Sylvester and the emperor Constantine.[39] By adding the 1,260 days of Daniel to either Constantine's accession or the Council of Nicaea, Servetus came to contemporary dates for the consummation of history. As he was the one to see this, it was no leap to cast himself as the manifestation of the archangel Michael, ready to do battle for God on earth against the antichrist and the four horsemen of the apocalypse, whom he identified as the pope, the cardinals, the Dominicans, and the other orders.[40] Though he was not an Anabaptist in the sense of desiring an end to the rule of the magistrates and kings, he proclaimed the overthrow of both Romanism and Protestantism in the imminent apocalyptic judgment. Servetus's apocalyptic creed, his assumption of a key role in this eschatological drama, renders his subsequent actions in confronting Calvin all the more understandable.

Servetus found no one in Vienne who would publish his work, but in Lyons it was different. There, two men agreed to publish it privately, Servetus underwriting the whole affair. One of the two printers, Guillaume Guéroult, had been banished from Geneva for sexual improprieties. Servetus assured them both that the doctrines were aimed at the Reformers and that all names would be kept secret.[41] Soon enough a copy arrived in Geneva, and it was no secret who the author was, for Servetus published in it some thirty of the letters he had written to Calvin.[42] Guillaume de Trie, a friend of Calvin, was

---

38. Cf. Joseph Farrell, trans. and ed., *The Disputation with Pyrrhus of Our Father among the Saints: Maximus the Confessor* (South Canaan, PA: St. Tikhon's Seminary Press, 1990), 15.

39. In an appendix that Servetus titled "Seventy Signs of the Reign of Antichrist," in number 17 he writes: "Although the mystery of Antichrist arose soon after Christ, nevertheless it truly emerged quickly, and his reign established at the time of Sylvester and Constantine. It was this time that soon the Son of God was ripped from us by an ecumenical council, the church was put to flight, and all the abominations were decreed by law" (*Christianismi restitutio*, 666). This is also in CO 8:715.

40. Servetus, *Christianismi restitutio*, 408–9.

41. Bainton, *Hunted Heretic*, 148.

42. Bainton, *Hunted Heretic*, 151–53.

in 1553 exchanging letters with a Catholic cousin in Lyons named Arney. In a polemical thrust, de Trie wrote that Protestants would never harbor arch-heretics, and especially would not allow one to serve as a physician to their clergy as Servetus did to the archbishop of Vienne.[43] Arney immediately brought this to the Inquisition and, under orders, wrote back to de Trie for further information. De Trie coaxed (as he put it) several of Servetus's letters from Calvin, those same ones published in the *Christianismi restitutio*, in Servetus's hand. Calvin, according to de Trie, felt he should take no part in punishing heresy by the sword.[44] Servetus was arrested and held in the episcopal palace. At his trial he maintained his identity as de Villeneuve and claimed that he only used Servetus's name as a way to write to Calvin. On April 7, Servetus, doubtlessly knowing what awaited him, made good his escape by jumping off the roof of a garden outhouse that was against the palace's garden wall. Condemned in absentia, he was burned in effigy, along with a bundle of blank papers, signifying his books.[45]

Servetus decided for Italy, or so he said, but he went via Geneva. Clearly, other routes existed. Having known of Calvin's complicity in Vienne, Servetus could not have thought that Calvin would harbor him. It must have been, as Calvin said, "a fatal madness."[46] Perhaps Servetus knew from Guéroult of Calvin's troubles in Geneva and thought the time propitious to confront him and perhaps even to unseat him. Calvin found himself in a struggle (explained in chap. 6 on the Enfants de Genève) with the opposition party then controlling the syndics, who, according to Calvin, desired to subvert church discipline. But, as Parker has put it, the Libertines (so named by Calvin) wanted a submissive Calvin, not a martyr running free in Zurich or Basle.[47]

Servetus stayed some days in Geneva without detection, but on August 13, 1553, he attended service at St. Pierre. Congregants from Lyons recognized him, and on Calvin's prompting, he was arrested and charged under the Genevan *Ordinances* for blasphemy and heresy.[48] While Calvin would be the chief theological prosecutor—he drew up the indictments, which included pantheism, denial of the soul's immortality, denial of the truthfulness of the Scriptures (his denial that Palestine was a land flowing with milk and honey), denial of the Trinity, and denial of paedobaptism—it would be Calvin's political enemies, the so-called Libertines of the council, who would judge Servetus.

43. Parker, *Calvin*, 141.
44. Parker, *Calvin*, 141.
45. Bainton, *Hunted Heretic*, 164.
46. Schaff, *Swiss Reformation*, 763.
47. Parker, *Calvin*, 116.
48. Parker summarizes the points at issue in *Calvin*, 144–45.

Indeed, many historians and commentators have seen the trial of Servetus as the high tide of Calvin's enemies, and his own personal nadir, proposing that the "Libertines" sought to embarrass him by Servetus, and use Servetus as a bludgeon.[49] But in fact, Calvin's enemies were just as concerned with Servetus as was he. And it was not foregone that Servetus would be executed, which was a decision of the Small Council, for just three days prior to his arrest in Geneva, the city had banished Jean Baudin of Lorraine for teaching that Jesus was but a man and the Bible just a book.[50] This is not to say that the outcome of the trial was ever in doubt. Servetus's assumed guilt guided the actions of the city; he was given no lawyer—though he requested one—for Calvin and the syndics considered him capable enough of lying without one.[51] Servetus was no drunken local or migrant émigré who shot off his mouth; he was notorious, and though clearly out of most people's sight and mind, he had not been out of Calvin's. Even though their correspondence had broken off in 1547, and thus perhaps had been an end to their relationship, Calvin had called special attention to Servetus in his 1550 treatise *On Scandals*, in which he named Servetus as the pretended Doctor Villaneuve (though not where he lived), an insane megalomaniac and mad dog.[52]

Though assumed guilty, Servetus was not sentenced right away. The final act was a letter to the other leading Swiss Reformed cities—Schaffhausen, Berne, Basle, and Zurich—asking them for their opinions on the matter.[53] A courier began the trip on September 22 and returned on October 18. Calvin sent his own letters to the pastors of these cities, especially to Johannes Haller in Berne and Simon Sulzer in Basle, prodding them to look with severity on Servetus. Calvin wrote as well to Frankfurt, relating the horror that was Servetus, ending the letter with "[He] is imprisoned by our magistrates, and soon punished, I hope; but it is your duty to ensure that his bile spreads no further."[54] It does not seem that Calvin's encouragements were necessary, for in the eyes of the Swiss, Servetus was insufferable. A year afterward Melanchthon

---

49. Bruce Gordon intimates this (*Calvin* [New Haven: Yale University Press, 2009], 219), and Parker asserts it (*Calvin*, 144), but Naphy argues against this reading in his *Calvin and the Consolidation of the Genevan Reformation* (Manchester: Manchester University Press, 1994), 183–84. See chap. 6 below on this point.

50. Naphy, *Consolidation*, 183. In July of 1553 Robert de Moynne of Normandy was banished for saying that prostitution and fornication were not prohibited by the Bible.

51. Gordon, *Calvin*, 220.

52. *De scandalis* (CO 8:47): "mordendi latrandique rabies"; *Des scandales qui empeschent auiourdhuy beaucoup de gens de venir a la pure doctrine de l'Evangile, et en desbauchent d'autres* (Geneva: Jehan Crespin, 1551), 89.

53. Gordon, *Calvin*, 220. One letter had already been sent on September 8.

54. CO 14:599–600; Gordon, *Calvin*, 221.

wrote to Calvin commending him and the Genevan magistrates for their actions and saying that both the present and the future owe, and will owe, them a debt of gratitude for ridding the world of such blasphemy.[55] Haller, the pastor in Berne, in a letter to Bullinger, said that if Servetus had shown his face in Berne he would have tasted the flames.[56]

Servetus did not have to go to Berne: the council, having heard from the Swiss churches, met on October 26 and sentenced him to die at the stake the next day. When notified, he shrieked for mercy, pleading that a lighter sentence be given lest in his agony he lose his soul. Calvin asked that he be beheaded, as was the custom.[57] The council was unmoved in both cases. Calvin visited Servetus in prison, where he reminded him that he had tried to meet with him sixteen years before at the peril of his life,[58] but Servetus maintained his creed. Due to illness, and perhaps because the matter was too painful, Calvin asked Farel to attend Servetus on his last day. Farel wrote an account of the event in the front page of his copy of *De Trinitatis erroribus*. The elder Reformer vainly tried to persuade Servetus of his error, but as with Calvin's attempts, Servetus remained unconvinced. It took a half-hour for the flames to do their job. Servetus's last words were, "Jesus, son of the eternal God, have mercy on me."[59] Farel noted that had he moved the adjective, he would have been saved.

No one should think Servetus's horrific fate at the hands of the Genevans alone established his place in history, for the brilliant Giordano Bruno (among thousands of others) faced the same fate in 1600 in Rome, and he has never obtained the same reputation, though like Servetus he has a monument to his memory. Rather, Servetus's name was preserved largely by those who indicted Calvin on Servetus's behalf, even if they did not follow Servetus's theology. Thus Servetus became the cause célèbre, or perhaps better put, the *casus belli* for several of the subjects of this book in their conflicts with Calvin, while for others he marks the first break from the trinitarian orthodoxy of the Catholic past that the Reformers still professed. While Calvin was busy with some of his interlocutors well before Servetus, and while Servetus serves only in some regards as an archetype for Calvin's enemies, their relationship

55. CO 15:247.

56. Bainton, *Hunted Heretic*, 201–2.

57. CO 14:657; and Parker, *Calvin*, 122–23.

58. It is a matter of some controversy what this meeting was. Beza in his *Life of Calvin* says that in 1534 Servetus had tried to meet with Calvin in Paris, but failed to show up for the rendezvous. See Jean Dupèbe, "Michel Servet à Paris (1537–1538). Questions Biographiques," in *Michel Servet (1511–1553): Hérésie et pluralisime du 16e au 21e siècle* (Paris: Honoré Chapman, 2007), 53–72.

59. John T. McNeill, *The History and Character of Calvinism* (Oxford: Oxford University Press, 1954), 176.

actually predates, with the exception of du Tillet, all of Calvin's other adversaries, dating back to 1536, when both were students in Paris, a year before
Calvin's first confrontation with Caroli. Calvin came late to the game as one
of Servetus's detractors, but he became the one Servetus latched onto, probably because Calvin by 1553 had survived all the others, and it would seem
that in Servetus's mind Calvin assumed the role of his own archnemesis, for
nemesis he was indeed for Servetus.

5

Sebastian Castellio

Colaboring Admirer to Belligerent Vilifier

Cordial friendship marked the first years of Sebastian Castellio's relations with Calvin; acrimony and mutual recriminations defaced the
last. Castellio, however, unlike others of Calvin's erstwhile friends,
always maintained his Protestant faith and a confession of orthodoxy, even
though he wore it lightly. And while these may not have always been to Calvin's
satisfaction, they were not the basis of the storms that disfigured their final
relations. These tempests arose with the execution of Servetus. Like Servetus,
Castellio spent a number of formative years in Lyons, some of them overlap-
ping Servetus's time there, though we have no evidence that they knew each
other. Also like Servetus, Castellio affected a pseudonym, though unlike the
Spaniard, he never went into hiding or exile, even though some seemingly
wished this for him. He always affected the annoying, compromising Gamaliel
to Calvin's Boanerges.

Castellio was born in western Savoy in 1515, in the village of Saint-Martin-
du Fresne, about forty miles to the east of Lyons, thirty miles west of Geneva.[1]
Although from peasant stock and the victim of an impoverished childhood,
his unlettered but virtuous father provided him the rudiments of school. By
1535 Castellio had gone to Lyons to the College of the Holy Trinity. As with

1. The most recent and most thorough biography of Castellio is that of the late Hans Guggisberg, *Sebastian Castellio, 1515–1563: Humanist and Defender of Toleration in a Confessional Age* (Aldershot, UK: Ashgate, 2002). But see also Roland Bainton, "The Remonstrator:
Sébastian Castellio," in *The Travail of Religious Liberty* (New York: Harper, 1951), 97–124.

all who studied the liberal arts, or the *studium humanitatis*, he endured a rigorous grounding in both Greek and Latin rhetoric and oratory, the basis of which was Cicero, Aristotle, Plato, and the poets. But for Castellio, as was becoming common, it also meant a rigorous curriculum in the third ancient language, Hebrew. By 1540 Castellio had embraced evangelicalism, if not the Reformation, which had come via Marguerite of Navarre's court preacher, Michel d'Aragnde, whom she had placed as bishop at St. Paul-Trois-Châteaux.[2] As a commercial town with multiple printers, Lyons made it easy to obtain humanist and Protestant literature. But while Francis I fluctuated in his attitudes toward evangelicals and sacramentarians (the usual words for French Protestants), and the length of his reach varied, by 1540 his wrath had arrived in Lyons, and the first judicial executions happened in that year. Castellio thought the better of staying and headed to Strasbourg in search of Calvin, for like everywhere, Calvin's name had come to Lyons in 1536 with the publication of his *Institutes*. The slight first edition functioned as an apology for French evangelicals, whom Calvin wished to distinguish from the Anabaptists, a word made loathsome by the radical Anabaptist kingdom of Münster, where Anabaptists had seized the city, expelled its Catholic and Lutheran inhabitants, and declared a commonality of property, even to the sharing of wives. This episode ended when the bishop of Münster stormed the city, putting most of the Anabaptist rulers to the sword. Calvin claimed that the French evangelicals were catholic, and he set forth the faith they professed using the Apostles' Creed as an outline. He dedicated the work to Francis I as a plea for toleration. That Calvin's plea to Francis I for toleration played a part in Castellio's seeking him out can only be surmised, but in 1540 Calvin certainly had attained a high status among the French Reformers. Castellio and Calvin shared basic humanist interests; like Calvin, Castellio had an immense esteem for Marthurin Cordier, Calvin's former teacher, even calling him, though never having formally had him as a teacher, his mentor.[3]

Castellio found Calvin serving as the pastor of the French refugees in Strasbourg, and he quickly became an integral part of Calvin's household, playing the keeper of Calvin's company. On at least two occasions Castellio ministered to people resident there during the plague.[4] Yet also on two different occasions, Calvin asked him to leave to make room for someone else. The first time was for a family so troublesome that Calvin regretted he had asked Castellio to leave. The second time was when Calvin married. Nevertheless,

---

2. Jonathan A. Reid, *King's Sister—Queen of Dissent: Marguerite of Navarre (1492–1549) and Her Evangelical Network* (Leiden: Brill, 2009), 1:74.

3. Guggisberg, *Castellio*, 31–32.

4. Bainton, *Travail*, 99.

Sebastian Castellio

Calvin valued Castellio and brought him with him when he returned to Geneva in 1541, employing him as the master of the grammar school, the Collège de Rive, and tasked him with teaching Latin, Greek, and French to the children of Geneva's citizens.[5] Castellio also became the preacher, though never the ordained minister (Geneva's company of pastors refused to ordain him), at the parish church of Vandœuvres, up the south shore of Lake Leman (Lake

5. Bruce Gordon, *Calvin* (New Haven: Yale University Press, 2009), 156.

Geneva) from Geneva, and ministered there for his whole time in residence.
Castellio also ministered in the plague hospital, a job that the members of
the company of pastors seemed disinclined to do, with some of them even
avoiding it when appointed to take Castellio's place. He also threw himself
into translating, seeking Calvin's advice and permission to publish his translations of Scripture, but Calvin, who looked at Castellio's interpretations and
translations with contempt, refused. Calvin wrote to Viret telling him that
Castellio had often corrupted the meaning of the text.[6]

Castellio's affections for philology indicate that he believed himself called
to more than the Christian ministry and the teaching of the elements of
grammar to the youth, for the humanist interests of translation and commentary occupied his life. Possessing skills in Latin, Greek, and Hebrew, he
bent his efforts to instruct his wards in both Scripture and Latin. To this end
he devised an increasingly difficult series of pedagogical dialogues, all based
on the biblical narrative, beginning with Eve's dialogue with the serpent in
Genesis.[7] The first simple dialogues had an accompanying French text so that
the students could see how the Latin language worked, but this apparatus
disappeared as the dialogues progressed. Castellio's *Dialogues* proved wildly
popular, went through at least 134 editions (the most recent in 1965), and were
used throughout Europe. In one sense the work seems counterhumanist, in
that most humanists would teach Latin via the examples of the classics, but
some Reformers had already sought more pious alternatives; for example,
Jacob Sturm had sought to rid his students of the bad influences of Terence.
But that motivation was hardly Castellio's, as the sequel proved, for his life
in Geneva grew increasingly troubled. Whatever virtues he had as a teacher,
and Calvin and the Genevans seem to have been satisfied with his students,
it was Castellio the translator and theologian with whom they had problems.
Castellio himself, moreover, was not happy with his living arrangements.
Having married upon his arrival in Geneva, he had to live on 400 florins a
year until complaining got his salary raised to 450.[8] Out of this he still had
to pay two assistants at the school: they were paid a mere 82 florins a year. By
contrast, the city paid Calvin 500 florins a year, and beyond this he received
food, wine, and cloth. The city also renovated Calvin's house. Calvin was paid
more than many of the magistrates, but as Gordon points out, as in Zurich
and Wittenberg, Calvin's house was an extension of the church, and there

6. CO 11:436–39.

7. Sebastian Castellio, *Dialogorum sacrorum liber secundus et tertius: Per Sebastianum
Castalionem* (Geneva: Jean Girard, 1543).

8. William G. Naphy, *Calvin and the Consolidation of the Genevan Reformation* (Manchester: Manchester University Press, 1994), 88–89.

were expectations about the entertaining and even boarding of students and guests. But Castellio's problems were more than his perceived slight in pay, for Calvin seemed quite nettled by his precocious schoolteacher.

Castellio differed from most of his contemporaries on the Song of Songs, and his handling of the text made no one in Geneva happy. For Castellio, the Song of Songs was merely a profane love poem that had no deeper theological meaning. Calvin, however, saw it as a form of prophecy about Christ's relationship to the church, or as an allegory, in the tradition of Bernard of Clairvaux, who read it as the union of Christ with the soul. Quite appropriately, then, Castellio, when he translated the Song into Latin, did not scruple to use the poet Catullus as his model, setting the Hebrew into Catullian Latin.[9] Castellio also dissented from Calvin on the *descensus* clause of the creed. In Calvin's mind, Christ's descent into hell was part of his humiliation and part of the suffering of being separated from God the Father in order to satisfy God's wrath. For Castellio, this was a ludicrous and stretched reading. The rancor of this disagreement is seen in a letter Calvin wrote to his friend Viret asserting that Castellio mocked him.[10] The truth, however, is that Calvin seemingly harbored a deep disdain for Castellio, for here was someone who had not scrupled to take any task set before him in his labors for Geneva; was paid poorly for it; and clearly, with Calvin excepted, was as learned as (and probably more learned than) anyone else in the company of pastors. Despite all this, as Bruce Gordon points out, Calvin and the company of pastors made life unbearable for Castellio.[11]

The ax fell in 1544, when Castellio was again turned down in his request to be ordained, the company of pastors writing to him that since the Reformation was in constant danger in Geneva, his dissent from Calvin could not be countenanced. Further, he made a scene after Calvin upbraided the Genevan pastors for their failures in ministering to the sick in the plague hospital, which Castellio had already shown himself willing to do. Castellio had again volunteered to do it, but he either changed his mind or was forbidden to take it on. Those among the pastors who were appointed to do so said that they would rather "go to the devil [*estre aux diables*]."[12] After Calvin's admonition, Castellio rose and unleashed a bitter screed against the company of pastors that doubtless had been building over the last two years. It was his swan song.[13]

9. Max Engammare, *Qu'il me baise des baisiers de sa bouche: Le Cantique des Cantiques à la Renaissance; Ètude et Bibliographie* (Geneva: Librairie Droz, 1993), 9–18.

10. CO 11:688.

11. Gordon, *Calvin*, 157.

12. *Registres*, Juin 1543, cited in Guggisberg, *Castellio*, 33.

13. Guggisberg, *Castellio*, 35.

Castellio, after inquiries, moved to Basle, working for the printer Oporinus. In many ways Oporinus was good to him, but Castellio's life now returned to the penury he had known as a child, a life of abject, even grinding poverty. He had to take employment as both a gardener and a water carrier, he had to fish to provide food and money for his family, and he had to scrounge for firewood, using a rope with a grappling hook to drag driftwood from the Rhine to take home to dry. Years later Calvin used this last fact as the basis of an accusation that Castellio was a thief: "I was employed in the translations of the Bible, which have gained me the envy and hatred of those men, whose love I deserved. Thus is the world wont to reward benefits. While I was wholly bent upon that study (so that I chose rather even to beg my bread, than desist) and dwelt on the bank of the Rhene [Rhine], sometimes at spare hours, I caught and gathered with a drag, sticks and fardles of wood the overflowing River used to bring done, to keep my house warm. This you interpreted and made theft."[14]

He labored at Oporinus's shop, producing as his first work a translation of the Pentateuch, which he titled *Moses Latinus*.[15] What Castellio had done in his translation of the Song of Songs he did again with *Moses Latinus*, though in a slightly different key. Unlike his treatment of the Canticles, Castellio did not take Moses's books for profane works. Rather, Castellio saw Moses as a master of all the ancient arts, cutting a grand, indeed classical, figure as a poet, orator, and lawgiver. Thus, he determined that Moses's words must not retain the Hebraic idioms, which were so foreign to the Latin ear. Moses's status demanded that he be translated into the proper Latin form, and this meant into classical prose.[16] Castellio had done this to a degree with his *Dialogues* by rendering biblical terms with classical analogies—for example, using *genius* for *angelus* and *Jova* for *Deus*. Castellio continued work on his *Dialogues*, but he also labored on two large translation projects. The first was of the whole Bible into Latin, retaining to a large degree his use of proper humanist idioms and style of Latin, though he wrote to Edward VI that the language was but the dress worn by the text, and he the dressmaker.[17] In 1551

14. Sebastian Castellio, *A Conference of Faith Written in Latin by Sebastianus Castellio* (London: J. R. for John Barksdale, 1679), 142.

15. Sebastian Castellio, *Mosis Institutio Reipublicae Graecolatina: ex Iosepho in gratiam puerorum decerpta, ad discendam non solum Graecam, verum etiam Latinam linguam, una cum pietate ac religione* (Basle: Johannes Oporinus, 1546).

16. "Moses, in Castellio's translation, was presented to the reader as a prophet, but also as a rhetorician, poet and philosopher; he was a charismatic *uomo universale* who excelled in . . . learning and whose literary skills surpassed . . . Homer" (Guggisberg, *Castellio*, 51).

17. Sebastian Castellio, *Biblia Interpretate Sebastiano Castalione una cum eiusdem Annotationibus* (Basle: Ioannem Oporinus, 1556 edition), f. i: "ad latinitatem attinet, est oratio nihil aliud quam rei quaedam quasi vestis, et nos sartores sumus."

he finally published his Latin translation of the Bible, which he dedicated to Edward VI. The *praefatio* is notable in that Castellio appeals to Edward VI as a prince to practice both clemency and a measure of moderation toward dissent. This same approach is used in his French translation of the Bible, dedicated to Henry II. In the French edition, he framed his efforts as had Jerome in the Vulgate, with an eye to the laity, and with a simple idiom, plain and understandable: "As to the French language, I have above all been concerned for the unlearned, and so have employed a common, unadorned idiom, the most understandable at my disposal."[18] Castellio had finished his French translation while in Geneva, but Calvin wanted to edit it; when Castellio refused to let him alter his text, Calvin denied him permission to have it published. In 1546 he published a translation of the Sibylline Oracles.[19] In 1554 he published extracts from Josephus that accompanied his new edition of the Bible.[20]

Castellio may have dedicated his Latin translation of the Bible to Edward VI in the hope of a post in England, as by 1551 he was still employed only by Oporinus. This was not his only source of money, however, for there were powerful families within Basle who supported him, including Bonifacius Amerbach, a lawyer and the executor of Erasmus's estate, who on several occasions gave Castellio money.[21] Finally, in 1553, although having no degree, Castellio was made a professor of Greek at the University of Basle. He would in course receive his MA, but this was perfunctory given the level of Castellio's abilities. This work did not hinder Castellio's literary productions: in 1558 he translated from the German the *Theologia Germanica*;[22] in 1562 he published an edition of *The Imitation of Christ*, which he had rendered in classical, "elegant Latin."[23]

For all his erudition, Castellio found multiple detractors, and that from diverse corners, and not only from Calvin in Geneva. In August 1554 the

18. "Quant au langage Francois, j'ai eu princialement égard aux idiots, et pourtnat ai-je usé d'un langage commun et simple, et le plus entendible qu'il m'a été possible," as quoted in Guggisberg, *Castellio*, 69–70.

19. Sebastian Castellio, trans., *Sibyllina Oracula* (Basle: [Oporinus?], 1546).

20. Irena Backus, "Moses, Plato, and Flavius Josephus: Castellio's Conceptions of the Sacred and Profane in His Latin Versions of the Bible," in *Shaping the Bible in the Reformation: Books, Scholars and Their Readers in the Sixteenth Century*, ed. Bruce Gordon and Matthew McLean (Leiden: Brill, 2012), 143–66.

21. Hans Guggisberg, "Tolerance and Intolerance in Sixteenth-Century Basle," in *Tolerance and Intolerance in the European Reformation*, ed. Ole Peter Grell and Bob Scribner (Cambridge: Cambridge University Press, 2002), 151.

22. Sebastian Castellio, trans., *Theologia Germanici* (Basle: Oporinus, 1557).

23. *The Christian's Latin Companion Containing The Imitation of Christ Rendered into Elegant Latin by Sebastian Castellio* (London: Souter, 1840).

Censura Generalis contra errores, issued by the Inquisition in Valladolid, Spain, took what appears to be a special aim at Castellio's Latin Bible. The *Censura* begins with a list of printers (e.g., *Basileiae, ex officina Frobeniana*) who had published the Bibles from which were then drawn the short index of condemned propositions. After the list, there is a note that "all these errors are contained in the margins, or in the Titles of the chapters in various annotated Bibles, which ought to be obliterated as it is decreed in front of this Censura." Following this there is then a whole extra page given just to Castellio's text. The reason for this attention, and for its placement at the end of the book, is that the censors only got their hands on Castellio's Bible after they had completed all their other work. Castellio's text certainly contains Protestant material, but the censors particularly noted that he had altered the sense of the text by his use of classical forms, which, said the censors, the fathers of the church had never countenanced.[24]

For all his learning, Castellio emerged most dramatically, however anonymously initially, in the aftermath of Servetus's execution in Geneva. Following Servetus's death, Heinrich Bullinger wrote Calvin that the Genevan needed to defend what the city had done.[25] In February of 1554 Calvin published his *Defensio orthodoxae fidei.*[26] For Calvin, while many offenses call for excommunication or exile, those that assault the honor of God call for capital punishment. The shepherd defending the sheep cannot be merciful to the wolf. Calvin also answered the objection that if Protestants killed heretics they would be no different from the papists by asserting that Rome killed for the sake of falsehoods and that their use of torture amounted to cruelty. Rome's abuse of the capital penalty, however, did not destroy its right use. Further, while it is true that no one can be compelled to faith and that princes cannot judge the heart, princes do have the duty to defend the church. Lastly, while it is true that Christ is loving, the countenancing of heretics was unloving to ordinary people, who were incapable of discernment. Bullinger complained that the book was poorly written. More recently, Owen Chadwick called it "probably the least clear-headed book by this so clear-headed author."[27]

24. Sebastian Castellio, *Censura Generalis contra errores, quibus recentes haeretici saram scripturam asperserunt, edita a supremo senatu inquisitionis adversus hereticam pravitatem et apostatiam in Hispania, et aliis regnis, et dominiis Cesareae Magestatis constituto* (Cordoba: Valladolid, 1554).

25. CO 14:683.

26. John Calvin, *Defensio orthodoxae fidei de sacra Trinitate, contra prodigiosos errores Michaelis Serveti Hispani* (Geneva: Robertus Stephanus, 1554), CO 8:457–644.

27. Owen Chadwick, *The Early Reformation on the Continent* (Oxford: Oxford University Press, 2001), 388; but see all of his chapter titled "Toleration."

Less charitable reactions came from Basle. One of the city's administrators, Nikolaus Zurkinden, an acquaintance of Calvin, wrote him that support for Geneva's actions was strong in Basle, but that he was writing privately, not seeking a public confrontation. Zurkinden had witnessed the execution in Strasbourg of an elderly lady and her daughter, a mother of young children, for holding Anabaptist beliefs. Were these two *misérables* threats to the society, threats to the faith?[28] Zurkinden continues, calling for moderation by the magistrates, asserting that "I freely confess to you that I am among those who either by lack of experience or by fear, desire that the sword hardly ever be used to coerce the enemies of the faith, whether erring from assumption or ignorance. . . . I prefer in this regard that both the magistrate and I use too much clemency and timidity acting from ignorance, than be quickly inclined to the severity of the sword."[29]

But a more public challenge from Basle was issued by one Martin Bellius in his *Whether Heretics Ought to Be Punished*. Bellius published the book in March 1554, ostensibly in Magdeburg, but actually in Basle. After his preface, Bellius drew on a number of authors, even citing Calvin, on why heretics should be tolerated. Besides Calvin, Bellius quoted Luther, Sebastian Franck, Johannes Brenz, Konrad Pellikan, and even Castellio's 1551 preface to Edward VI. The last author in the book was one Basil Montfort. Bellius's identity was unknown and remained unknown. When Theodore Beza took up the quill in Calvin's defense, he titled his own book the *Antibellium*, and referred to *Whether Heretics Ought to Be Punished* as the *Ferrago Bellii*. Bellius, of course, was Sebastian Castellio, as was Basil Montfort, though Calvin had divined as much about Montfort early on, complaining to Bullinger about the Basle ministers, wondering why they would not rein in Castellio.[30]

Castellio made his appeal mainly on the grounds of the last two objections Calvin had addressed in the *Defensio orthodoxae fidei*, the compulsion to faith and Christian charity. Castellio did not argue for full-blown religious liberty in the sense of pluralism, but only for at best a narrow tolerance, urging that beyond expulsion for the most notorious of blasphemers, heretics should be left unharried and allowed to live freely in their commonwealths. For him, Paul's admonition about heretics was nothing other than Christ's words about Christians overcome by a fault (Matt. 18). In neither case were Christians called on to destroy life. The final part of the Bellius preface made an anguished appeal to Christ:

28. CO 15:20.
29. CO 15:20.
30. CO 15:93–96.

O Christ, creator of the world and king, do you see all this? Have you changed from what you were, to become cruel? When you walked the earth, no one was more gentle and none more full of compassion. Cut with whips, derided, spat upon, crowned with thorns, and with the greatest insults you were crucified among thieves, yet you prayed for all those who scorned you. Have you now changed? I beseech you . . . have you ordered all these drownings, burnings, beheadings, tortures . . . ? Did you really order and approve these things? Are the people who do these acting for you [*vicarii tui*]? Do you eat human flesh? If so, what have you left for Satan?[31]

Castellio calls for moderation both in defending dogma and in dogmatic assertions. In the person of Montfort, Castellio closes, "It is clear from this that when they begin as paupers and without power, they detest persecution; the same having obtained strength imitate the persecutors, and putting aside the weapons of Christ, they take up the weapons of the Pharisees without which they would be unable to defend their power."[32] Castellio's description here may well be contradicting Calvin with his own plea to Francis I, in the first edition of the *Institutes*, that the king accept the French sacramentarians as Catholics.

Roland Bainton noted that *Whether Heretics Ought to Be Punished* marks a critical juncture in the history of religious toleration. Here, for the first time, serious debate about religious toleration, however acrimonious, actually begins, and Bainton draws a direct line from Castellio to the English Acts of Toleration.[33] The book certainly has its rhetorical elements, but as literature, and as an eloquent piece of writing, it misses the mark. It reads more like a bill of indictment or a florilegium of quotations that one would use in a debate. Castellio wholly depends on the work of others and simply tries to bury his critics in words, sometimes with his critics' own words. Though Castellio's effort had seemingly little effect in his day, as Europe stood on the brink of almost ninety years of religious wars, and as Castellio himself lamented in his *Advice to a Desolate France*, his endeavors were for the future, and few people have had as much impact on a question as has Castellio on the matter of religious toleration. In this he joins, in his own century, such prominent thinkers as Erasmus before him and Montaigne after. All to say, however outstanding his acts may have been, Castellio was still very much alone. Geneva hardly took the matter lightly, and Calvin's lieutenant, Beza, responded with his *De*

---

31. Martin Bellius (S. Castellio), *De haereticis an sint persequendi et omnino quomodo sit cum eis agendum, Luteri et Brentii, aliorumque multorum tum veterum tu recentiorum sententiae* (Magdeburg [Basle]: Ioanis Caroli Typographia, 1554), 27.

32. Castellio, *De haereticis*, 138.

33. Bainton, *Travail*, 97.

haereticis a civili magistratu puniendis libellus, in which he accuses "Bellius" of being an academician (a reference to the ancient skeptics who spewed an undogmatic and skeptical theology), without moorings, and blown by the wind and tides. In brief, Bellius had offered not well-articulated thoughts and arguments but a farrago of snippets that collectively missed the mark.[34] According to Beza, by asserting a doctrine of "not knowing," the authors of *Whether Heretics Ought to Be Punished* threw the weak into doubt and the peril of perdition. Doubt, to Castellio, was hardly the horror it was to Beza, for as Castellio would attest in his last, but unpublished, work, doubt keeps us from acting hastily and from haste's frequent deadly consequences.

Castellio in due course responded with two shorter works that treated specific criticisms (that he had misused both Calvin and Erasmus). But in his third book, the *Contra libellum Calvini,* Castellio took special aim at Calvin's defense of his triumph in Geneva in 1555 and asserted that Servetus had simply been a victim of Calvin's lust for power. Though not published in Castellio's lifetime, the book did circulate as a manuscript, and would actually find friends and a publisher among the Arminian Remonstrants of the Netherlands. The *Contra libellum Calvini* is important for another reason beyond its take on toleration, for it provides a great deal of biographical material for the historian, in that Castellio believed he had to defend himself against accusations from Calvin (e.g., that he stole firewood).[35] It is also from the book that we learn of Castellio's father's virtue. That the text was not published during Castellio's life should not surprise us. Calvin had many friends in Basle, and Castellio had already felt Calvin's unwanted hand in the editing of his books published there. Castellio's publisher, Oporinus, at the instigation of Castellio's friend but Basle's censor, Martin Borrhaus, had removed from the 1551 *Biblia* several pages of commentary on Romans 9 that were highly critical of Calvin's doctrine of predestination.[36]

Castellio stayed the course, for there were those in Basle (such as Zurkinden) who sympathized with him and protected him from those who sought to silence him. Both Calvin and Beza were in contact with the Basle ministers asking them to shut Castellio up, but this never happened. While Erasmus before and Montaigne after pleaded for toleration, in the mid-century the closest minds to Castellio's were those of the *moyenneurs,* men such as François Baudouin

---

34. Theodore Beza, *De hæreticis a civili magistratu puniendis libellus, adversus Martini Bellii farraginem, et novorum Academicorum sectam, Theodoro Beza Vezelio auctore* (Geneva: Robert I Estienne, 1554), 6.

35. Sebastian Castellio, *Contra libellum Calvini in quo ostendere conatur haereticos jure gladij coercendos esse* (Amsterdam: n.p., 1612); and Castellio, *Conference of Faith,* 142.

36. Guggisberg, *Castellio,* 102.

(who will be discussed in chap. 7) and George Cassander, who sought to reconcile the Protestants with the Catholics through debate and colloquy. But what Castellio sought was not rapprochement with the Catholics as much as ultimately a legitimization of dissent. What are heretics, he asked in *De haereticis*. Nothing but those who disagree with us.

Castillio's agenda for toleration comes out fully in one of his last published works, written in French in 1562, on the eve of the Wars of Religion in France, his *Conseil à la France Désolée*. In the modern edition, the editor cites three events that compelled Castellio to write: the failure of the Colloquy of Poissy, the Edict of January (the so-called Edict of Toleration), and the massacre at Vassy.[37] Mario Turchetti argues that Castellio moved from a simple legal moderation in his 1551 preface to Edward VI, to a doctrine of toleration of heretics who were not seditious in 1554, to a full-blown legitimization of competing creeds in *Conseil*. Peace would never come to France without the willingness of the two sides to tolerate the other. This idea was as loathsome to Calvin as it was to Castellio's Catholic detractors, for while it would allow the French Protestants to exist in peace, Calvin still held to the dictum of "one king, one law, one faith" ("un roi, une loi, une foi," but for him the one faith was "une foi reformée").[38]

Castellio's last work was an unpublished piece, his *Concerning the Art of Doubting* (*De arte dubitandi*), something he was working on as his health declined from what seems to have been a bleeding ulcer. What Castellio expressed in this text was reminiscent in many ways of items already touched on in the beginning of his *Moses Latinus*. Castellio put great store by reason. Reason is a gift from God that guided the lives and ethics of Abraham, Noah, and Enoch before books and ceremonies, and it will be reason that guides when books and ceremonies are no more. He came very close to saying that even special revelation would cease, and to sundering reason from revelation. But he stopped short. He actually equated reason with the eternal law of God, and further affirmed that Christ, the Logos of God, both operated by the law and was himself God's eternal wisdom: "Finally, reason guided Jesus Christ, the son of the living God—who is called in Greek Logos, which means reason or word, which are the same thing, for reason is like an inner and everlasting word of

---

37. Sebastian Castellio, *Conseil à la France Désolée*, ed. Marius F. Valkhoff (Geneva: Librairie Droz, 1967), 10; trans. Wouter Valkhoff, *Advice to a Desolate France* (Grand Rapids: Acton Institute, 2016).

38. "Calvin contradicted the proponents of concord (the moyenneurs), and the contrivers of tolerance (the followers of Castellio)." Mario Turchetti, "Calvin face aux tenants de la concorde [moyenneurs] et aux fauteurs de la tolérance [castellionistes]," in *Calvin et ses contemporains: Actes du colloque de Paris 1995*, ed. Olivier Millet, Cahiers d'Humanisme et Renaissance 53 (Geneva: Librairie Droz, 1998), 43–56.

truth within us. It was by her that Christ taught others and refuted the writings and ceremonies, to which the Jews attributed more authority than to reason."[39]

But despite his valorization of reason, Castellio really wrote in praise of doubt, insisting that far too often people fell into sin and error because they believed when they should have doubted and doubted when they should have believed.[40] His targets here were those who took themselves as oracles of the divine will. Certitude brings action that may or may not be right; doubt brings hesitation and deliberation, and with that the exercise of reason. What Castellio maintained was not wholly different from what he had said in other texts, and indeed Calvin had already accused him of letting reason supplant Holy Scripture.

Castellio died on December 29, 1563, fighting another attempt to silence him, this time from Adam Bodenstein—the son of Andreas Bodenstein von Karlstadt—who was prosecuting him for heresy and for having translated Bernardino Ochino's tract on polygamy.[41] As the heresy charges echo Beza's complaints, they may have been inspired by Geneva, but this is supposition at best. Castellio was buried with honors, and his pension was paid out to his widow (his second wife, his first having died some years earlier). Had the magistrates of Basle aught against him, they never expressed it.

Castellio was no theologian, even though he was well read in theology. He was instead a humanist, a philologist whose chief interest was language. While never imbibing Renaissance Platonism to the extreme we find in Servetus, his assertions about reason echo it. In this notion of human nature as rational but not omniscient, we see the basis for his thoughts on toleration. In this regard, there were a great many people in the sixteenth century who would agree with him, even though they never stuck their heads out as far as Castellio had. He had friends in Basle who supported him, and he was even invited to live in Poland, where toleration had been materially in effect since 1557. But perhaps a measure of justification for his troubles was realized when he received a note dated February 1, 1557, one he never publicized, from Philip Melanchthon (the letter became public upon publication of Melanchthon's letters) stating, "As I consider your writings though unknown to you, I would be your friend . . . for if I live I would speak with you face-to-face about many things."[42] Melanchthon's sentiments no doubt bolstered Castellio. His belief

---

39. Sebastian Castellio, *De arte dubitandi*, trans. Elizabeth Feist Hirsch (Leiden: Brill, 1981), 224–25.

40. Guggisberg, *Castellio*, 221.

41. Guggisberg, *Castellio*, 202.

42. Philip Melanchthon, *Corpus Reformatorum*, ed. Karl Bretschneider (Halle: C. A. Schwetschke and Sons, 1842), 9:359–60.

in the unity of divine revelation and the created order, which would include reason, all subjects he treated from his *Moses Latina* to his *De arte dubitandi*, shows why he believed himself justified, whether with the Pentateuch or the *Imitatio Christi*, in synthesizing the two. It also shows why he could play skeptical of hardened dogmas that absolutized one reading of Scripture or one school of thought. In this he was of a mind with Sadoleto, even if the two stood in some ways on either side of Calvin.

6

Calvin and the Enfants de Genève

Flatulence in a Purely Reformed Church

Calvin doesn't want us to cough [during the sermon]? We'll fart and belch."[1] Philip (or Philibert) Berthelier's 1547 disdainful justification for his interruption of one of Calvin's sermons, occasioned by a supposed fit of coughing, crudely expresses the rancor between Calvin and many of the Genevans, Berthelier certainly prominent among them. His malady struck him more than once. But less than ten years later, John Knox in a letter to Harry Locke could write: "I . . . cannot cease to wish, that it would please God to guide and conduct you to this place; where I neither fear, nor am ashamed to say, is the most perfect school of Christ that ever was in the earth since the days of the apostles."[2] The change that occurred in Geneva by 1556, from one that endured Berthelier to one that welcomed Knox, came not from the labored, disciplined harvest of reform per se but from Calvin's emerging victorious from a rancorous conflict that would test his commitment not only to Geneva but also to his ideas of discipline as a mark of the church. In 1553, so vitriolic had become those elements within Geneva that sought to oust Calvin that he actually preached on Paul's farewell discourse in Acts 20 to the Ephesian elders, applying it to himself, and steeled himself to oppose the Genevan government, which he feared

1. *Annales Calvini*, in CO 21:417, for November 28, 1547.
2. Knox to Locke, December 9, 1556, in *Writings of the Rev. John Knox* (Philadelphia: Presbyterian Board of Publications, 1842), 454.

would provoke his second banishment.[3] What both subjected Calvin to the flatulences of his parishioners and transformed Geneva into the Reformed Elysium that Knox proclaimed had their origins in Genevan history as well as in Calvin's surety of vision for his prophetic ministry, inculcated in his first confrontation with Geneva's magistrates in 1538 and illustrated in his responses to Louis du Tillet.[4]

In 1500 Geneva formed part of the duchy of Savoy and had been ruled till the 1520s by its duke Charles III. Even when exercising sovereignty, the house of Savoy governed Geneva through the local prince-bishop, often a scion of the house. When Geneva finally broke from Savoy, Pierre de la Baume, the gifted though politically tone-deaf prince-bishop, still governed it.[5] The initial struggles between Geneva and Savoy came to a crisis in 1519, when some eighty-six members of Geneva's bourgeoisie obtained co-citizenship with Fribourg, with whom a pact was made, and an army from Fribourg appeared outside Geneva. But Savoy was able to influence the Genevan citizenry to repudiate the pact, the Fribourg army had to be paid off, and an amnesty was declared. Then in August of that year the bishop breached the amnesty and executed the leader of the faction, Philip Berthelier (father of the above cougher), and declared that the city's executives, the four syndics, operated by his good pleasure.

The sequel saw two factions emerge, both having as their goal the breaking of the power of the prince-bishop, though one wanted to remain under Savoy, while the other wished to keep the bishop but sought political power in confederation with the Swiss. The first called themselves the Monseigneuristes, though labeled the Mammules by their opponents (for the Mamelukes, who had freely placed themselves in slavery); the other party, remembered by history as the Eidguenots (from which the word "Huguenot" may derive) from the Swiss Eidgnossen, or confederates, called themselves "les Enfants de Genève." Desiring freedom from Savoy, they saw themselves as the heirs of Berthelier, whose last words had been of Genevan liberty.[6] By 1527, with the aid of Fribourg and Berne, the Enfants had gained independence from Savoy and had broken the power of the Monseigneuristes. Geneva still functioned

3. Bernard Cottret, *Calvin: A Biography*, trans. M. Wallace McDonald (Grand Rapids: Eerdmans, 2000), 194.

4. See chap. 1.

5. This chapter depends on several biographies of Calvin, but is heavily indebted to what the author considers one of the excellent books on Geneva published in the last few decades, William G. Naphy's *Calvin and the Consolidation of the Genevan Reformation* (Manchester: Manchester University Press, 1994). Taking my cue from Naphy, I have tried to stick closely to the sources as well.

6. Naphy, *Consolidation*, 15.

under the prince-bishop, and most of the clergy of the city were Savoyard; and Geneva also saw this foreign, ecclesiastical authority as an encroachment on its liberty. Thus, the Enfants contemplated moves against the Genevan church long before the Reformation became an issue, for the wealth of the church in the city was immense, and the city itself was feeling an economic pinch from Lyons. With such wealth in the hands of those who were not Genevans, the question obviously took on practical importance as regards Geneva's liberty: the ecclesiastical control of so much wealth could only be seen as detrimental to Geneva, and insofar as the bishop still paid homage to Savoy, he could only be held as a threat to the new republic. In this regard, conflict between the city and the church as an institution within the city predated Calvin's arrival in 1536. Nor were the city's moves motivated by anticlerical sentiments or greed, for the spoils of the church were used to civic ends: for example, monies collected from the sale of ecclesiastical lands were used for hospitals and the defense of the city.

While Geneva was technically part of Savoy, Savoy itself had for some time been in an alliance with France, which alliance Savoy ended when in 1524 Charles III aligned himself with the emperor Charles V. This allowed France to move against Savoy, carving off bits of its territory, and Savoy's preoccupation with France allowed for the territorial expansion of the large Swiss canton of Berne. The town of Berne was one of the three largest Swiss cities, along with Basle and Zurich, each having about ten thousand citizens, which in 1535 was roughly the same number as Geneva. But Berne was also the largest of the cantons, nearly encircling its neighbor Fribourg to the north, east, and south. Berne, like France, also sought to expand, but could do so only to the west, or to the very southwest, beyond Fribourg (Geneva, at the southwestern end of Lake Leman, is on a line extending to Berne in the northeast, about seventy miles distant, with Lausanne, also on Lake Leman, twenty miles up the line, and Fribourg another thirty beyond that, but below Berne; see map on p. ii). Berne looked to take Savoy's territories north of Lake Leman, which included both Geneva and Lausanne, and Savoy, now entangled with the French, was largely powerless to do anything about it. Further, Geneva lay just off the main route of what was called the Spanish Road, the main route for soldiers under Charles V to move from Italy to the Low Countries. Geneva's geography played an important role in its later history as regards its relations with France. Ironically, had not France sought to plunder Savoy following 1524, Savoy might have been able to thwart both Geneva's and Berne's ambitions, and the Reformation might never have been allowed to flourish in Geneva, a situation that would have changed the course of the French Reformation as well.

Protestantism appeared in Geneva by 1532, when Guillaume Farel and Pierre Robert Olivétan arrived and held clandestine meetings. Summoned before an ecclesiastical court, they were roughly evicted from the city.[7] Farel returned at the end of 1533, soon joined by Pierre Viret and Pierre Caroli, and they found a city far more receptive to the Protestant message than the one that had expelled Farel. Caroli (see chap. 2), a Sorbonne doctor of theology who, like Farel, had been one of the Reformers associated with Briçonnet at Meaux, took a prominent role in disputations with the jailed Dominican priest and also a Sorbonne doctor, Caroli's former student Guy Furby.[8] Jeanne de Jussie, a nun of the convent of the Poor Clares, gives a vivid picture of the chaotic and belligerent city in her *Chronicle*. Even given her obvious attachment to her creed, the unsettling picture that emerges from her text is of a city riven along religious lines. But what does not come out so clearly is the coincidence between the program of the Reformers and that of the Enfants, which came to maturity in 1535, the year the nuns abandoned Geneva. When Guy Furby was arrested, one of the charges against him was that he had defamed the rulers of Berne, something only tangential in Jeanne de Jussie's *Chronicle*. De Jussie used the term "Eidguenots"—"that means in French 'good allies.'"[9] However, the real villains for de Jussie were the "Lutherans" (all Protestants were Lutherans to her). De Jussie seemed wholly ignorant of the key role that Furby would play in the drama. Originally from Savoy, he had obtained a dispensation that allowed him to be ordained in 1509 when he was but twenty-three. He had acquitted himself well in Paris and had been, apparently to good effect, a Lenten preacher in Geneva in 1531, the same year he obtained his doctorate. His return to Geneva in Advent of 1533 was not so happy. He had made mention in his sermons of the dangers of the religion of Berne and had warned Genevans against the Bernese government in particular. Berne was quick to pounce on this affront, demanding repayment of a large loan from Geneva and threatening to end their alliance unless both a retraction came from Furby and, more importantly, an evangelical would be allowed to preach openly in the city. Caught now between Catholic Fribourg, their ineffectual prince-bishop, and the more powerful Berne, Geneva fell in with Berne. Henri Naef concludes: "Geneva had no more than one protector, and it was Zwinglian."[10] Furby remained in prison for twenty-seven months, despite

7. Jeanne de Jussie, *The Short Chronicle*, ed. and trans. Carrie F. Klaus (Chicago: University of Chicago Press, 2006), 72–74.

8. De Jussie, *Chronicle*, 96. The *Chronicle* states that when Furby saw Caroli he sank down in despair that his former teacher had become a heretic. De Jussie calls him Furbity.

9. De Jussie, *Chronicle*, 42–43.

10. "Genève n'a plus qu'un protecteur, et il est zwinglien." In James K. Farge, *Biographical Register of Paris Doctors of Theology, 1500–1536* (Toronto: Pontifical Institute of Medieval Studies, 1980), 177.

Guillaume Farel

the appeals of both the Duke of Savoy and King Francis I (who had released French evangelicals, including the future Genevan minister Antoine Saunier). Finally Furby's brother, Guillaume, suffragan of Belley, convinced Furby to write a retraction that would placate the magistrates but still save face.[11]

And so in 1535 the Genevans effectively threw off government by the bishop (and implicitly that of Savoy) and aligned themselves, at least nominally, with the Swiss Confederation, and specifically with Berne. This alignment with Berne instead of with Catholic Fribourg entailed the presence of the already-mentioned French ministers Farel, Olivétan, Viret, and Caroli, among others, and they proved effective instruments in stripping Geneva of the vestiges of Catholicism. De Jussie's *Chronicle* ends its history before Berne's and Farel's triumph, but so dangerous and hostile had the situation become that the nuns of the convent fled the city to reestablish themselves at the Convent of the Holy Cross in Annecy, and thus she makes no mention of Calvin. All the same, she depicts a Geneva in chaos, one dominated by violence, iconoclasm, and mendacity.

To this Geneva came Calvin in August of 1536; his friend Louis du Tillet was there already. Farel's projection of urgency in the well-known confrontation

11. The above comes largely from Farge, *Register*, 175–77, but see the larger discussion in Henri Naef, *Les Origines de la Réforme à Genève*, 2 vols. (Geneva: Librairie Droz, 1968).

with Calvin gives a sense of what Farel thought himself up against. Since Geneva had acted against the Catholic Church not from a sense of religious obligation but from that of Genevan self-interest and liberty, it could hardly be called a Protestant stronghold. It should be thought odd, therefore, that Geneva, so recently liberated from the Savoyard clergy, should now want to relinquish that liberty to the French, for from France had come most of the Protestant ministers now in Geneva. Calvin's arrival in the city coincided with Farel's desire for a book of church order, and the implementation of church order became the great struggle that defined much of Calvin's interaction with the city, even when Farel was no long there. This quest by the Protestant clergy for such a device should not be thought odd, since what had governed the moral and religious life of Geneva previously—the entire apparatus of canon law—had now been jettisoned with little to replace it. What little church structure did exist came through Geneva's alliance with Berne.

The dependence on Berne also became the cause of new factions within the city, for the Genevans divided themselves over how close their relationship with Berne should be: having thrown off one "foreign" power, were they to replace it by another? The Genevan government did see the Bernese ecclesiastical model as an exemplar for its own, and all the better since Berne's ministers served at the pleasure of the Bernese government. The Genevan ministers in the wake of the city's siding with the Reformation drew up both a confession and a book of church order and asked the magistrates to enforce an oath to the confession. Berne discouraged enforcement of the oath, counseling that this would only result in massive perjury, and many citizens balked at having their citizenship depend on their subscription. But for Farel and Calvin the matter was one of the purity of the sacraments and the preached Word. Calvin and Farel had no enthusiasm for Bernese forms, using neither unleavened bread for the Eucharist nor the Bernese form of service. The confrontation over who administered discipline led ultimately to Farel and Calvin excommunicating the entire city by refusing to administer Communion on Easter Sunday of 1538, asserting that they could not expose the Lord to such wickedness. On the two days following, the magistrates banished Calvin and Farel. Not waiting to appeal, they both left, Farel settling in Neuchâtel, and Calvin heading to Strasbourg, his original destination before his detour in Geneva eighteen months previously. While on the road to their destinations, Calvin and Farel stopped at Berne to protest their innocence in the whole matter and to assert that they had never resisted using the Bernese forms of worship. Representatives from Geneva soon followed and told a completely different story. Berne was not amused. Later that month and into early May, a synod at Zurich, which included Bucer despite his difficulties with Bullinger, framed Calvin and Farel as the problems in Geneva rather than the magistrates.[12]

What role had Calvin played in his first exile? Was it his stance for the independence of the church from the republic and for the right of the ministry to guard the Lord's Table via excommunication that had brought about his and Farel's decision to cancel the Eucharist on Easter morning of 1538? Or rather was he but a side note in a larger play that concerned how closely to follow Berne in all things ecclesiastical, and was it this conflict that swept him away, Calvin being but the ecclesiastical expression of the Enfants' desire for political liberty? Berne itself was not happy with the eviction of Calvin and Farel, for while they had little sympathy for the ministers' actions, the two represented order and a stable ministry. There was fear in Berne that Calvin and Farel's failed confrontation with the government could throw Geneva back to Rome (and back to Savoy), so Berne supplied ministers to take up the mantle that Calvin and Farel had discarded by their ultimatum. The two ministers Berne sent to Geneva were Antoine Marcourt (author of the infamous placards of October 1534) and Jean Morand. But this did not bring the factionalism of Geneva to an end, for the city still had to deal with Berne. In aiding Geneva, Berne had hazarded war with Savoy, and to a degree with France; thus they sought some form of say in Geneva's life in return. The expulsion of Calvin and Farel still left the city in two factions: the Guillermins (so called for their loyalty to Guillaume Farel) and the Articulants (derisively called the Artichokes, so labeled for their agreeing to a twenty-one-article alliance with Berne). The defeat of Calvin and Farel did not conclude the Reformation but rather stymied Calvin's and Farel's vision of a church independent of the magistrates, for many of the moral reforms that the Reformers had wanted were put into effect, but the pastoral ministry of the Genevan church suffered.

In any event, the Articulant syndics bollixed the politics of the negotiations with Berne in the eyes of most Genevans, for the whole agreement conceded to Berne's interests, granting its expectations regarding religion and turning over to Berne what might be thought Genevan territory. The dismissal of two other pastors loyal to Farel and Calvin, Mauthurin Cordie and Antoine Saunier, only further deteriorated ecclesiastical life. The Guillermins, who included Ami Perrin, kept the exiles informed by a continuous correspondence, particularly with Farel in Neuchâtel. Calvin, for his part, urged those loyal to him in Geneva to amity, patience, and restraint. Such advice paid off with the collapse of the Articulant program. The Articulants and others did brandish the charge of

---

12. Bruce Gordon, *Calvin* (New Haven: Yale University Press, 2009), 82–83.

lack of patriotism and too-close affinity to France at the Guillermins, but the Guillermins were able in turn to distinguish themselves as the ones interested in independence from Berne. By February 1540 the alliance with Berne had been materially repudiated when two Guillermin candidates captured two of the syndic posts. More importantly, in June of that year the two remaining Articulant syndics, Jean Philippe and Claude Richardet, got involved in a brawl that led to the death of their opponent. Jean Philippe was executed the following day; Claude Richardet fell to his death while trying to escape through a window. Subsequently, the Bernese ministers, Mourand in June and Marcourt in September, returned to Berne. The two remaining ministers, holdovers from the time of Calvin's first stay, Henri de la Mare and Jacques Bernard, wrote Calvin, who had already shown himself a champion of the city in his reply to the letter from Sadoleto in 1539, imploring him to return.[13]

After some wavering about the matter,[14] particularly on the part of Martin Bucer, the chief minister of Strasbourg, who had made great use of Calvin in the colloquies and diets in 1540 and 1541 and valued his mind greatly, Calvin determined to return to Geneva. In September of 1541 Ami Perrin, with an armed escort, arrived in Strasbourg to bring Calvin south. Calvin's party took a rather circuitous route home, going first to Basle, and then Zurich and Berne, and lastly by Neuchâtel to visit Farel. Calvin must have still had some reservations, for he left his wife, Idelette de Bure, in Strasbourg (he had married Idelette, a former Anabaptist, on the recommendation of Bucer).[15]

Calvin's wariness of Geneva can be seen in other matters as well: he let it be known that the book of order was to be enacted; indeed it was of the utmost importance, the seemingly necessary thing for his return. The *Ecclesiastical Ordinances* would encompass all citizens within its purview, from highest to lowest, and essentially ensure, at least Calvin so thought,

---

13. Philip Schaff, in *History of the Christian Church* (New York: Charles Scribner's, 1910), 8:428, notes that this was a tribute to de la Mare's and Bernard's character that they would write Calvin, even though they were his "enemies." All this betrays Schaff's basic assumptions that the fighting in Geneva pitted true religion against dissimulation and that those not with Calvin must be opposed to him. Such thinking Gordon labels "Tolkienesque" (*Calvin*, 216), though in Schaff it comes across as almost Manichaean. The sad fate of Henri de la Mare will be touched on in the conclusion.

14. Calvin had been adamant in his letters that he could think of no worse death than to return to Geneva, telling Viret, who wrote from Lausanne encouraging his return: "Would I rather not consider Geneva a desirable place? Why not rather directly to the cross? Indeed it would have been preferable to perish at once, than on that rack again be twisted. Therefore, my Viret, if you desire my health, stop this advice." CO 11:36: "Genevamne, ut melius habeam? Cur non potius recta ad crucem? Satius enim fuerit semel perire quam in illa carnificina iterum torqueri. Ergo, mi *Virete*, si salvum me esse cupis, consilium istud omittas."

15. Gordon, *Calvin*, 123.

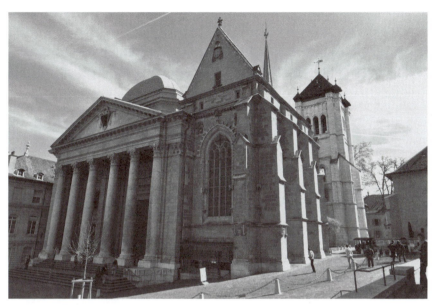

St. Pierre's Cathedral, Geneva

the independence of the church from the magistrates. This theme so colored Calvin's thought and disposition that he would later tell even Ami Perrin, his chief advocate and champion among the Guillermins, that he would never grant him any special measures when it came to church discipline.[16] Calvin's adamant disposition on this matter cannot be understated, though it should also be noted that whatever goodwill Perrin might have obtained from Calvin was largely dissipated through his wife, that inveterate lover of dancing Françoise Favre.

The city gave Calvin a house near St. Pierre's Cathedral and paid him the handsome salary of five hundred florins a year. This enormous sum was not all in cash, but some in wine and cloth. All the same, this salary was given with the intent that Calvin's home was to be one of hospitality for students and ministers. Idelette did join him later and kept his home until her death in 1549. Calvin counted Idelette a great benefit to his life and ministry, for his ministry completely comprehended every aspect of his life. He preached almost every day, and a perusal of his sermons shows that these were works of rhetorical art, objects crafted from his humanist education in legal studies and rhetoric. Apart from preaching, Calvin produced numerous commentaries and a massive number of letters; his entire corpus, however numbered, runs over fifty volumes.

16. Cottret, *Calvin*, 191–92.

One of the most important elements of Geneva's new order was the Consistory. Loosely modeled on Bucer's polity in Strasbourg, the Consistory had the duty of moral supervision of the various parishes; while members of the company of pastors attended it, it was largely made up of lay elders drawn from the city's governing bodies. Essentially a lay Christian court, one of the syndics oversaw it. The group met every Thursday except when Communion was to be offered on a Sunday, and then they would meet the prior Tuesday as well. Calvin saw the Consistory as one aspect of the moral reform of Geneva, and it certainly proved contentious, to both Geneva's government and its citizens, who frequently chafed under the moral strictures the Consistory imposed: no dancing, censorship of the theater, and regulations on drinking and other aspects of life.[17] With respect to the magistrates, the Consistory challenged them as to who possessed the authority of excommunication—that is, who possessed authority over legal standing in the city: the Consistory or the councils? The Consistory as a board of lay elders is one of the hallmarks of Calvin's church polity, later turned into the notion of "ruling elders," as distinct from ordained or teaching elders. Calvin drew this novel distinction from his interpretation of 1 Timothy 5:17.[18]

Calvin used the daily sermons as another means for moral improvement, and Genevan ministers preached in every parish of the city, every day of the year. The demands this made on the clergy did not always sit well with them. But whatever burden this placed on the company of pastors, the toll this took on the faithful could border on the maddening, for ministers in their sermons would sometimes call out particular people for their sins, and the delicacy of the matters treated seemed to offer no brake to the ministers' pronouncements, such that people feared matters private could all too often become public. At one point someone left a note in the preacher's lectern in St. Pierre's threatening death if the marital problems of Ami Perrin and his wife came up in a sermon. The sermon in Geneva, among other things, functioned as the public arm of the Consistory's moral duties. But the sermon served a greater purpose in Calvin's mind than moral correction, and indeed, the process of citing individuals from the pulpit was no mere way to inform the town of someone else's sin. For Calvin, a minister needed to take care not to make his sermons mere orations to an audience, but needed to break into a conversational style appropriate for private admonitions; sermons should be done with the intent of accompanying biblical exposition with private admonitions. Beyond this,

17. See Gordon's discussion of the organization of the Consistory in *Calvin*, 133–35.
18. See especially Scott M. Manetsch, *Calvin's Company of Pastors: Pastoral Care and the Emerging Reformed Church, 1536–1609*, Oxford Studies in Historical Theology (New York: Oxford University Press, 2013).

care should be taken that sermons were not flippantly delivered, and the auditors should know they were as much in the presence of God as the original
hearers of the day's lectionary reading.[19] By the power of the Spirit (in a way
analogous to the Spirit's action in the Eucharist), the time from the "then" of
the text to the "now" of the hearers' day was bridged. Thus preaching was a
means of grace. Preaching, the Eucharist and baptism, and the disciplinary
work of the Consistory composed Calvin's marks of the true church.[20]

The tale of the collapse of Calvin's opposition can be condensed to the
years from 1552 to 1555. Troubles existed prior to that, most famously the case
of Ami Perrin and his wife, along with other notable people of their circle,
who were cited to the Consistory in 1546 for dancing at the April wedding of
Antoine Lect's daughter. This grand affair included guests from Berne who
the Genevans asserted had prompted them to dancing, since such activities
were not banned in Berne. Françoise Favre, Perrin's wife, for her part showed
no contrition about the whole matter, asserting that she had done nothing
wrong. Incensed, Calvin wrote to Farel of his anger and subsequently denounced dancing from the pulpit. Besides his wife, Ami Perrin himself and
the head of the Consistory, Amblard Corne, were cited before the Consistory
for their gamboling offenses. Corne submitted, but Perrin blew off the whole
affair. This ambivalence elicited a letter from Calvin that led Perrin to soften,
but the seeds of the later conflict were already germinating, for whatever the
resolution to the troubles in 1546, the circle around Perrin chafed under the
Genevan ministry. Perrin's father-in-law, François Favre, found himself before
the Consistory for calling Calvin Geneva's bishop and a devil and asserting
that one had to rehearse his sins to Calvin and ask for his pardon.[21]

Calvin had little regard for Perrin, the captain general of Geneva, labeling
him "Caesar comicus" to Farel,[22] even though Perrin arguably had the greatest hand in Calvin's return to Geneva. Doubtless Perrin saw Calvin as part of
the solution to severing unwanted ties with Berne, but other ministers whose
personalities and dispositions may have better suited Perrin's tastes (he was
widely known for his appetites) certainly were to be found. Perhaps he thought
he could control Calvin. Yet for all the contention within Geneva between
the Consistory and some of the citizens, the late 1540s and the opening of

19. Ronald S. Wallace, *Calvin, Geneva, and the Reformation* (Grand Rapids: Baker, 1988),
172–74.

20. Thomas J. Davis, "Preaching and Presence: Constructing Calvin's Homiletical Legacy,"
in *The Legacy of John Calvin*, ed. David Foxgrover (Grand Rapids: CRC Product Services,
2000), 84–106; see 96–98.

21. CO 21:431, proceedings for September 20 and 23, 1547.

22. CO 14:657.

the 1550s seem relatively free of the factionalism that had dominated the city up until 1540.[23]

The most spectacular confrontations between the ministers and Perrin's circle, whom Calvin dubbed "the Libertines" but who called themselves Enfants, harkening back to those who had stood for the liberty of Geneva,[24] came in 1552, when those who opposed Calvin ascended to power in multiple offices in elections across the city. The confrontation centered on the case of Philip Berthelier, whom the Consistory had barred from Communion. Berthelier, the son of the Enfant Philip Berthelier, who had been executed in 1519, is the same Philip Berthelier who had interrupted Calvin's sermons with his coughing. Berthelier found himself in an unhappy marriage (he thought he had married money but had not), showed little constraint about adultery, and thus found himself before the Consistory on several occasions for philandering and drunkenness. In October 1552 he got into an altercation with Raymond Chauvet, one of the ministers, threatened him with violence, and took after him, chasing him through the streets until the minister found refuge in St. Pierre's. Berthelier was summarily excommunicated.[25] This rancorous case coincides with the Enfants' accession to the government of the city, but it was hardly the only cause of dissension, for the posture of the ministers to the citizens, the growing number of French émigrés in the city, and the correlative fact that the chief ministers and their allies (Farel in Neuchâtel and Viret in Lausanne) were also French all played a part. Probably the single election that tells the most about the public mood concerning the French involved Philip Berthelier, who but three days removed from his release from prison and still under excommunication, was elected as an auditeur, an assistant to the lieutenant of the city.[26]

Behind the struggles stood the growing question of the émigrés, who overwhelmingly supported Calvin and the company of pastors. Many of them had materially attained the status of bourgeois within the city, though having not been formally declared such, and thus they lacked the franchise. In this regard, the concerns animating much of the disquiet in Geneva in 1553 were the same as those in 1530—namely, the presence of foreign interests and foreign clergy—only this time the clergy were far more involved in almost every

23. This is a sustained argument of Naphy, and he notes the reemergence of factionalism on the part of the Enfants or Perrinists in 1552 (*Consolidation*, 172).

24. Naphy, *Consolidation*, 182.

25. T. H. L. Parker, *John Calvin* (Hunts, UK: Lion, 1975), 136; and Wallace, *Calvin*, 61 (Wallace gives the date as 1551); CO 21:520. Berthelier was not the chief instigator in the fracas, but Philip Bonna, who had been reprimanded by Chauvet for making advances on a married woman. They were joined in the chase by Balthazar Sept.

26. Naphy, *Consolidation*, 173.

aspect of life, from the shuttering of the theaters to the closing of taverns and their replacement with pious wine dispensaries used for the discussion of theology and the singing of Psalms. That innovation did not go over well, and the taverns soon reemerged. Actions were taken against the French émigrés, including disarming them, with the exception of personal swords, and even these they were forbidden to carry in public. Beza saw this as the disarming of the godly to keep them from defending themselves.

In September 1553 the Small Council overturned the decision of the Consistory and informed Philip Berthelier that he could receive Communion that coming Sunday, but someone apparently warned him not to go. Calvin, not knowing Berthelier's intentions, and more defiant than ever, blasted the decision from the pulpit and warned that no one under excommunication should dare approach the table, for Calvin would give his life to make sure they did not receive Communion. That afternoon Calvin preached the sermon referenced above on Paul's farewell in Acts 20. He had already asked the Small Council to accept his resignation, but they had refused, and now he was convinced that they would act. But Calvin survived. To some, his continuance rode on the back of the Servetus affair (Servetus had come to Geneva in early August and was arrested on August 13).[27] Miguel de Serveto, or Servetus, had come knowing that Calvin faced opposition, and Calvin himself was sure his enemies were using Servetus against him. This assertion that Servetus was a tool in the hands of Calvin's enemies, made at the time only by Calvin but repeated by Beza, is groundless, in that no one stood up for the Spaniard.[28] The only hesitation from the council came not in any delay of the prosecution of Servetus but rather to seek advice from the other Swiss churches and Melanchthon (all of whom concurred that Servetus should be executed). Servetus's hunch that Calvin was weak got him sent to the stake, with all of Geneva, including the syndics and the Small Council, which at this point was composed of a majority of Calvin's enemies, concurring. Indeed, the whole trial was a civil affair, Servetus never appearing before an ecclesiastical court, with Calvin only being called in as an expert for the theological arguments. The prosecution fell to the lieutenant Pierre Tissot, but he handed it over to Philip Berthelier, still excommunicate, who did his duty by Genevan law.[29]

Calvin actually survived the confrontation with Berthelier because he had the backing of the company of pastors, who had closed ranks behind him.

27. Parker, *Calvin*, 147. Parker depicts the reaction to the case as Calvin being the champion of Christendom, and the Libertines its enemies.

28. Cf. Wallace, *Calvin*, 177; and Parker, *Calvin*, 144.

29. See Naphy, *Consolidation*, 183–84; and for the makeup of the council and their handling of the Servetus case, see also chap. 4.

There was also the matter that about half the citizenry and the whole of the émigré community stood with him. The magistrates and Calvin sought the views of the other Swiss churches, but they uniformly placed excommunication in the hands of their magistrates. The only non-Genevan pastor to support Calvin was Farel, who full of sound and fury blundered his way through a sermon accusing Geneva's "youth" of, among other things, murder, lewdness, robbery, and atheism.[30] While in law the Small Council had the right of excommunication, and while the rest of the Swiss churches, especially Berne and Zurich, backed the magistrates, Perrin and his allies did not have the power to thwart Calvin on this issue.

In the spring 1554 elections, the city demonstrated no desire for change, and the results fell to neither faction's favor, an outcome that certainly does not suggest that the Servetus affair had hurt the Enfants; in fact the November elections heavily favored the Enfants. What did hurt them was the use made by the ministers of some spectacular cases involving sodomy and sacrilege, with capital punishment meted out to three offenders. Even though the culprits were all French, the cases were used by the ministry to highlight, according to them, what sort of town the Libertines (i.e., the Enfants) wanted to make Geneva. A more serious matter, because of its proximity to the elections, occurred in January of 1555, when a group of youths, some of them scions of the Enfants, marched through the streets late at night mocking the Psalms. In his sermon on the next Sunday, Calvin thundered from the pulpit: "Alas! Our Lord has indeed given occasion to weep and moan, both to you, children of Geneva, and to me with you. For it is needful that a pastor, when there is some scandal in the church, should be the first to cry out to ask pardon of God so that all the people may follow him."[31] Public opinion seems to have turned toward the pastors, and the Enfants were turned out in the 1555 elections.

The success of the Reformers brought with it measures to ensure that their political opponents were barred from power. By May a number of the French émigrés were made bourgeoisie; when even more were admitted, the Enfants started to grouse, demanding that the matter be sent to the Council of Two Hundred, which recommendation the Small Council promptly brushed aside. On the night of May 16, after having too much to drink, a

30. Naphy, *Consolidation*, 185, notes that the sermon was against the youth of Geneva (and Farel does use the word "jeunesse"), but Parker took Farel's sermon to be aimed at the Enfants, and the record of the council, reproduced by Amédée Roget in *Histoire du peuple de Genève depuis la réforme jusqu'à l'escalade* (Nieuwkop: B. de Graaf, 1825–83), 4:134, notes that Farel's words were "à grande injure des enfans de la ville." All the same, Farel was cited by the Small Council, and he returned to Geneva and apologized.
31. Quoted in Cottret, *Calvin*, 198.

number of the Enfants took to the streets, and a "riot" ensued. Many writers give the event an apocalyptic tone, claiming that it spoke of revolution and that this is what ended the Enfants' power in Geneva.[32] Ami Perrin did actually grab a syndic's baton of office, but at the moment, and actually for some days following, no one seems to have thought anything of it. Indeed, Perrin was still attending council meetings on May 24. It only seems to have dawned on the Reformers over the summer to use the incident to their advantage. Numerous Enfants, or Perrinists as they have also been labeled, were publicly admonished, and they were the fortunate ones; seven of them were executed, including François Comparet, who was in prison at the time of the riot. Another five were banished, numerous were fined or beaten, and another sixteen, including Perrin, Philip Berthelier, and Claude Sept, escaped with death sentences over their heads.[33]

The actions of the Reformers were met with uniform disapproval in Zurich, Basle, and Berne. François Hotman, though certainly one of Calvin's most ardent admirers, wrote that Calvin was as popular in Basle as he was in Paris.[34] The Enfants—who had held themselves to be the defenders of Geneva's liberty and independence; who saw the burgeoning of the French refugees, despite their diligence and prosperity, as a threat; and who doubtless were not averse to acting violently—nonetheless did not banish Calvin or the ministers when they had the opportunity. This was not the case once Calvin's party came to power. Ultimately the Consistory was granted the power of excommunication, and Geneva became the lone Protestant city whose church exercised such power. Calvin's arrangement, of course, suited his followers in France, where the godly magistrate was hard to find, and it speaks to how Thomas Cartwright in England could seek a church disentangled from the prince and without bishops, who were obviously (in critics' eyes) agents of the queen.

Calvin's view on the independence of the church, redolent of the Gregorian Reformers,[35] became a hallmark of his thought, in that discipline stands as one of the marks of the true church. Calvin's vision of a godly society, one whose theaters performed only such plays as *The Acts of the Apostles*, and one without dancing and taverns, does not mean that Calvin disdained pagan learning; he saw the liberal arts as gifts of God given to humans via the pagans—that is to say, Calvin saw a place for the secular that was not merely

---

32. Parker, *Calvin*, 149–50; Cottret, *Calvin*, 198; Wallace, *Calvin*, 67.

33. The whole list is given in Naphy, *Consolidation*, 195–96.

34. Naphy, *Consolidation*, 197.

35. See H. E. J. Cowdrey, *The Cluniacs and the Gregorian Reform* (Oxford: Oxford University Press, 1970).

negative.[36] Where Calvin differed from his coreligionists was in granting a redemptive place to the godly magistrate. Luther had taken the fourth commandment, to honor father and mother, and applied it to the godly prince (as opposed to the clergy). The rest of the Reformers followed Luther's lead, leaving the ban in the hands of the magistrates. Calvin's position set him apart on this point, and doubtless his enthusiasm for moral austerity informed him that the Genevan magistrates, seeking their own liberty from the church, were never going to produce the godly Jerusalem that Calvin envisioned, that most perfect school of Christ as seen by Knox hardly more than eighteen months after the flight of Perrin and Berthelier. Calvin's making discipline a mark of the church automatically set him on a course for the confrontations that ensued (in any city his uncompromising position would have created problems), and clearly in Geneva's specific situation, the implications of his doctrine entailed the strife that ensued. The austerity that Calvin expected of Geneva, the strictures he expected the citizens to accept, far from creating a church at liberty from the magistrates, made the church instead the conscience and reformatory of even the magistrates, de facto making the entire city into a catechetical school, and one that had no room for humanists such as Castellio, let alone such sinners as Françoise Favre and Philip Berthelier.

36. CO 49:325: "Indeed what is nobler than human reason, by which man excels other animals? How rightly does liberal learning deserve honor, which refines humans that they might be truly civilized?"

7

François Baudouin

An Odyssey of Werewolves and Brothel Keepers

And behold . . . [Calvin's] notorious pamphlet appeared in French, besotted with an atrocious yammering (for he employs this marvelously eloquent language for cursing): and not as a witty buffoonish rake, but adorned with the repetitions one gets from the decorous dives of a raucous obscene brothel keeper, and at the same time armed with bolts of anathemas . . . that by reason of such strength he can conquer with a single hiss, for this is his art of choice when treating with others.[1]

Though at first possessed of filial devotion to Calvin, François Baudouin, with his love of the law and the tools necessary for legal study (grammar, philology, and history), developed a doctrine of the church wholly at odds with that of Calvin. While Baudouin's transformation occurred over the course of years, his final break with Calvin came with a swift ferocity and a violent animosity. François Baudouin's early life mirrored Calvin's: both began their higher education in the study of law, both had the same legal and humanist influences, and both subsequently embraced the Reformation, resulting in their exiles. The trajectory of Baudouin's Protestant pilgrimage

1. François Baudouin, *Fr. Baldvini responsio altera ad Ioan. Calvinum* (Paris: Morelius, 1562), 2–3.

reached its zenith in 1547, when he served as Calvin's secretary, living in Calvin's home. The denouement of Baudouin's journey, however, like that of Louis du Tillet, took him back to the Catholic Church, only for Baudouin the return proved more circuitous, informed far more by humanism than theology. As with du Tillet, the move also included a strong ecclesiological bent, one that produced rancorous diatribes between Baudouin and Geneva. But unlike du Tillet's case, the break with Calvin came even while Baudouin still openly embraced Protestantism. The epithet Nicodemite plays in Baudouin's story as well, but for Baudouin and those of like mind, Calvin even coined a new term: *moyenneurs* (those irresolute compromisers in the middle).[2]

Baudouin spent his early years in the town of his birth, Arras, and there took in the basic elements of the arts before following in the footsteps of his father in the profession of law, studying jurisprudence at Louvain. In 1540 he went to Paris, where he fell in with Charles Dumoulin, a jurist and friend of Calvin,[3] who practiced law in Paris; Baudouin also made his first acquaintance with François Hotman, who would play a large role in his life.[4] Though civil law was not formally taught at Paris, nonetheless lectures on it were given as they touched the study of canon law. In 1542 Baudouin published his first book, a study of the emperor Justinian's agricultural legislation. This was followed in 1545 with a preface to a larger work that marked what Donald R. Kelley has called "the first history of Roman legal science."[5] Unlike Calvin, Baudouin never abandoned his study of law, and he left an indelible mark not only on legal studies but also on the study and discipline of history. Having finished the first part of his university training, Baudouin returned to Arras practicing law, and there fell under the sway of the Reformed minister Pierre Brully, who had for a while succeeded Calvin as minister of the French congregation in Strasbourg.[6] During this time in the early 1540s, Baudouin roomed with the future martyrologist (and future friend of Calvin) Jean Crespin. But in 1545 the ecclesiastical and temporal authorities cracked down on heresy in Flanders

2. Mario Turchetti, "The 'Moyenneurs' Pursue Conciliation," in *Reformation, Revolt and Civil War in France and the Netherlands, 1555–1585* (Amsterdam: The Royal Netherlands Academy of Arts and Sciences, 1997), 165–83.

3. Little has been done in English on Dumoulin, but see Donald R. Kelley, "*Fides Historiae*: Charles Dumoulin and the Gallican View of History," *Traditio* 22 (1966): 347–402.

4. Donald R. Kelley, *Foundations of Modern Historical Scholarship: Language, Law and History in the French Renaissance* (New York: Columbia University Press, 1970). For Hotman, see Kelley, *François Hotman: A Revolutionary's Ordeal* (Princeton: Princeton University Press, 1973). See p. 40 for Baudouin and Hotman's early Calvinism.

5. Kelley, *Foundations*, 118.

6. Jean Crespin, *Histoire des martyrs persecutez et mis a mort pour la vérité de l'Évangile, depuis le temps des apostres jusques à présent* (Toulouse: Société des livres religieux, 1885), 1:427–40.

and placed both Crespin and Baudouin under the ban, expelling them from Arras and confiscating their properties. Two days after this action, Brully was burned at the stake, and Baudouin fled back to Paris.[7]

From Paris Baudouin began writing Calvin, and later that year appeared in both Strasbourg and Geneva, drinking in the world of Rhenish and Swiss Protestantism. Baudouin's correspondence gives the details of his mind as he progressed in the Reformed faith. But the letters contain more than just his incipient creed, for they reveal an almost fawning exuberance, labeling Calvin "mi pater," exclaiming that he would be an ingrate if he did not pay Calvin proper thanks for his admonitions, and declaring that he was bolstered by a perpetual filial devotion to Calvin.[8] The religious connotations of this devotion are reinforced by the fact that Calvin was hardly more than ten years Baudouin's senior. He generally addressed Calvin by his frequently used epistolary pseudonym, Charles d'Espeville; Baudouin would sign himself Petrus Rochius (Peter the Rock) when the letters originated from France, but when writing from Strasbourg he addressed Calvin by name and signed with his own.[9] Baudouin referred to their friends by pseudonyms as well—for example, Crespin being Burgundus.

He visited Calvin in 1546, and in 1547 took up residence in Calvin's house, acting as his personal secretary. During the first of his sojourns he translated the treatise of his personal acquaintance Jacques de Bourgogne, sieur de Falais, *Excuse de noble Seigniur Iacques de Bourgoinge. S. de Fallez et Bredam* into Latin.[10] Since fleeing Arras in February of 1545, Baudouin had led a bohemian life, and while certainly gifted and possessing deep legal knowledge, he had no teaching appointment; perhaps he was awaiting one from Calvin or within Calvin's sphere of influence, though he never obtained this despite his labors and all his services.[11]

Failure to obtain an academic appointment brought with it a need to change his living arrangement and to seek what employment he could find. In 1548 he took work with the publisher Sebastian Gryphius in Lyons.[12]

7. For the documents and record on Brully, with reference to Crespin and Baudouin, see Charles Paillard, *Le Procès de Pierre Brully, Successeur de Calvin comme Ministre de l'Èglise Française Réformée de Strasbourg* (Paris: Sandoz et Fischbacher, 1878), 95; and the text of their expulsion, 171. Brully's passion is also recorded in Crespin, *Histoire*, 1:439.

8. CO 12, cols. 122–24, and CO 14:406–9.

9. Cf. Epistle 709 in CO 12, cols. 184–86.

10. Irena Backus, *Life Writing in Reformation Europe: Lives of Reformers by Friends, Disciples and Foes* (Aldershot, UK: Ashgate, 2008), 171.

11. Kelley, *Hotman*, 37.

12. For Gryphius, see Ian McLean, "Competitors or Collaborators? Sebastian Gryphius and His Colleagues, 1528–1556," in *Learning and the Market Place: Essays in the History of the Early Modern Book*, Library of the Written Word (Leiden: Brill, 2009), 9:273–89.

Mario Turchetti sees this as Baudouin's entrance into the broader world of humanism, even though doubtless the air of northern Europe in almost all its schools would have had whiffs of it. Employment with Gryphius brought Baudouin directly into the world of the Erasmians, for Gryphius had published the Erasmians and other humanists, including Rabelais, Alciato, Sadoleto, Claude Baduel, Emilio Ferretti, Etienne Dolet, Hector Froest, and Clément Marot.[13] For Turchetti, this marked for Baudouin a sea change in vision and perception, awakening in him what Turchetti calls a new religious language, one that was his own version of the *Institutes*.[14] In the strict sense of the term, Baudouin was already a humanist, gifted in philology and the use of both Latin and Greek, but the new element included manners and patterns of thought beyond the simple polarity of Catholic or Protestant. Lyons was also the second city of France, and as such was still subject to the whims of the king. When Henry II cracked down on heresy after his accession in 1547, the royal reach extended to Lyons. Baudouin had up till then been attending the Protestant church in the city, but with this, as he wrote Calvin, he began attending Catholic Mass.

In autumn of 1548 Baudouin finally obtained an academic appointment to teach jurisprudence at Bourges, the leading law school in France, having already turned down an offer to teach at Grenoble. The appointment in Bourges also marked the year of his mother's death, and he was with her at the end. As she lay dying, his mother pleaded for him to return to the Catholic Church.[15] There seems little evidence that he had any intention of acquiescing to her request, for while he did attend Mass in Bourges, and thus bolstered his credentials as a Nicodemite, throughout the 1550s he always maintained himself as a confessor of the Reformed faith, not only at Bourges but also in both Strasbourg and Heidelberg. Certainly Baudouin knew before ever taking the position at Bourges that this move necessitated Nicodemism, as Bourges had been the site of *autos-da-fé* (the acts of public penance by heretics, followed by their execution at the hands of the temporal authorities, almost always by burning at the stake).

For the next twelve years Baudouin threw himself into the study of both law and history, as he saw the latter as that most necessary thing in understanding law. For him the study of law demanded the study of its history, using the tools of humanism, and in particular philology, to liberate law from

13. Mario Turchetti, *Concordia o tolleranza? François Bauduin (1520–1573) e i "Moyenneurs"* (Geneva: Librairie Droz, 1984), 71.

14. Turchetti, *Concordia o tolleranza?*, 71–72.

15. Michael Erbe, *François Bauduin (1520–1573): Biographie eines Humanisten* (Gütersloh: Mohn, 1978), 57.

all the extraneous flotsam and jetsam that the years had piled up around it. Thus for Baudouin, history joined itself to philology and philosophy for a proper understanding of law: "There were three subjects indispensable for the understanding of civil law, each prescribed by a seminal title of the Digest. . . . 'On natural law' required . . . philosophy, so that 'On the meaning of words' required philology, and that 'on the origin of law' required history."[16] The study of law in France was not associated with the University of Paris (indeed, a royal edict had proscribed its teaching there), and so two law schools emerged separate from the capital, first at Bourges, and then at Orléans. At Bourges Baudouin took up the mantle of the jurist and humanist Andrea Alciato, his predecessor, in championing the use of humanism in the understanding of law; he looked more and more to ancient Rome for the origins of European law, for only by beginning with Rome could law be understood. This led to his prodigious output of commentaries and studies on both republican and imperial Roman law. In 1548 he published on Justinian's *Novellas*,[17] followed in 1550 by a study of the twelve tablets,[18] then in 1554 both a commentary on Justinian's *Institutes* and a treatise on the Roman jurist Papinian,[19] and in 1555 a study of Cato.[20] Then in 1556 came his work on the ecclesiastical legislation of Constantine, a project that marked a significant turn in his life.

When Baudouin had first come to Bourges, the memory and work of Alciato dominated the school, a legacy his colleagues Eguinaire Baron and François Le Douaren maintained. Although Baudouin had dedicated his 1548 work on Justinian to Le Douaren, he admired Baron more, and he edited Baron's works following the latter's death in 1550. Between Baudouin's arrival in 1548 and Baron's death, Le Douaren had left Bourges, but returned following the latter's demise, and this began a period of trouble for Baudouin that resulted in his leaving Bourges in 1555. While, as Kelley points out, faculty squabbles are sometimes hard to figure out, in the back of Baudouin's mind was also the religious question. He had complained more than once to Dumoulin about "idolatry," and these sentiments Dumoulin had related at least

16. Kelley, *Foundations*, 120.

17. François Baudouin, *In praecipuas Justiniani Imp. Novellas: sive Authenticas constitutiones: Idem ad Aedilitium Edictum* (Lyons: Sebastion Gryphius, 1548).

18. François Baudouin, *Libri duo ad Leges Romuli Regis Rom. Leges XII Tabularum. Ejusdem conscilium de nova juris civilis demonstratione, singularumque eius partium consideratione* (Lyons: Sebastian Gryphius, 1550).

19. François Baudouin, *Commentarii in libros quatuor Institutionum Iuris Civilis et eiusdem libri duo ad leges Romuli et leges XII Tab.* (Paris: Iakobus Dupyus, 1554); *Ad Paulum de cautione lecta in Auditorio Papiniani* (Lyons: Antony Vincent, 1554).

20. François Baudouin, *Cato, Sive Commentarivs Ad Regvlam Catonianam* (Strasbourg: Christian Mylius, 1555).

to Bullinger.[21] In 1555 Baudouin made his break with Bourges, and by 1556 through the interventions of Jakob Sturm was teaching in the one chair of law at Strasbourg to much acclaim.

Whatever the squabbling between Baudouin and his compeers among the jurists, no formal breach had occurred between him and Calvin, and Baudouin had never repudiated his affection, love, and filial appreciation for Calvin, even though, it should be noted, that while he had a letter of recommendation to Strasbourg from Dumoulin, he did not have one from Calvin, the same situation he had faced in 1547. And while Michael Erbe ponders that a breach may have at least been simmering since 1551, when Baudouin's friend Jacques de Bourgogne had opposed Calvin on the banishment of Bolsec from Geneva over the question of predestination,[22] it was 1556 that marked the formal end of their relationship (the material end would come in 1561), all stemming from the publication of Baudouin's aforementioned work on Constantine, *Constantinus Magnus: sive de . . . Legibus Ecclesiasticis atque civilibus Commentariorum.*[23] The text painted a picture of an early church in sharp contrast to that regnant in Geneva, one that seemed rather soft on the question of ecclesiastical discipline. Constantine's empire never prosecuted heretics at the level or to the expectations of the sixteenth century—that is, with the sixteenth century's level of exacting and near ferocious diligence to protect God's honor and the holiness and purity of the church. "But the most clement emperor," Baudouin claimed, "in all the affairs of the Church wished to act moderately, not violently or fearfully."[24] At the end of book 1, Baudouin wrote: "Happy the empire of Constantine, which had written such canons. Happy the canons, which had such a champion and defender. . . . We should turn our eyes to the age of Constantine [in thinking about laws and councils] and the judgment of his age."[25] Baudouin's lectures in Strasbourg emphasized the tolerance of Constantine's church.[26] Coming on the heels of the execution of Servetus and the initial controversy with Castellio, with confessional lines becoming increasingly sharper in France and the distinctions between Protestant and Catholic more pronounced, Baudouin's *Constantinus* spoke of reconciliation, of the power of the past to shape the present—that is, of the binding

21. Kelley, *Foundations*, 125.

22. Erbe, *François Bauduin*, 49.

23. François Baudouin, *Constantinus Magnus: sive de Constantini Imp. Legibus Ecclesiasticis atque civilibus Commentariorum libri duo* (Basle: John Oporinum, 1556).

24. Baudouin, *Constantinus*, 59.

25. Baudouin, *Constantinus*, 117–18.

26. Erbe, *François Bauduin*, 82–91.

character of tradition and custom.[27] Calvin could only view this, as Kelley notes, as "heresy, as well as betrayal."[28]

But contention with fellow Protestants hardly characterizes the entirety of Baudouin's brief time in Strasbourg, for in early 1556 he received an invitation from Matthias Flacius Illyricus to join the humanists of Magdeburg in producing a history of the church from the time of Christ onward. Baudouin declined the invitation, but he and Flacius took up a revealing correspondence on the nature of historical method, particularly as it relates to the composing of ecclesiastical histories. Baudouin proved a beneficial influence on the Centuriators, so called after the fruits of their labors, *The Centuries*.[29] The letters, which Baudouin addressed to the members of the Fünfmännerkollegium, which included Flacius, directed the Centuriators on what sources to use for setting context (e.g., secular histories and legal statutes) and what sources to avoid or treat with skepticism.[30] From their correspondence, Flacius drew up a list of thirty-seven points to guide the writing of *The Centuries*.[31] Flacius admired Baudouin, although Flacius hardly saw toleration, let alone concord with Rome, as an option. Indeed, for Flacius the arc of history was one set by the conflict of the Christ's true church with that of antichrist's— that is, Rome. Flacius's invitation to Baudouin came to him in Strasbourg, but Baudouin did not get to respond to Flacius from Strasbourg but from Heidelberg, as his tenure at Strasbourg came to an end due to the machinations of his adversaries.

In his inaugural lecture at Strasbourg, Baudouin took a swipe at Le Douaren, and in his subsequent book he took one also at his old acquaintance François Hotman.[32] Le Douaren met Baudouin's swipes with unmeasured animus, and Hotman joined him in this, as it was Hotman who had informed Le Douaren of Baudouin's incivility. Le Douaren wrote Calvin that Baudouin was nothing other than an "Ecebolius," an epithet of apostasy, for Ecebolius had been

27. Cf. Mario Turchetti, "Costantino il Grande al tempo della Riforma protestante e nel trattato 'Constantinus Magnus' di François Bauduin (1557)," in *Costantino il Grande tra Medioevo ed età moderna*, ed. Giorgio Bonamente et al. (Bologna: Il Mulino, 2008), 235–55.

28. Kelley, *Foundations*, 125.

29. François Baudouin, *Ecclesiastica Historia, integram Ecclesiae Christi ideam, quantum ad Locum, Propagationem, Tranquillitatem, Doctrinam, Haereses, Ceremonias, Gubernationem, Schismata, Synodos, Personas, Miracula, Martyria, Religiones extra Ecclesiam et statum Imperii politicum attinet, secundum singulas Centurias, perspicue ordine complectens: singulari diligentia et fide ex vetustissimis et optimis historicis, patribus et aliis scriptoribus congesta* (Basle: Ioanem Oporinum, 1559–74).

30. There are three letters edited and reproduced in Erbe, *François Baudouin*, 263–69, 270–76.

31. Gregory B. Lyon, "Baudouin, Flacius, and the Plan for the Magdeburg Centuries," *Journal of the History of Ideas* 64, no. 2 (April 2003): 253–72, and see 260.

32. Kelley, *Hotman*, 78.

Julian the Apostate's teacher. Hotman hardly settled for inciting Le Douaren against Baudouin. In the years since Baudouin had left Geneva, Hotman had first taken up residence as his replacement in Calvin's house, and then had taught not law but grammar for some years in Lausanne, chafing from the lack of an appointment to teach law. Hotman was, like Baudouin, a brilliant humanist and jurist, and they agreed on much concerning the study and value of law. But Hotman had never played the Nicodemite, never hidden his light under a basket; he never scrupled to point out these facts to Calvin, almost always with a reminder that Baudouin most certainly had done so, at one point labeling him a sometime frequenter of idolatrous temples.[33] Hotman had sat for years teaching grammar in Lausanne while Baudouin obtained the reputation as a distinguished teacher. Hotman not only wrote to the faculty at Bourges of Baudouin's words against Le Douaren, with the help of Calvin and Johannes Sturm (not to be confused with Jakob Sturm, who had been a patron of Baudouin), but he also hatched a plot that eventually won him Baudouin's position in Strasbourg. Hotman held the post for eight years, championing the Huguenots' cause and contending against anything having to do with Baudouin's attempts at Protestant and Catholic concord. Baudouin would, however, land on his feet as he ended up in the service of the Palatine elector at the University of Heidelberg, from where he would continue his prolific output of legal commentaries and essays, but even more importantly, where his ecclesiastical horizon greatly expanded, an enlargement of perspective that set him on course for a final, vitriolic confrontation with Calvin.

At Heidelberg he fell into the orbit of other irenic-minded thinkers: in 1557 at the Colloquy of Worms, acting as the Palatine elector's agent, he met both Philip Melanchthon and a fellow refugee from the Low Countries, Georg Cassander, the leader of the second wave of German Erasmians. In Heidelberg he also met George Witzel and James Omphalius, both of whom had known Erasmus, and Pietro Paulo Vergerius, the former papal nuncio and humanist. Of all of these it was Cassander who gave ideological contours to the mid-century irenic movement as he strove to implement reforms along the lines of the first five or six centuries of the church. To this end Cassander produced a number of works seeking to simplify the Mass, including two that were placed on the Index, *Hymni Ecclesiastici* and *Liturgica de ritu et ordine Dominicæ coenæ celebrandæ*.[34] His vast reading and antiquarian scholarship gave him the status necessary to draw ideas from the ancients

33. Kelley, *Hotman*, 144.

34. Georg Cassander, *Hymni Ecclesiastici, Praesertim qui Ambrosiani dicuntur* (Cologne, 1556); and Cassander, *Liturgica de ritu et ordine Dominicæ coenæ celebrandæ* (Cologne: Arnold Birkmann, 1558).

and present them for debate to his contemporaries, and his views strongly appealed to Baudouin's "new historical perspective," as H. O. Evennett put it.[35] Cassander more than anyone steered Baudouin's mind not toward a notion of toleration (what Castellio preached) but toward one of concord, of a vision of a church that, *mutatis mutandis*, could comprehend both Catholics and Protestants. Essentially Cassander and his vision, and its coincidence with the tragedy about to unfold in France, was the powder that ignited Calvin's and Baudouin's explosive confrontation, when Baudouin found himself swept into what Kelley calls "the maelstrom of ecclesiastical politics."[36]

Protestantism in France had been a growing movement for decades, despite harsh treatment at the hands of Henry II, and over these years the French Protestants, the Huguenots, had looked to Geneva for aid, particularly in the training of their ministers. Calvin's triumph over the Genevan patriots in the mid-1550s only strengthened the tie between Huguenot France and Geneva. With the untimely death of Henry II in a jousting tournament in 1559, France descended into turmoil, as the throne passed to Francis II—only fifteen at his father's death—and the queen mother, Catherine de Medici, though a foreigner, took the lead in governing a nation on the verge of civil war. Catherine was pinched from all directions, for powerful factions within the nobility supported both ecclesiastical sides. Catherine desired Catholic answers to the situation, but far too many interests ranged against her pacific designs. The Huguenots, besides being a force in their own right, had powerful allies and many useful cobelligerents, including Elizabeth of England; for the Catholic side, both the Spanish and the Austrian branches of the House of Habsburg stood forth, but especially the Spanish as the rebellion within their provinces of the Low Countries unfolded. Philip II of Spain would become the backbone of the French Catholic League both militarily and financially. Hoping to find some way forward, some way of saving her son's kingdom from the ravages of war, Catherine initially placed her hopes on a proposed colloquy in Poissy.[37]

Baudouin also, unfurling his colors with the rump of the Erasmians, openly sided with the colloquy. In many ways the Colloquy of Poissy replayed what had happened in the run-up to the first sessions of the Council of Trent, when such individuals as Giovanni Morone, Reginald Pole, George of Saxony, and even Emperor Charles V had looked to the thought of Erasmus and Gasparo

35. H. O. Evennett, *The Cardinal of Lorraine and the Council of Trent* (Cambridge: Cambridge University Press, 1930), 245–46.

36. Kelley, *Foundations*, 126.

37. See Donald Nugent, *Ecumenism in the Age of the Reformation: The Colloquy of Poissy* (Cambridge, MA: Harvard University Press, 1974).

Contarini for a way to end the religious conflict. But, as Evennett points out, much had changed in just fifteen years:

> Circumstance, however, gave to the French movement even smaller chances of success than those enjoyed by its forerunner. The rock of Calvinist theology and organization presented to eirenic endeavour a problem very different from the shifting sand and uncoordinated being of Lutheranism. The theological emphasis had passed from Justification to the Holy Eucharist; nor did such great names arise to guide what was in all respects a less powerful movement.[38]

Indeed, the naysayers were not only Calvin and the Huguenots but so too the Parlement of Paris, the papal envoys in France, most of the French Catholic hierarchy, and the University of Paris. But then Charles of Guise, the cardinal of Lorraine, threw his support behind the colloquy and was joined by several other bishops and clerics, some of whom would end up converting to Protestantism. In the midst of this, one of the leaders of the Huguenots, Antoine of Navarre, a prince of the blood and a man of some Machiavellian tendencies, appealed to Baudouin, seeking for what he called moderate counsels.[39] Baudouin responded from Heidelberg, championing Cassander's views, and thus did Baudouin enter the French arena. In 1561 he traveled to France, and with the help of Paul de Foix, Anthony of Navarre's agent whom Baudouin had known since meeting him in 1557 in Strasbourg, gained access to Navarre. Navarre had been approached already by Hotman and had initially taken his stance with Geneva's agenda, but after his meeting with Baudouin this tie was severed, and the prince turned away from the Huguenots and toward the positions championed by Baudouin and Cassander.[40] Upon hearing firsthand what Baudouin had to say, Navarre made him his agent and wrote the ruler of Heidelberg, the increasingly Calvinist Frederick III, to allow Baudouin more time in France.[41] Navarre got Baudouin an audience with Catherine de Medici, and she introduced him to Charles of Lorraine.

Baudouin's studies of history had already led him to abandon Calvin's precision, both in his theology and in his vision of the godly society. Baudouin desired a church built on a broader set of assumptions than those in Geneva; he demonstrated this in 1561 when he championed the *Augustana* to Catherine de Medici and the cardinal of Lorraine as a way to achieve concord. Baudouin, certainly no Lutheran—he had actually taken Calvin's side in the

38. Evennett, *Cardinal of Lorraine*, 239–40.
39. Evennett, *Cardinal of Lorraine*, 246.
40. Kelley, *Hotman*, 137.
41. Evennett, *Cardinal of Lorraine*, 248.

eucharistic conflict with Joachim Westphal[42]—employed the *Augustana* not as his own confession but rather as a basis for concord, through which war could be averted and peace restored to the church. Unlike his friend Castellio, who preached toleration, Baudouin actually still held out hope for some rapprochement between the factions.

Baudouin's hopes for a reconciliation collided with Calvin's pure-church model: Calvin's theology of discipline as a mark of the church dominated the Huguenot party and rendered peace impossible. Further, Calvin rightly saw that Baudouin was not of one mind with Castellio, for Baudouin did not want some form of toleration, which spoke of two churches, but of concordance, which led to but one. This via media that Calvin designated in Latin as *mediator*, in the French translation as the *moyenneur* position, elicited his full wrath on Baudouin, for he saw his and George Cassander's church as a betrayal of the gospel. Further, Calvin saw the *Augustana* as the means that the cardinal of Lorraine would use to undermine the Gallic Confession, making the *Augustana*, in Calvin's eyes, a Trojan horse to destroy unity among the French Protestants.[43] Charles of Lorraine, however, saw it as a way to draw the Huguenots to Baudouin's middle position. Calvin and Beza had advised the Huguenots to be prepared for such an overture at the colloquy. Ultimately, Poissy effected none of the ends for which either the queen mother or Baudouin had hoped; what it did show was the stark distance not only between the Huguenots and Catholics of France but even between the Huguenots and those who hoped for some form of cordial coexistence. The main result, the edict of January 1562, struck a blow at Baudouin's hopes, for it established the division, and not concord, between Protestants and Catholics in France in law. The *moyenneurs* could still have hope in that it was but provisional, for this was the interpretation of the law by the Parlement of Paris.[44] All the same, the end of the colloquy found Baudouin as the champion of both moderation and the idea of tolerance, which may have stood him in good stead with the Erasmians and such as the chancellor Michel l'Hopital and the cardinal of Lorraine, but in Geneva, his name became a byword of disgust.[45]

The Colloquy of Poissy saw the end of any decorum between Baudouin and Geneva. Calvin wrote to Antoine of Navarre, upbraiding him for listening to Cassander's counsels through the former papal nuncio Pietro Paulo Vergerio

42. Evennett, *Cardinal of Lorraine*, 247; and chapter 9 in this book, on Joachim Westphal.

43. Mario Turchetti, "Calvin face aux tenants de la concorde (moyenneurs) et aux partisans de la tolérance (castellionistes)," in *Calvin et ses contemporains: Actes du colloque de Paris 1995*, ed. Olivier Millet, Cahiers d'Humanisme et Renaissance 53 (Geneva: Librairie Droz, 1998), 54–55.

44. Turchetti, "'Moyenneurs' Pursue Conciliation," 172.

45. Turchetti, *Concordia o tolleranza?*, 226.

and also for taking up with Baudouin, "who has three or four times apostatized from Christ."[46] Not even the innocuous could be excused: Baudouin had left France before the colloquy started and returned only to find it disbanding, but he had brought with him Cassander's short treatise *De officio pii viri*, which Calvin took to have been Baudouin's own composition, a further testament to his opportunism. Baudouin's possession of the short treatise formed the occasion for Calvin's first printed treatise against Baudouin, the *Responsio ad versipellem quendam mediatorem*.[47] Kelley translates *versipellem* as "renegade," though the word has the strict connotation of shape changer, not like Proteus but, according to Pliny, like werewolves (*Naturalis historia* 8.34). Calvin saw the *De officio pii viri* as more evidence of Baudouin's irresolute character, in the same manner that Calvin had taken his adoption of the *Augustana* as just another step in his former disciple's wayward ways, a clear indication of his confessional instability. His meetings with the Catholic Charles of Lorraine also spoke of Baudouin's want of a theological anchor and willingness to betray the gospel. Calvin vented almost fifteen years of anger and frustration on Baudouin.

Baudouin embraced Calvin's mistake, owning Cassander's tract, and published a short apologia for *De officio pii viri*,[48] but more fulsomely "struck back under cover of a [legal] commentary" that contrasted Calvin and Beza's catalog of "laws" with the far more tolerant world of the ancient church.[49] Baudouin's efforts brought the full measure of Geneva's indignation, for Calvin mustered seemingly the whole of his network from France through the Rhineland, from Beza and Hotman to Le Conte, and even Baudouin's old friend Jean Crespin.[50] Calvin answered with his *Responsio ad Balduini convicia*, in which Crespin, then a printer in Geneva, not only printed Calvin's short response but also reproduced a number of letters, including Baudouin's fawning ones to Calvin, that painted Baudouin as the opportunistic shapeshifter that Calvin claimed him to be.[51] Crespin included the open letter from Le Douaren six years before in which Le Douaren had labeled Baudouin Ecebolius. The book also contained an anonymous letter from Hotman rehearsing Baudouin's theological peregrinations, and then attacking his views on

46. CO 18:660: "qui a desia este trois ou quatre fois apostat de Jesus Christ."
47. CO 9:529–60.
48. François Baudouin, *Defensio insontis libelli, de officio pii viri, adversus iniquum et importunum castigatorem* (Paris: H. Franciscum, 1562).
49. Kelly, *Hotman*, 143.
50. Turchetti, *Concordia o tolleranza?*, 201.
51. John Calvin, *Responsio* (Geneva: Crespin, 1562), in CO 9:565–80, is only Calvin's part, folios 3–40 in the original.

jurisprudence, displaying all his books for criticism.[52] Calvin's initial attack in 1562 was translated into French, which prompted Baudouin's *Responsio altera ad Ioan. Calvinum* (from which the initial text of this chapter is taken). Baudouin answered with vibrant invectives, responding to Le Douaren with more from the early church on the treatment of heretics, and citing Castellio, Bucer, and Melanchthon, among others, in his defense. For Baudouin, Calvin was the one guilty of corrupting the faith, having seduced all his lackeys into committing Calvinolatry. Further, as for his time with the cardinal of Lorraine, it was far more edifying, Baudouin maintained ("with God as my witness"), than any time he had ever spent with Calvin.[53]

Baudouin's most brazen apologia came in his anonymous *Religionis et regis adversus exitiosas Calvini, Bezae et Ottomani conjuratorum factiones defensio prima*.[54] Addressed to the Parlement of Paris, it cited Hotman (whose family was part of the nobility of the robe and stood to lose a great deal were Baudouin's accusations true), along with Beza and Calvin. For Baudouin, Calvin and Geneva through their theology formed a political faction that threatened the peace and well-being of France. Baudouin linked this agenda to the Conspiracy of Amboise of 1560. The Huguenots had hoped to kidnap Francis II and arrest both Henri Duke of Guise and Baudouin's new patron, Charles cardinal of Lorraine, the Duke of Guise's brother, but it had been a colossal failure, resulting in the execution of the conspirators and the discrediting of the Huguenots. Here Baudouin made his most sensational accusation, that the "most cruel and atrocious conspiracy" had Calvin as its instigator (*authorem*), Beza as its leader, and Hotman as its cosignatory (*subsignatorem*).[55] Baudouin particularly took the measure of Hotman, whom he condemned for his characterizations of the cardinal of Lorraine and in particular his activities in the Rhineland that undermined the Colloquy of Poissy.[56]

52. François Hotman, *De officio tum in religione tum in scriptionibus retinendo*, in Calvin, *Responsio*, 81–99. Le Douaren's epistle, 55–69. Crespin closed the text with his own backhand, a cataloging with commentary of the fourth-century laws against apostasy from Constantine and Theodosius, *Ad legem tertiam, Codice Apostatis, commentarius Io. Crispini, ad Iurisconsultos*.

53. Baudouin, *Responsio altera*, 37–38: "I met with the Cardinal of Lorraine who was then in Paris, concerning the controversial religious questions, which, with God as my witness . . . this conversation was more devout than any ever was which I had ever had with you."

54. François Baudouin, *Religionis et regis adversus exitiosas Calvini, Bezae et Ottomani conjuratorum factiones defensio prima* (Cologne: Werner Richwine, 1562). Though the work is anonymous, I follow Donald R. Kelley here in ascribing it to Baudouin, who alone possessed the knowledge the book contained; it also follows closely the rest of both his apologies and invectives against Geneva.

55. Baudouin, *Religionis et regis*, 22b.

56. Baudouin, *Religionis et regis*, 23b–25a.

Calvin's response came via his preface to Beza's *Ad Francisci Balduini apostate Eceboli convicia* of 1563. Beza continued his polemic in his *Vita* of Calvin, and other Calvinists piled on.[57] Baudouin ended his direct part in the dispute, though some of his students—two brothers—took up the mantle: Michael Fabricius published *Responsio Calvinum et Bezam pro Francisco Balduino* in 1563, and his brother, Gabriel, a response to Beza in 1567, his *Responsio ad Bezam.*[58] Ironically, perhaps the last volley of this fight was fired by one of Baudouin's last students, Jean-Papire Masson. The whole debacle had poisoned Baudouin's life at Heidelberg, as the elector had gone over to Calvinism in early 1561 and had turned against Baudouin owing to the inveterate imprecations of Hotman. Baudouin spent the next several years in Paris, and through the interventions of the cardinal of Lorraine was received back into the Catholic Church in 1563. He eventually obtained another faculty appointment in law at the University of Angers, which he held until his death in 1573. Masson was Baudouin's student at Angers, and following Baudouin's death—Masson was Baudouin's literary executor—penned a short biography of Calvin based on Calvin's writings, Baudouin's recollections, and the recollections of one of Calvin's cousins in Paris.[59] One might take Masson's account of Calvin as remarkably evenhanded given the vitriol between Masson's subject and his mentor; but perhaps even more significantly, we should see Masson as the dutiful student of his master, faithful to the discipline of history that Baudouin had preached to the Magdeburg Centuriators. Masson's *Vita Ioannis Calvini*, though short and though critical of Calvin, purposefully slighted the one de rigueur element in Catholic polemics of the 1570s, Jerome Bolsec's tale of Calvin's having been branded for sodomy.

François Baudouin's appointment to Angers marked a return to his past, in that he had been banned from the Low Countries by decree in 1545, and now through the interventions (again) of Charles of Lorraine was able to return. His odyssey had certainly carried him through the legal and cultural world of humanism, only to land him back nearly where he had started. Willing to face exile for his faith, he at some point, while willing to keep it even if in a compromised form, turned his back on what he saw as some of its more rigorist elements of his creed—namely, those aligned with Geneva's disciplinary regimen. Whether this change came at Lyons at the presses of Sebastian Gryphius, as Turchetti thinks, or due to his admiration for the

---

57. Kelley, *Hotman*, 147.

58. Michael Fabricius, *Responsio Calvinum et Bezam pro Francisco Balduino Iuriscons., cum Refutatione Calumniarum de Scriptura et Traditione* (Cologne: Werner Richwine, 1564); Gabriel Fabricius, *Responsio ad Bezam Vizeliam Eceboliam* (Paris: n.p., 1567).

59. For Masson and his influence, see Backus, *Life Writing*, 170–83.

opinions of Jacques de Bourgogne as they pertained to the Bolsec affair, per Erbe, Baudouin came to see the political character of his early faith to be at odds with what the church had traditionally maintained. Baudouin believed the Genevan pastors had arrogated powers the early church would not even have granted its emperors.[60] Such stringencies could hardly be maintained in Geneva without the greatest of civil unrest; how could they be expected of all of Christendom?

60. See Turchetti, *Concordia o tolleranza?*, 111.

8

Jerome Bolsec

No Insult or Vicious Defamation Good Enough

On June 21, 1581, during the University Act, a three-day event at the end of Oxford's academic year, students entered the University Church of St. Mary the Virgin to find a Latin tract titled *Rationes decem* distributed throughout the pews. Had they reached the third section, they would have found ribald and scurrilous descriptions of various Reformers, such as Zwingli, "Helvetus gladiator," and Luther, "infelix Monachus incesto connubio votam Deo virginem funestasset" (the unhappy monk defiled with murder his vow of chastity to God by an incestuous marriage), and Calvin, "stigmatus perfuga," a branded deserter.[1] Ribald satire marked the University Act—in 1670 the university moved it from the church to a more suitable place, the Sheldonian Theatre—and the students may well have taken this for part of the day's wit, but in fact the tract was written by the Jesuit (and soon-to-be Catholic martyr) Edmund Campion, and his purpose was deadly earnest.[2] His use of the term "*stigmatus perfuga*" arose from a 1577 biography of Calvin that he may have read at Douai, one penned by the physician and erstwhile Protestant Jérôme-Hermès Bolsec, who in the text asserted that Calvin as a youth had been caught *in flagrante dilecto* with another boy, and instead of being sent to the stake for sodomy was merely branded by the mercy of the

---

1. Edmund Campion, *Rationes decem quibus fretus certamen Anglicanae Eccl. Ministris obtulit in causa fidei* (Ingolstadt: David Sartorius, 1583), 19. The tract was reprinted across Europe, with editions coming out in Würzburg, Antwerp, and Vienna.

2. Gerard Kilroy, *Edmund Campion: A Scholarly Life* (Farnham, UK: Ashgate, 2015), 201–2.

bishop of Noyon with a fleur-de-lis on his shoulder.[3] Edmund Campion's salacious reference, for all its prurient import, had its genesis in an argument over predestination, an inflammatory altercation that Calvin's friend and colleague Theodore Beza could not leave without comment in his biography of Calvin. Clearly the doctrine of predestination was not without its critics in Geneva, as seen in July 1553, when the French expatriate Robert Le Moynne de Unfleur pronounced his disdain for "fottue predestination,"[4] a crass gerund that could have either a verbal or adjectival sense (for Le Moynne it obviously was adjectival). Bolsec had two years earlier hoped indeed to give the term its full verbal import, to defile and bring shame on the doctrine that for many remains synonymous with Calvin's name, the doctrine of double predestination. Bolsec exposed Calvin on the question of predestination, though not so much on a theological level (for while possessing some theological acumen, he certainly did not get the better of Calvin), but by revealing the indifference and even alarm with which many of Calvin's Swiss Protestant allies held the doctrine. Indeed, apart from Beza in Lausanne and to a lesser extent Farel in Neuchâtel, Calvin found that his views had little support among the Swiss. But it was not just the other Reformed cities—Berne, Zurich, and Basle—for even Calvin's close friends suddenly seemed shocked that he could hold the views that he did, and that with unreserved certitude he would not only brook no dissent but even have those who disagreed—that is, Bolsec—put in prison. But Bolsec would have his revenge, for he would join with others whom Calvin had alienated to produce a biography that spared no salacious innuendo in its depiction of Calvin and that stands as the source of Campion's defamation.

The doctrine of predestination as Calvin understood it grew up in Latin Christendom, arising from Augustine's disputes with Pelagius over the relationship of free will and grace.[5] From Augustine's time onward, predestination did not want of defenders in the Latin church, and indeed the church's most notable theologians—for example, Anselm and Aquinas—can be counted as its apologists. Predestination plays a prominent role in Dante's *Divine Comedy*.

---

3. Jerome Bolsec, *Histoire de la vie, moeurs, actes, doctrine, constance et mort de Iean Calvin* (Paris: Gervais Mallot, 1577), 6b: "fut surprins ou conuaincu du peche de Sodomie, pour lequel il fut en danger de mort par feu . . . Mais que l'Evesque de laditte ville par compassion feit mòderer laditte peine une marque de fleur de lys chaude sur l'espaule."

4. CO 21:545.

5. Indeed, Calvin slighted all the Greeks, especially John Chrysostom, and thought that Augustine alone spoke with any clarity on the matter. CO 2:188, *Institutes* 2.2.4: "Moreover although the Greek more so than others, and among them Chrysostom especially, have excelled measure in extolling the ability of the human will, yet all ancient theologians, Augustine excepted, speak so variously, vacillatingly, and confusedly on this subject, that nothing certain can be had or obtained from their writings."

Even those on the margins of Latin Christendom—such as John Wyclif and Jan Hus—also supported the doctrine. Among the Reformers Calvin was not the doctrine's first champion, for both Zwingli and Luther took up the matter, Zwingli in his book on providence[6] and Luther more famously in his dispute with Erasmus over the freedom of the will.[7] Luther's arguments, while not slighting the primacy of the divine will as the initiator of salvation, focused on the inability of the will in humans to function righteously or virtuously apart from regeneration, for "since we are all under sin and damnation by the single offense of a single man, Adam (Rom. 5:12), how can we attempt anything that is not sinful and damnable?"[8] Erasmus had taken the contrary stance on the question in 1524, argued even for the possibility that pagans may also act virtuously, and contended that Luther had first maimed the will by cutting off its arm and then slit its throat to get rid of it altogether.[9] Luther responded to this in his 1525 *The Enslaved Will*.

Calvin's own doctrine of predestination had a definitive though unsettled position in his works. Briefly stated, Calvin taught that God by the good pleasure of his will before all time determined who would be those fitted for bliss and heaven and who would be those fitted for wrath and damnation apart from any consideration of foreseen merit or vice; however, there is much to consider within these terms. Does the last clause of the definition—for instance, Calvin's *decretum horribile*, that God determined in some way the number and means of the damned—entail that God, before decreeing creation, decreed that certain individuals were predestined to hell (reprobation); or rather, does God decree creation, and with it the fall, and then "pass over" those who will remain in their wretchedness (preterition), while electing others for salvation? Calvin scholars and Calvinists themselves have come to a range of different conclusions.

Calvin first tamely stated his doctrine in the 1536 edition of the *Institutes,* but gave a more robust statement in the 1537 French confession of the Genevan church:

> In such a difference [between those who seek God by faith and those who seek him otherwise] the great secret council of God is necessarily to be considered: because the seed of the word of God plants roots and is fruitful in those only

6. Huldrych Zwingli, *Ad Illustrissimum Cattorum Principem Phiippum, Sermonis De Providentia Dei* (Zurich: Christopher Froschauer, 1530).

7. Clarence H. Miller, ed., *Luther and Erasmus: The Battle over Freewill*, trans. Clarence H. Miller and Peter Marcadle, with introduction by James D. Tracy (Indianapolis: Hackett, 2012).

8. In Miller, *Luther and Erasmus*, 107.

9. Miller, *Luther and Erasmus*, 29.

whom the Lord by his eternal election has predestined for his children and heirs of the celestial kingdom. To all the others, who by the same council of God before the foundation of the world are reprobate, the clear and obvious preaching of the truth would be nothing other than the fragrance of death to death. Now, why the Lord uses his mercy for some, and exercises the rigor of his judgment towards others, we must leave to his knowledge alone, which he has desired us all to celebrate, and not without very good cause.[10]

Calvin linked both reprobation and election to the inscrutable will of God, and later in the same section stated that both election and reprobation are from God's sovereign bounty.[11] In the 1539 *Institutes*—and this continued through the 1554 edition as well—Calvin linked his discussion of the topic with preaching, for the proclamation of the gospel manifested the grace of God in election. This changed in 1559 when Calvin expanded on the contents of his thought by removing his discussion of providence, previously treated with predestination, and linked the former with his final thoughts on the doctrine of God proper (1.16–18).[12] Predestination he treated at two places, the first (2.17), where he touched on the merit of Christ, affirming that the merit accepted by God on behalf of Christians was not intrinsic to Christ but was accepted only by the choice of God due to his predestination of Christ to this end. Calvin maintained that nothing created (here Christ's righteous keeping of the law) can have standing before God except by God's expressly willing it so.[13] The fuller treatment of the subject Calvin placed at the end of book 3 (21–24), which concludes the discussion of the benefits and effects of the Christian's obtaining the grace of Christ.[14]

Perhaps Calvin's clearest statements on the matter came in his commentary on the Epistle to the Romans, the first edition published in Strasbourg in 1540.[15] Calvin, as Gordon maintains, was just coming into his own as a serious theologian, emerging from the dark events of 1538 to take his place among the front rank of Reformers. His taking up Romans was thus a natural event, Romans being a book so central to the Protestant cause that it had already been treated by Luther, Bullinger, Melanchthon, and Bucer, and as well by Erasmus and Jacques Lefèvre d'Étaples. Gordon proposes that Calvin kept

10. CO 22:46 (*Instruction et Confession de Foy*).
11. CO 22:47: "God has a right to so act, and in those whom he withdraws from perdition one cannot observe anything other than his sovereign goodness."
12. CO 2:144–74.
13. CO 2:386–87. Calvin's theology here will be discussed in chap. 10.
14. CO 2:678–728.
15. For the chronology of the various editions, see Wulfert de Greef, *The Writings of John Calvin*, trans. Lyle D. Bierma, expanded ed. (Louisville: Westminster John Knox, 2008), 75n20.

Melanchthon's treatment at hand, using it as a light post, rhetorically and otherwise.[16] But on the doctrine of predestination Calvin took his own path. For Luther the primary concern in his arguments with Erasmus had been to champion God's will as the merciful agent of grace to the undeserving and impotent sinner. Luther's discussion of predestination did not arise from the necessity attendant on God's sovereignty, although it certainly was coincident with it. But the sovereignty of God, as Calvin would come to formulate it, was not the obvious matter of dispute between Luther and Erasmus. For Calvin, the divine will's inscrutable ways assumed primacy, and Paul's Epistle to the Romans—particularly chapter 9, Paul's theodicy on the divine justice and why some of the Jews of Paul's day had accepted the gospel while others had not—provided an apt vehicle for that topic.

Quite naturally, when Calvin turned to this passage, the voluntarism that characterized his approach to merit in the *Institutes* (2.17) was also present here. Commenting on Paul's reply to his putative interlocutor's question, "Why does God find fault with sinners, if they are only doing what God has ordained for them to do?" Calvin has Paul remove all concern about merited justice that would stand within a created framework of justice:

> Thus speak the Sophists here, "What cause does he have why he is angry with us? as he formed us as we are, since he guides us for his own will where he wishes, what else in destroying us is he doing but punishing his work in us?" . . . What does Paul say to these things? But, O man! who are you? etc. . . . In this first answer, he does nothing but blunt shameless blasphemy by an argument taken from the human condition: he will soon add another, by which he will vindicate the righteousness of God from every recrimination. Indeed he points out that nothing is adduced higher than the will of God. Since there is no obvious answer, that the difference depends on just reasons, why did not Paul use so brief an answer, but place the will of God as the chief cause that it may alone satisfy us instead of all other causes?[17]

Calvin's 1540 edition, briefer than the later 1550 French edition and the 1551 and 1556 Latin revisions, all the same gave the basic contours that would be followed in subsequent texts, and what is more, also gave his beliefs in such sharp relief that when Albertus Pighius took up the matter of free will and predestination in 1542, ostensibly aiming at Luther, he placed Calvin with Luther front and center in his arguments.[18] Calvin had met Pighius at the 1541

16. Bruce Gordon, *Calvin* (New Haven: Yale University Press, 2009), 105–6.
17. CO 49:185.
18. Albertus Pighius, *De Libero hominis arbitrio et divina gracia libri decem, nunc primum in lucem editi, autore* (Cologne: Melchior Novesian, 1542).

Regensberg Colloquy. Pighius, professor of theology at Louvain, had been
associated with the Catholic Reformers around Contarini, and—picking up
on a suggestion made by Erasmus in his last book, the 1536 *On the Mending
of the Peace of the Church*—Pighius proposed a double-righteousness model,
one that saw initial imputed righteousness as the formal cause of justification, albeit a righteousness always accompanied by the works of Christians,
accepted by God's good pleasure as meritorious even if inherently not so.[19]
Pighius's was the sole doctrine on which the participants at the colloquy could
come to any agreement, though Luther later rejected it, and the whole matter
became academic in that the colloquy could produce no agreements on any
other matters. Pighius's *De libero hominis arbitrio* came out the next year,
and Calvin responded with his *Defensio Sanae et Orthodoxae Doctrinae de
Servitute et Liberatione Humani Arbitrii*, a text that addressed itself to the
question of the corruption and potency of the will, yet left unaddressed the
larger questions of providence, predestination, and election.[20] This silence
ended with the Bolsec controversy of 1551.

Obscurity blankets much of Bolsec's early life.[21] Prior to his arrival in Geneva
in 1550, he had been a Carmelite monk, though whether a priest is unknown.
Erik de Boer states that he had a doctorate in theology from the Sorbonne,
but gives no citation, and no one else asserts this.[22] At some point in 1545,
one of Bolsec's sermons, preached at the church of St. Bartholomew in Paris,
drew the attention of the Sorbonne.[23] Flight took Bolsec to Ferrara, where
he lived for almost five years and there took up both medicine and further

19. Christopher Ocker, "Double Justice," in *The Oxford Handbook of the Protestant Ref-
ormations*, ed. Ulinka Rublack (Oxford: Oxford University Press, 2017), 35–36.

20. CO 6:225–404; John Calvin, *The Bondage and Liberation of the Will: A Defence of the
Orthodox Doctrine of Human Choice against Pighius*, ed. Anthony N. S. Lane, trans. G. I.
Davies (Grand Rapids: Baker Academic, 2002); see also Kiven S. K. Choy, "Calvin's Defense
and Reformulation of Luther's Early Reformation Doctrine of the Bondage of the Will" (PhD
diss., Calvin Theological Seminary, 2010).

21. The largest study of Bolsec and the whole of his conflict with Calvin and Geneva is
Philip C. Holtrop, ed. and trans., *The Bolsec Controversy on Predestination, from 1551 to 1555:
The Statements of Jerome Bolsec, and the Responses of John Calvin, Theodore Beza, and Other
Theologians*, 2 vols. (Lewiston, NY: Edwin Mellen Press, 1993), and see especially his treatment
of the trial and the translation of the documents pertaining to it. Holtrop's volumes are not
without their critics on a number of matters: for a critique of the volumes as finished works of
scholarship, see Brian G. Armstrong's review in *Sixteenth Century Journal* 25, no. 3 (Autumn
1994): 747–50; for a critique of Holtrop's argument (which runs very favorably for Bolsec), see
Richard Muller's review in *Calvin Theological Journal* 29, no. 2 (November 1994): 581–89.

22. Erik A. de Boer, "The Presence and Participation of Laypeople in the Congrégations of
the Company of Pastors in Geneva," *Sixteenth Century Journal* 35, no. 3 (Fall 2004): 651–70
(here 660).

23. Eugène Haag, *La France Protestante ou Vies des Protestants Français* (Paris: Bureaux
de la Publication, 1847), 2:360.

studies in theology. As Ferrara's university had no medical faculty, it must be assumed that he traveled elsewhere for his training and medical studies, for he certainly showed himself a capable physician later in Geneva. Bolsec also apparently furthered himself in the evangelical faith to such a degree that he felt he would be comfortable living near Geneva. François Wendel notes: "He was a fervent advocate of the Calvinist doctrine, except in respect of dual predestination."[24] Bolsec took up residence in the village of Veigny, just a few miles outside Geneva though under Bernese authority, where he practiced medicine, proving himself a valuable physician to the close friend of Calvin Jacques de Bourgogne, sieur de Falais, whose son he had helped. By 1550, regular sermons and doctrinal training were available in Geneva, and Bolsec began attending the Friday meetings of the company of pastors, meetings set up for the teaching of doctrine, and, while the meetings were attended by the laity—and it seems that often the majority there were laypeople—the eighteen ministers of the city and its villages were always present.[25] Bolsec had written to one of them, Abel Poupin, asking for some clarifications on the doctrine of predestination and, perhaps at Poupin's invitation, started attending meetings. When Bolsec received no satisfaction at the meeting he attended, he returned on a Friday in October to hear both Jean de St. André and Guillaume Farel teach on John 8:47, "Whosoever is God's, hears God's words, but you don't hear them, for you are not of God." Beza later records that Calvin was not present when the meeting started but entered at some point after Bolsec had already risen in response. To read Beza, Bolsec expressed himself freely, perhaps thinking Calvin absent.[26] Whatever the basis of Bolsec's liberty of expression, he asserted that the Genevan church's doctrines of election and reprobation proceeding from God *ab aeterno* were false propositions. "And speaking with grand protestations and exhortations that one ought not to recognize any election or reprobation than that only which one sees in belief or unbelief; and that those who put an eternal will in God by which he has ordained some to life and others to death makes a tyrant or an idol of God as do the pagans, making him into a Jupiter."[27]

Bolsec then protested that to hold such heretical things as Geneva confessed could only cause scandal, that Augustine never held such views, and that one

24. François Wendel, *Calvin: Origins and Development of His Religious Thought* (New York: Harper & Row, 1963), 90. This is an overstatement, as will be seen below.

25. De Boer, "Presence and Participation," 653.

26. Theodore Beza, *Ioannis Calvini Vita*, in CO 21:144.

27. CO 8:145 (*Actes du Procès Intenté pár Calvin et les Autres Ministres de Genève a Jérome Bolsec de Paris. Procès—Verbal de la congregation du 16 octobre 1551*). The process against Bolsec is contained both in CO 8:145–247 and in Jeffrey R. Watt et al, eds., *Registres du Consistoire de Genève au temps de Calvin. Tome I* (Geneva: Librairie Droz, 1996), 1:80–131.

had to twist Scripture to come up with such "faules et perverse" doctrines. He cited what he claimed were mistranslations of Proverbs and Romans, the latter's text on Pharaoh having been "depravé et corrompu."[28]

Once Bolsec had finished, Calvin took to the floor and answered point by point. More importantly, one of the lieutenants of Geneva then present, Iehan de la Maison, immediately had Bolsec arrested for the slander that the doctrine of Geneva had made an idol of God. The company of pastors, based on Bolsec's statements, drew up articles of his faith to present against him in proceedings, for his arrest meant that he was now liable to criminal prosecution in Geneva, even though not a citizen. The whole affair lasted for more than two months, and Bolsec, though lacking precision in addressing the theological questions at hand, admitted to holding the propositions that the company of pastors had drawn up against him, including that Calvin and Zwingli essentially taught Manichaean doctrine in making God the author of sin. Bolsec also, as Richard Muller points out, ruled out the will of God as predestinating acts in time, since the will of God existed in eternity, outside of time.[29]

The magistrates—the ones actually handling the trial—wrote letters to the Swiss cities seeking their advice on what to do with Bolsec. The responses were, with the exception of Farel and the church in Neuchâtel and Viret and Beza in Lausanne, if not critical of Calvin, certainly far short of the indictments that Calvin and the Genevans had hoped they would receive. Wendel muses that the Genevans actually wanted to do the Swiss a favor by executing Bolsec.[30] Perhaps most disappointing to Calvin was Bullinger's response, which showed him almost completely sympathetic to Bolsec. Certainly, wrote Bullinger, "We add that Jerome [Bolsec] erred, if he thinks that Zwingli made God the author of evil, or that God compels us to sin." Despite this defense of Zwingli, Bullinger did not leave Calvin blameless: "For you ought to believe me that many are offended by your words in your *Institutes* on the matter of predestination, and Jerome has collected from it the same that he collected from Zwingli's book about providence." Bullinger continued that this was something the apostles had treated gingerly, and that people would be more drawn by the free offer of the gospel than by Calvin's teaching.[31]

28. CO 8:145.

29. Richard Muller, "The Use and Abuse of a Document: Beza's *Tabula praedestionis*, the Bolsec Controversy, and the Origins of Reformed Orthodoxy," in *Protestant Scholasticism: Essays in Reassessment*, ed. Carl R. Trueman and R. S. Clark (Carlisle, UK: Paternoster, 1999), 41–42.

30. Wendel, *Calvin*, 91.

31. CO 14:214–15; and see Gordon, *Calvin*, 206–7; and also Cornelius Venema, "Heinrich Bullinger's Correspondence on Calvin's Doctrine of Predestination, 1551–1553," *Sixteenth Century Journal* 17, no. 4 (Winter 1986): 435–50.

Geneva received letters from more than just the Swiss churches, for Calvin's friend de Falais also wrote the magistrates seeking Bolsec's release, citing the imprisoned physician's service to his family. De Falais's letter was not something private, for as already noted, François Baudouin knew of it. Bolsec's imprisonment also marked a rift between de Falais and Calvin that ended with de Falais severing ties with Geneva and, following 1557, moving to Basle. It is difficult to say what Bolsec's stay in prison entailed, and he was visited several times by Calvin. Bolsec turned the ordeal into an occasion for a lamentation, basing his plaint, it would seem, on Psalm 22. Both in the first and last stanzas this comes out:

I

My god, my king, my strength and my betrothed
My only support, and my only hope
Send me your servant, who demands your grace
Turn thy eyes, and show me thy face.

X

Sustain then, my heart, restore strength and vigor;
Remove sorrow, and the effort of singing.
Praise God, who for your salvation watches over you!
It is for your sake that He watches the evil;
Chase away crying, flick away bitter pain,
That you may praise God and call him Father.[32]

In the end, Geneva released Bolsec from prison and banished him from Genevan territory. The Bolsec controversy would prove costly, for Bolsec became a crusader against Calvin, Geneva, and even Beza; he would prove, via his polemics, to be a thorn in the side of not only Geneva but also the Huguenots, a cause dear to Calvin.[33] The controversy helped ensure that Calvin's name, and certainly not without his consent, would stand linked to the doctrine of double predestination.

Using the language of later Protestant scholasticism, Calvin's doctrine, which involves not merely the doctrine of special election of the righteous to eternal bliss, but also the doctrine of special providence, falls between

---

32. Jerome Bolsec "Complainte de Bolsec, 1551," *Bulletin historique et littéraire (Société de l'Histoire du Protestantisme Français)* 15, no. 8 (1866): 372–74.

33. Muller, "Use and Abuse," 36–37; and as regards the Huguenots, see Chiara Lastraioli, "D'un texte inconnu de Jérôme Bolsec contre Calvin," *Reformation and Renaissance Review* 10, no. 2 (2008): 157–74.

supralapsarianism and infralapsarianism.[34] The former holds that, logically prior to the fall, God ordained and predestined everyone to their particular ends, the redeemed or saved to everlasting bliss and the reprobates to everlasting torment. This decree, which then adumbrates the fall as a means of the reprobate's destruction, most easily lends itself to the charge that God is thus the author of sin, since he not only decreed its occurrence in each individual's life but also determined that the human race would be ruined in Adam and Eve's primordial lapse, even apart from the concupiscence that now besets the human race. Infralapsarianism, conversely, holds that God permitted the fall and then from the *massa damnata* (to use Augustine's phrase) chose who would receive the grace of Christ, and then "passed over" the others, leaving them in their sins, and thus their reprobation was by the divine act of preterition, or passing over. For the first, God acted without or beyond consideration of the fall, in that it was but a means to bring about the salvation of the elect; for the other, God acts in redemption as a logical but not necessary consequence of the fall.

In both positions, the actions of God are eternally wrought and denote no time in God: God does not act in consequence of historical actions on the part of his creatures. Calvin's doctrine does not fall too neatly into either category for the simple reason that he was not addressing the concerns that gave rise to this later scheme of categorization.[35] Since Calvin worked off a different set of ideas from those of his heirs, his theological horizon limited his own writings, doctrines, and words; as a consequence, some passages and phrases can appear to lend aid and comfort to one side of the later debate, and some to the other. But any close reading of Calvin, despite what might be drawn from certain places by imprecise language (not to say careless, for Calvin was seldom careless, even in his most passionate passages)—for example, that God ordained the damned to their end—reveals a theology that taught that God passed over the reprobate, who were already in the throes of their sins, left there by the desolation of the fall, which had happened certainly within the providence of God, but that had its immediate cause in the will of Adam. Thus, the damned are justly punished for their own sin,

34. These terms, though certainly not without application to Calvin, come from seventeenth-century controversies. See Richard A. Muller, *Calvin and the Reformed Tradition: On the Work of Christ and the Order of Salvation* (Grand Rapids: Baker Academic, 2012), especially chap. 1, "Reformation and Orthodoxy: The Reformed Tradition in the Early Modern Era," and 44–45.

35. The Louvain theologian Thomas Stapleton did, in fact, take Calvin up on this question, though also apart from the seventeenth-century debates; see my "Thomas Stapleton: Loathes Calvin, Will Travel," in *From Rome to Zurich, between Ignatius and Vermigli: Essays in Honor of John Patrick Donnelly, SJ*, ed. Kathleen R. Comerford, Gary W. Jenkins, and W. J. Torrance Kirby (Leiden: Brill, 2017), 75–76.

even if in the providence of God, God had so ordered, ordained, and pre-destined the course of the world that they would perish. Calvin's comments noted above on Romans 9, especially those on verse 20, bear this out: "The impious object that men are exempt from blame if God's will holds primacy in both salvation or perdition. Would Paul deny this? On the contrary his answer confirms that God orders as it seems good the concerns of men, and men vainly and madly rise to contend with God, since he appoints, by his own right, whatever he pleases to what he made."[36] Further, his statements in the *Institutes* bear directly on this: that God had by a *decretum horribile* established the unbelieving in their unbelief.[37]

Doubtless Bolsec garnered his view that Calvin taught God as the author of sin from such passages, even though Calvin objected to this reading of his doctrine.[38] Bolsec's conclusions should not be seen as some obdurate and intractable willfulness on his part, born of some inveterate contentiousness, for Bullinger had come to similar conclusions. As noted, Bullinger and Calvin had corresponded over the matter when the Genevans wrote to the Swiss churches. The letters were prompted by Bolsec's assertion that Bullinger agreed with him (he also cited Martin Chemnitz and Melanchthon), and when the Zurich pastors replied, Bullinger responded to Calvin personally. Bullinger reprimanded Calvin for Geneva's treatment of Bolsec, asserting that if the physician held that God's grace alone saved the sinner, he should be let go. Further, he upbraided Calvin for his language in the *Institutes* that, according to Bullinger, clearly implied that God was the author of sin; Bullinger stated that he dissented from this view, for it made God less than the lover of the human race and curtailed the universal application of the gospel. Calvin, by way of response, requested that Bullinger keep their correspondence private for the sake of unity. Bullinger, ever cautious and circumspect, agreed, but noted that "the origin of evil and the cause of sin, this manner of speaking, that God not only foresaw but also predestined and effected Adam's fall, it seems that by this it can turn God himself into its author."[39]

One clear consequence of the Bolsec affair, and coupled with the several cases of those who even as Genevan citizens or residents took umbrage at the

36. *CO* 49:185: "Obiiciunt impii, reatu eximi homines, si in eorum salute vel exitio primas partes tenet Dei voluntas. An negat Paulus? imo sua responsione confirmat, Deum quod visum est de hominibus statuere: frustra tamen ac furiose insurgere homines ad litigandum, quia figmentis suis Deus quamcunque voluerit sortem iure suo assignat."

37. Calvin, *Institutes* 3.23.7 (*CO* 2:704): "Decretum quidem horribile, fateor."

38. For a full treatment of this, see Richard Muller, *Christ and the Decree: Christology and Predestination in Reformed Theology from Calvin to Perkins* (Grand Rapids: Baker Academic, 2008), especially 35–38.

39. *CO* 14:289.

doctrine of predestination, was Calvin's more detailed response to Pighius, his *Concerning the Eternal Predestination of God*.[40] Calvin takes on both Pighius and one Georgius, a monk of Sicily, in a book that contains the Reformer's longest sustained comments on the question of predestination. Calvin sought not only to answer the two Catholics on predestination but also to address the questions and concerns raised by both Bolsec and Bullinger through an extended treatment of providence and a direct discussion of the relationship of the sovereign will of God to sin. (It should be noted that Calvin never mentions Bolsec in this book.) For Calvin, God orders both the means and ends of all things, and it is through the order of the universe—that is, his ordering of all the things he has created—that God effects the eternal ends of his elections. The human will is part of this secondary order of contingency and, as such, is a proximate or immediate cause, but not the ultimate cause, within the working of providence. Thus, though God has by his eternal will effected all that comes to pass, because the human will is a secondary cause and the immediate cause of sin, God cannot be called the author of sin. Sin is necessary in that its consequences are what the elect are saved from by God's special election, but God is not its author. Calvin may seem to be wanting to have his cake and eat it too, but he responds:

> God in ordaining the fall of man had an end most just and right, which holds the name of sin in abhorrence. Though I affirm that He ordained it so, I do not allow that He is properly the author of sin. Not to spend longer on the point, I am of the opinion that what Augustine teaches was fulfilled: In a wonderful and ineffable way, what was done contrary to His will was yet not done without His will, because it would not have been done at all unless He had allowed it. So He permitted it not unwillingly but willingly.[41]

Calvin's treatise represents his most fulsome statement on the matter of predestination, but it did not end the unpleasantries occasioned by Bolsec, for upon his banishment he continued his offensive against Calvin, joined by the Bernese pastors John Lange and Andrew Zebedee.[42] Having been barred from Geneva, Bolsec resided until 1555 in Thonon, across Lake Leman from Lausanne; in that year he was banished as well from all Bernese territory, for

40. The first iteration was a short treatise by Calvin delivered to the company of pastors in 1551, *Sur l'Election Eternelle* (CO 14:93–118); with the Latin edition in 1552, *De Aeterna Praedestinatione* (CO 14:257–366). For the English translation, see John Calvin, *Concerning the Eternal Predestination of God*, trans. and introduction J. K. S. Reid (Edinburgh: James Clarke, 1961).

41. Calvin, *Concerning Eternal Predestination*, 123.

42. Holtrop, *Bolsec*, 771.

from 1551 onward, as recorded by the company of pastors, Bolsec continued in his denunciation of the Genevan creed.[43] Eventually Berne gave in to the entreaties of the church of Geneva and banished Bolsec. Having removed to Paris, he sought entrance into the French Reformed churches, hoping to function as a minister, but his theology on predestination traveled with him, and he was denied an office when he refused to produce the necessary statement of faith. Conjecture alone can supply how Bolsec imagined he could undertake a life among those followers of Geneva, but whatever aspirations he entertained turned to a distinct level of animus, as evinced by his 1556 satirical tract *Le double des lettres envoyées à Passevent Parisien, par le Noble et excellent Pasquin Romain, contenant en vérité la vie de Jehan Calvin.*[44] The tract contains a 546-line poem that labels Geneva a new Rome, Calvin a new pope, and therefore Calvin as antichrist. The invective gives hints of what Bolsec would eventually publish in 1577, containing among other choice stories one in which Calvin's valet is allowed by the Reformer to rob him and then escape, as Calvin feared what stories the boy could tell.[45] Bolsec remained in Paris for eight years, until he attempted to go back to Bernese territory in 1563; the government made his signing of the Bernese confession a condition of his residence, and declining from this, he returned to France. Shortly thereafter he went back to the communion of Rome. Little is known of him till after Beza in his Latin life of Calvin decided to include a salacious bit of information about Bolsec, which prompted Bolsec to reply in kind. Beza in his 1565 biography of Calvin took especial note of the controversy with Bolsec. Beza cited the whole matter to note how God used Satan's wiles to bring greater clarity to the doctrine of the Genevan church. Beza also disparaged Bolsec, claiming that when expelled by Berne, he had feigned his desire to be reconciled with Geneva in order to obtain a post with the French Reformed church, but seeing persecution on the horizon, he forsook the Protestants to take up medicine again. Beza then added that Bolsec had "prostituted his wife to the canons of Autun" (in the Latin of the *Calvini Opera*, "uxore quoque canonicis Augustodunensibus prostituta"), and spent the remainder of his life railing against the true faith, having returned to his previous error in the fold of Rome.[46]

43. *Registres de la compagnie*, 2:122, October 1, 1553, in Lastraioli, "D'un texte inconnu," 164.
44. Lastraioli, "D'un texte inconnu," 165–66.
45. Lastraioli, "D'un texte inconnu," 167.
46. Beza, *Calvini Vita*, in CO 21:144; cf. the original French edition, *L'histoire de la vie et mort de feu Mr Jean Calvin, fidele serviteur de Jesus Christ* (Geneva: François Perrin, 1565), which does not mention his wife in conjunction with his trial, as the Latin life does. The Sibson

Bolsec's own biography of Calvin did not come out till 1577, and Bolsec returned more than measure for measure. He confessed that he could not allow Beza's biography of Calvin, which had turned Calvin into a saint, to pass without comment, for the real Calvin, asserted Bolsec, was wholly different from the one found within Beza's biography.[47] Bolsec depicted Calvin from the beginning of his life onward as a vicious and vile immoralist: Calvin deflowered, according to Bolsec, any young girl in Geneva who struck his fancy, and indeed his lechery extended even to married women. Bolsec asserted that the real reason that de Falais left the vicinity of Geneva was not a falling out with Calvin over the question of tolerance—the reason generally assumed, as de Falais was a correspondent of both Baudouin and Castellio, and differed markedly from Calvin on that issue—but because, Bolsec asserted, Calvin had seduced his wife.

As for the matter of Calvin's youth, Bolsec claims he got the story of Calvin's sodomy from one of Calvin's other tormentors, Philip Berthelier.[48] Both the French and the Latin versions of Bolsec's works were reprinted and widely disseminated, with these libels being picked up by Lutherans and, most especially, English Catholics.[49] The life of the sodomy accusation is a chapter unto itself, and its most famous iteration may have been that of Edmund Campion's *Rationes decem* and its sequel. Clandestinely printed in a secret press at Stonor Park, home of a recusant family, Campion distributed four hundred of the tracts at the university church. Almost all of them, however, were commandeered and destroyed, and Campion for his efforts as part of the Jesuit mission was hanged, drawn, and quartered. Nonetheless, among the English, both Protestant and Catholic, the tract took on a life of its own.[50] Responses appeared from the English Protestant divines, including Laurence Humphrey and William Whitaker.[51] The episode seemingly made it into the

---

translation ambiguously renders it "abandoned also his wife to the canons of Autun" (*The Life of John Calvin*, trans. Francis Sibson [Philadelphia: John Whetham, 1836], 53).

47. Jerome Bolsec, *Histoire*, and *De Joannis Calvini, magni quondam genevensium ministri, vita moribus, rebus gentis, studiis ac denique morte, historia* (Cologne: Jacob Soteris, 1582).

48. Bolsec, *Histoire*, 6b.

49. Peter Marshall, "Calvin and the English Catholics," *Historical Journal* 53, no. 4 (December 2010): 854–57.

50. Marshall, "Calvin and the English Catholics," 849–70, goes into the life of the slander among the English Elizabethan Catholic expatriates in fine detail.

51. William Whitaker, *Ad rationes decem Edmundi Campiani Iesuitae, quibus fretus certamen Anglicanae Ecclesiae ministris obtulit in causa fidei* (London: Vautrollier, 1581); Laurence Humphrey, *Iesuitismi pars prima sive de Praxi Romanae Curiae* (London: H. Middleton, 1582); and Humphrey, *Iesuitismi pars secunda etc.* (London: H. Middleton, 1584). Whitaker in 1606 published an English refutation of Campion, *An Answere to the Ten Reasons of Edmund Campion the Jesuit etc.* (London: F. Kingston). For Whitaker's quote of Demosthenes, see p. 40.

writings of the English expatriate and Catholic theologian Thomas Stapleton. Stapleton had made a life of contradicting Calvin's theology, and in one of his *Promptuaria Catholicae* he asserted that he had seen the records of Calvin's offenses in Noyon, and that they were there for all to see still. (Stapleton spent most of his time between Douai and Louvain, not far removed from Noyon.) This particular statement then was repeated in Edward Peach's *Remarks . . . to the Author of a Pamphlet . . . Entitled Reformed Religion Vindicated*,[52] from which it was picked up by *Harper's Weekly* in 1870.[53] A problem emerges when locating this quotation in Stapleton, as Peach simply gave an abbreviated title, *Promptuar. Cath.*, and a section with a page number, pars 3, p. 138, but nothing else. And herein lies the problem, for of the extant versions available, none match this reference. Stapleton's *Promptuaria* were commentaries on the lectionary, had numerous printings with varied titles, and also went through numerous editions, and so far this author has failed to track down the citation.[54] This casts the existence of the putative testimony of Stapleton, an otherwise careful and circumspect scholar, into grave doubt, especially considering that he was not above throwing insults at Calvin.[55]

This want of verification actually forms a commentary on the afterlife of the rift between Bolsec and Calvin. Irena Backus notes that Bolsec's biography was really aimed at Beza (and Bolsec would pen a *Vita* of Beza as well) and not really at Calvin, but this skews Bolsec's intentions.[56] Certainly he had no love for Beza, as seen in his biography of him, but Bolsec went out of his way to defame Calvin, and it would seem that he was not merely making things up, especially as regards the "stigmatus perfuga"—that is, that there was a Calvin who was a branded fugitive. Bolsec asserted that Philip Berthelier had given him the information, who has already been seen to have a deep grudge against Calvin (see chap. 6), and it may well have been that Bolsec took this most notorious of Enfants at face value. But when this is joined to the fact

---

52. Edwin Peach, *Remarks Addressed to the Author of a Pamphlet Lately Published by John Webster Jun., and Entitled Reformed Religion Vindicated* (Birmingham: W. Broomhall, 1825), 13.

53. Edward Peach, "Caricatures of the Reformation," *Harper's Weekly* 50 (December 1874–May 1875): 637–52, especially 649.

54. Upon consultation with Professor Peter Marshall, I learned that he had not found this citation either.

55. See my "Thomas Stapleton," 71n14, as Stapleton attributes, imputes, or contemns Calvin for blasphemy, dementia, and being foul or offensive (*teterrima*); he labels him the greatest of diseases, detestable, pestilential, a fraud, a horror, a dissimulator, and of course, a heretic.

56. Irena Backus, "Roman Catholic Lives of Calvin from Bolsec to Richelieu: Why the Interest?," in *Calvin and Roman Catholicism: Critique and Engagement, Then and Now*, ed. Randall C. Zachman (Grand Rapids: Baker Academic, 2006), 25–57. Professor Backus goes into far more detail about Bolsec's *Life* in her *Life Writing in Reformation Europe: Lives of Reformers by Friends, Disciples and Foes* (Aldershot, UK: Ashgate, 2008), 153–69.

that there had been a cleric in Noyon named Jean Cauvin who had been degraded of his ordination for his dissolute life, one can see how, fueled by his own animus, Bolsec's imagination would have gotten the better of his discretion. In fact, the Jean Cauvin of Noyon was not Jean Calvin of Geneva, and Berthelier never had the offices that Bolsec attached to him in the *Histoire*.[57] Yet the story came from somewhere, and it would seem to be from Berthelier, thus leaving the Enfants de Genève seemingly with the vile last word in their conflict with Calvin. Ironically, it was a word that Catholics, even ones who would have been horrified at such a man as Philip Berthelier, used to impugn Calvin's friends and coreligionists with the sin of their compeer, and a bludgeon adopted against him by none other than Cardinal Richelieu.[58]

The vast lacunae in Bolsec's life after his return to Rome present many problems, chief among them how he, a renegade religious, functioned in Catholic France. A clue comes from Bolsec's dedication of the *Life of Calvin* to Pierre d'Epinac, archbishop of Lyons. Bolsec thanks the archbishop for his many kindnesses, "consolation and succor in my afflictions," and says that he owes him "an obligation for your clemency and liberality."[59] It may have been the archbishop who paid for the publication of the *Vie*, as d'Epinac had no love for the Huguenots, and the *Vie* was published in 1577 in both Paris and Lyons; or the debt may have come in the form of aiding Bolsec to obtain the necessary permissions and dispensations attached to his irregular life. All the same, in the 1570s in France greater crimes than irregular monks were afoot. According to Eugène Haag, Bolsec died in Annecy in 1584.[60]

---

57. Backus, "Roman Catholic Lives," 31.
58. Backus, "Roman Catholic Lives," 54–57.
59. Bolsec, *Vie*, 5.
60. Haag, *France Protestante*, 755.

9

Joachim Westphal

Calvin the Reluctant Zuricher

How many and how considerable are the struggles effected across the world by the doubt touching the meaning of this syllable: *hoc*!"[1] Thus did Michel de Montaigne's 1580 observation, made at the height of the French Wars of Religion, illustrate how verbal polemics often turned to fire and sword as the preferred methods suitable for theological dispute. Nothing generated heat in sixteenth-century polemical exchanges like the Eucharist. While both Protestants and Catholics saw the question of justification as central, and treatises on that subject proliferated from the Reformation's very start, the Eucharist easily outstrips any other subject for both volume and intensity; this arises because it was a point that separated not merely Catholics from Protestants, but also Reformed from Lutheran, and even Reformed from Reformed. Other reasons for this fervid, voluminous output reside in the central place that the Eucharist holds in Christian worship

---

1. Michel de Montaigne, *Apologie de Raimond Sebond*, in *Essais de Montaigne* (Paris: Éditions Garnier Frères, 1962), 1:587. Montaigne a few lines on makes clear his targets as those who have been driven not by faith but by reason: "See how we can defend ourselves from this kind of talk, wholly irreverent. As regards the present controversies in our religion, if you put our adversaries to it, they will most emphatically tell you that it is beyond the power of God to make his body at once in paradise, on earth, and in several other places" (Voyez comment on se prevaut de cette sorte de parler pleine de ireverence. Aux disputes qui son à present en nostre religion, si vous pressez trop les adversaires, ils vous diront tout destrousséement qu'il n'est past en la puissance de Dieu de faire que son corps soit in paradis et en le terre et in plusieurs lieux ensemble), 588.

and in the divergent views among theologians over what is conveyed by, with, and through the elements.[2]

Joachim Westphal's conflict with Calvin sparked what has been called the second eucharistic controversy, though in fact Westphal would have seen himself as building very much on the first. Nor did he see what he had started as a fight with Calvin, though that is how it is remembered.

The first eucharistic controversy erupted in 1524 when the city of Strasbourg, ironically, requested of both Wittenberg and Zurich responses to the recent publication of Andreas Bodenstein von Karlstadt's five eucharistic treatises.[3] Luther and Zwingli responded nearly simultaneously, and their divergence on the question of the Eucharist inaugurated not only the controversy but also the rift between Lutheran and Reformed Protestantism that persists till this day. That Strasbourg initiated the controversy assumes an ironic character in that its chief Reformer, Martin Bucer, persistently sought harmony between the Lutheran and Reformed factions. Bucer had first met Luther at the 1519 Leipzig Disputation. Like Tetzel, the former indulgence seller who happened to be dying in Leipzig at the time of the disputation, Bucer had been a Dominican, but he had subsequently turned to Luther's ideas and seemingly embraced Luther's views on all things. But with the inauguration of the eucharistic controversy in 1525, it was clear he was cutting his own path as regards the nature of the Eucharist. Bucer repeatedly tried to mediate between the two camps, hoping for some form of rapprochement via his views. But the sundering of Zurich and Wittenberg over the question of Christ's presence in the sacrament of the Eucharist proved intractable, though it may have seemingly admitted of resolution with the death of Zwingli in the Cappel War of 1531. Bucer hoped to build

2. The bibliography on this is staggering, and the best place to begin is probably Lee Palmer Wandel's *The Eucharist in the Reformation: Incarnation and Liturgy* (Cambridge: Cambridge University Press, 2005), and also Wandel, ed., *A Companion to the Eucharist in the Reformation* (Leiden: Brill, 2014). See also for Calvin, Thomas J. Davis, *The Clearest Promises of God: The Development of Calvin's Eucharistic Teaching* (New York: AMS Press, 1995), but more readily available Davis's *This Is My Body: The Presence of Christ in Reformation Thought* (Grand Rapids: Baker Academic, 2008); also for Calvin see B. A. Gerrish, *Grace and Gratitude: The Eucharistic Theology of John Calvin* (Eugene, OR: Wipf and Stock, 2002). For the Lutheran view, see John R. Stephenson, *The Lord's Supper*, vol. 12, *Confessional Lutheran Dogmatics* (St. Louis: Luther Academy, 2003), and the older but still excellent Hermann Sasse, *This Is My Body: Luther's Contention for the Real Presence in the Sacrament of the Altar* (Minneapolis: Augsburg, 1959). The bibliography in Wandel's *Eucharist in the Reformation* runs almost twenty-five pages but is at best still only partial (e.g., there are no titles from Brenz and only one from Vermigli).

3. Amy Nelson Burnett, ed. and trans., *The Eucharistic Pamphlets of Andreas Bodenstein von Karlstadt,* Early Modern Studies 6 (Kirksville, MO: Truman State University Press, 2011), 110–218.

on the ambivalent admission of Luther at the end of the 1529 Marburg Colloquy about the mechanism and manner of corporal presence.[4] Luther did not hold himself bound by a strict identity of the body and blood of Christ with the elements as long as it was admitted that when the faithful ate and drank they were eating and drinking the body and blood in, with, and under the elements, though this was never to be considered some crass, corporeal eating, since the body of Christ had been transformed by the power of the Spirit, the Lord and giver of life.[5] But Bucer failed to see the essential and intractable place that corporeal eating had in Luther's thought. Further, the death of Zwingli raised him to near-martyr status, and Zurich with the calling of Heinrich Bullinger to be its chief minister signaled a retrenchment of its position, not a mollification of it.

By the time Calvin finally arrived in Strasbourg in 1538, Bucer had agreed to the Wittenberg Concord of 1536, which entailed confessing, inter alia, the Augsburg Confession of 1530 (the *Augustana*), whose Latin text might seem ambiguous on the question of the sacramental union of sign and signified (the body and bread, the blood and wine) but whose German text explicitly assumed the doctrine of Wittenberg. In its tenth article, the Latin version of the *Augustana* states: "Of the Supper of the Lord they teach that the Body and Blood of Christ are truly present, and are distributed to those who eat the Supper of the Lord; and they reject those that teach otherwise."[6] Whether Bucer could confess without dissimulation the text that Luther proffered can only be hesitantly answered, for Bucer certainly knew German (Strasbourg was a German city then, and Bucer was originally from Schlettstadt—now Sélestat, Alsace, then part of the empire). But however Bucer took the words, it seems to have been with the clear reservation that the impious never partook of Christ's body and blood, though he admitted that the unworthy did, for none have a claim to God's grace, and the unworthy include the humbly contrite, whereas the impious were brazen in their vices. The question is more fraught with Calvin, for disagreement exists whether he held to the 1530 *Augustana* or confessed to the later *Variata* of Melanchthon. Ultimately, however, both present problems, though not in the way perhaps thought. The *Variata* is actually far less of an Augustinian document as pertains to predestination,

4. Sasse, *This Is My Body*, 301–10.
5. This same note about no mere crass eating is sounded by Catholic apologists in their polemics against Calvin; see my "Thomas Stapleton: Loathes Calvin, Will Travel," in *From Rome to Zurich, between Ignatius and Vermigli: Essays in Honor of John Patrick Donnelly, SJ*, ed. Kathleen R. Comerford, Gary W. Jenkins, and W. J. Torrance Kirby (Leiden: Brill, 2017), 77.
6. Book of Concord, http://bookofconcord.org/augsburgconfession.php. For the German edition of the *Augustana* and the confession's meaning, see Sasse, *This Is My Body*, 298–300.

even though on the surface it may seem more amenable to Calvin's views on the Eucharist. But Calvin's views actually sit much closer to the early Melanchthon's than may appear, especially given how Calvin would have taken the terms *exhibere* and *representare*—that the first means "to hold forth," and not merely "to point out," while the second means "to present again," and not "to depict." Given this, Calvin could well have believed himself justified in holding to the 1530 *Augustana*.[7]

Calvin, despite his persistent denunciations of Luther's so-called ubiquitarianism (a word the Reformed used of the Lutherans, and not one the Lutherans used of themselves, nor did Lutherans accept that they taught what the Reformed asserted that they did), went out of his way to cite his fealty to the Wittenberg Reformer.[8] Other Reformers were sharply critical: the Zurichers in the 1545 *Warhaffte Bekanntunus*, countering Luther's assertions that Zwingli's position on the Eucharist was heretical, maintained that the Lutherans were the true heretics;[9] Peter Martyr Vermigli thought Luther's doctrines unchristian and even damnable, but asserted his belief that Luther repented at his death and thus hoped for his eternal salvation despite his sacramental theology.[10] Calvin, on the other hand, seemed almost sycophantic in his admiration of Luther: in a 1545 letter to Luther, Calvin referred to him three times as his "father in the faith." In truth, up to at least 1549 Calvin probably thought himself closer to Luther than to Zurich, for while at Strasbourg from 1538 to 1541 he had at least affirmed Melanchthon's *Variata* of the *Augustana*, if not the *Augustana* itself. Knowing what the Lutherans had confessed at Marburg in 1529, what "truly present [*vere adsint*]" in the *Augustana*'s tenth article entailed could not have been lost on Calvin. Calvin knew that his host in Strasbourg, Martin Bucer—while certainly no Lutheran even though he had professed the *Augustana* as early as 1534 and had found himself drawn more closely to Luther by the Wittenberg Concord of 1536 (which brought the Reformed of the Rhineland and the German Lutherans to the summit of their

---

7. Richard Muller, "From Zürich or from Wittenberg? An Examination of Calvin's Early Eucharistic Thought," *Calvin Theological Journal* 45 (2010): 243–55. My gratitude to Professor Muller for an exchange of emails on this question, and for his sending me this article.

8. See Sasse's discussion in *This Is My Body* for Luther and his understanding of the various ways Christ is present physically, 149–64, and for the Formula of Concord, 341.

9. Heinrich Bullinger, *Warhaffte Bekanntnus der dieneren der kirchen zu Zuerych* (Zurich: Froschauer, 1545); and in Latin, *Orthodoxa Tigurinae ecclesiae ministrorum confessio* (Zurich: Froschauer, 1545), accessed respectively at http://www.e-rara.ch/zuz/content/titleinfo/477770 and http://www.e-rara.ch/download/pdf/855784 and through Post-Reformation Digital Library, http://www.prdl.org/.

10. John Patrick Donnelly, SJ, ed. and trans., *Life, Letters, and Sermons of Peter Martyr Vermigli* (Kirksville, MO: Truman State University Press, 1999), letter no. 266: "To the Strangers' Church at London," 188.

Joachim Westphal

unity)[11]—had no sympathy with the Zurichers, apart from the fact that both denied any corporeal presence of Christ coincident or otherwise with the eucharistic elements. Perhaps for Calvin it was Bucer's take on the *Augustana* and the Wittenberg Concord that allowed him to affirm the former. This is the obvious basis of his exchange, at first via Bucer, with Luther's lieutenant, Philip Melanchthon, the key force behind the *Augustana*. Calvin seemingly believed that Melanchthon was close to affirming Calvin's own opinions about a spiritual eating.[12] Calvin's early views are fully expressed in his 1541

11. The Concord affirmed that the body and blood of Christ were truly and substantially present with the eucharistic elements, that the *manducatio impiorum* (the eating of the elements by the impious) occurred, and that through a sacramental union the bread is Christ's body and the wine his blood.

12. Randall C. Zachman, *Calvin as Teacher, Pastor, Theologian: The Shape of His Writings and Thought* (Grand Rapids: Baker Academic, 2006), 33.

Petit traicté de la saincte cène, his Latin edition appearing in 1545.[13] Therein Bucer's own beliefs about a spiritual nourishment from the body and blood of Christ through the instruments of bread and wine seem adopted whole cloth by Calvin, and certainly were Calvin's opinions throughout his life, even though constantly muted in the face of Zurich pressure. The question is complicated by Calvin's stance in the early 1560s against the introduction of the *Augustana* into the French church, as has been discussed when treating François Baudouin. Calvin's adamant resistance to the *Augustana*, however, should not be read as a commentary on Calvin's own understanding of it in the 1540s, but as to how by the 1560s it had come to be regarded by Lutheran and Reformed alike as emphatically contrary to Swiss eucharistic theology.

In Bucer's Strasbourg, Calvin refined his views on the structure of the church, with Strasbourg serving as a model for his four-office notion of church polity. It would seem that Calvin also tailored his eucharistic views along the lines of Strasbourg and Bucer, for it was in Strasbourg that he wrote his *Traicté,* and it was from Strasbourg that he also took the structure of the Genevan services after he returned in 1541.[14] The need for doctrinal uniformity upon his return to Geneva, as evidenced by his expulsion of Castellio, assumed a central place in Calvin's ministry, whether in his conflict with the Enfants de Genève or that with Rome. Before circumstances brought him relief from his enemies within Geneva, a relief that seemed so long in coming that at one point he was ready to leave the city in near despair (the sequel to the execution of Servetus being the downfall of the Genevan opposition), Calvin was pushed, though not to say forced, into a public change of views concerning the Eucharist, a change ultimately brought about by the very thing that had occasioned his last confrontation with Caroli—namely, the matter of the Schmalkaldic League. In the dispute with Caroli, the Sorbonne doctor got the best of Calvin, Farel, and the league by preventing the city of Metz from aligning with the league; in the case of Calvin's alteration in his eucharistic confession, it was the league's collapse in the Schmalkaldic War and the victory of Charles V at Mühlberg near Leipzig in 1547 that threw Calvin into a seeming panic for reconciliation on this question with the Swiss. The league's defeat brought into focus, in both Calvin's mind and that of other Swiss Reformers, the need for military alliance, if, as feared, Charles V were to move against them. Such a league would necessitate a common confession. Calvin and Zurich, and in particular Bullinger, exchanged a number of letters on the issue, Bullinger not giving in

13. John Calvin, *Petit traicté de la saincte cène* (Geneva: Michel du Bois, 1541); Calvin, *Libellus de Coena Domini* (Geneva: John Girard, 1545).
14. John Calvin, *Traicté de la saincte cène* (Geneva: Michel du Bois, 1541), CO 5:433–60.

to Calvin's view that the substance of the promises of God, the substance of Christ, was communicated to the faithful at the Holy Table through a faithful eating and drinking.[15] Calvin and Bullinger had been exchanging letters throughout the 1540s, and obviously Calvin's consonance with Luther was not at first fully realized in Zurich; neither did Bullinger champion his own disagreements with Zwingli, which were obvious even in 1524.[16]

The dialogue between Bullinger and Calvin began in earnest following the former's *Absoluta* or *de Sacramentis* of 1545. Penned secretly and distributed to a clandestine few, it was published in 1551 in London, and only four copies are now extant. It consists of sermons 6 and 7 (both amended) of the fifth of Bullinger's *Decades*; Paul Rorem points out the interesting emendations made between the 1545 work and that reproduced in the *Decades*, and significantly how Bullinger, obviously under the influence of Calvin, removed the entirety of his section dealing with the sacraments as not offering what they signify.[17] Already in 1545 Bullinger with the rest of the Zurich clergy had published the aforementioned *Warhaffte Bekanntunus*, but this represented only a slight alteration to Zurich's Zwinglianism, going beyond Zwingli only in asserting that at the Communion it was not only the faithful who were the active participants but that Christ was there also reminding the faithful of his grace, though certainly not imparting it. Calvin voiced his impatience with the tract to Melanchthon, calling it wholly meager and childish, and accusing it of more impertinently than learnedly defending Zwingli, all the while taking nothing from Luther.[18] But the *Absoluta* gave something more

15. The details of the correspondence and discussion leading up to the *Consensus Tigurinus* of 1549 are provided in Paul Rorem, "Calvin and Bullinger on the Lord's Supper, Part 1: The Impasse," *Lutheran Quarterly* 2, no. 2 (Summer 1988): 155–84; and Rorem, "Calvin and Bullinger on the Lord's Supper, Part 2: The Agreement," *Lutheran Quarterly* 2, no. 3 (Autumn 1988): 357–89. The two articles were published as a book, Rorem, *Calvin and Bullinger on the Lord's Supper* (Nottingham: Grove, 1989). All citations from Rorem are taken from the Grove edition. It should be noted that the notes that run consecutively in the *Lutheran Quarterly* articles are renumbered on every page in the book.

16. Rorem, *Calvin and Bullinger*, 14.

17. Rorem, *Calvin and Bullinger*, 23–24.

18. CO 12:98: "Indeed beyond this, as regards the whole book, it is barren and childish, and while they feebly explain and defend their Zwingli, on the other hand very stubbornly rather than eruditely they baselessly attack a considerable amount in Luther . . . in my judgment in this whole affair they have conducted themselves unhappily." (Praeterquam enim quod totus libellus ieiunus est et puerilis, quum in multis pertinaciter magis quam erudite, et interea parum verecunde *Zwinglium* suum excusant ac tuentur, nonnullaque *in Luthero* immerito exagitant, tum vero in praecipui capitis tractatione, id est in ipso causae statu, infeliciter meo iudicio se gerunt.) In Henry Beveridge and Jules Bonnet, *Selected Works of John Calvin. Tracts and Letters. Volume 4. Letters Part I, 1528–1545* (Philadelphia: Presbyterian Board of Publications, 1858; repr., Grand Rapids: Baker, 1983), 466–68, the volume completely leaves out this sentence from

for Calvin to work with, and a way to address constructively the differences between him and Bullinger. Yet while he got Bullinger to admit that the sacraments were not empty, Bullinger still maintained that they did not contain grace but only held forth or signified God's mercy, acting as signs and seals of grace. Calvin received the *Absoluta* from Bullinger when visiting Zurich in January 1547 and responded shortly thereafter. Bullinger's reply to Calvin's vast critique was silence, Calvin even writing to him wondering what had happened. By the time of Calvin's letter, the whole affair had become urgent, for Emperor Charles V had won the day at Mühlberg, and Calvin feared Strasbourg would be next, after which the whole Swiss Confederation would lie open before him. But Bullinger had taken great exception to Calvin's thought, and in particular his notion that in the Eucharist the Christian has a substantial participation through faith with the body and blood of Christ, the sacrifice of the new covenant, and thereby grace. While Bullinger's pointed response is lost, scholars have pieced together from Calvin and Bullinger what it contained. For Bullinger, it were better that the sacraments remain empty than that such an option as Calvin's be considered, and he thought Calvin virtually a Thomist on this point.[19] Despite the seeming impasse, Calvin and Bullinger continued their efforts and by late 1548 attacked the problem in earnest, each responding to the other twice and at length on several propositions, all points of divergence finding some form of reconciliation except Calvin's twofold insistence that God worked through (*per*) the sacraments and that the sacraments were instruments (*organon*) of grace. But by the spring of 1549, Calvin had dropped this language and instead proffered wording from the Genevan Form of Communion that the sacraments were signs and testimonies of God's grace. The Mutual Agreement, or *Consensus Tigurinus*, finalized in September of 1549, showed no evidence of Calvin's theology, and indeed those things that Calvin had maintained the *Consensus* denied. Rorem concludes that "the real resolution of their long-standing differences regarding the sacraments seems to have resulted from Calvin's willingness to omit certain phrases," and that "missing . . . were Calvin's usual references to the actual presenting [exhibiting] of what is signified, to the sacraments as 'instruments' although they are called 'implements,' and as that through which God acts in conferring grace."[20] Calvin had obtained one seeming concession with the assertion in his preface that the *Consensus* "does not contain everything which could usefully and aptly

the letter, rendering it a screed against Luther's "tyranny" as opposed to Calvin's exasperation with parties on both sides.

19. For Calvin's doctrine, see Gerrish, *Grace and Gratitude*, 129–33.

20. Rorem, *Calvin and Bullinger*, 46.

be said, and which otherwise perfectly fits their true understanding."[21] But when the Swiss churches published the *Consensus* in 1551, this preface was not part of it—an important point, as this is where the second eucharistic controversy began, with Westphal's response to the *Consensus,* taking it wholly as a Zurich-dominated document.

Joachim Westphal, born in Hamburg in 1510, received his earliest education at his parish school before going to Lüneburg and then eventually to Wittenberg, where he studied under both Luther and Melanchthon. In 1532 Melanchthon recommended him to a post in Hamburg, where he stayed till 1534, only to return to Wittenberg for more study. From 1537 to 1541 he lectured on philology at Wittenberg. That year he returned to Hamburg as minister of St. Catherine's parish. He assumed the role of acting superintendent of the city in 1562 and was elected superintendent in 1571, a post he held till his death in 1574.[22]

Westphal's initial publication on the matter, his short work *Farrago*, consisted first of extended quotations from various Reformed clergy demonstrating their confused and contradictory assertions on the question of how and in what way Christ was present in the Eucharist.[23] Westphal cited a long passage from Calvin's 1545 *Libellus*, not to align Calvin with the *Consensus* and the Zwinglians per se, but essentially to show in what way Calvin radically differed from the Zurichers and the other Reformed theologians already cited and was thus part of the *confusa* of the sacramentarians.[24] Westphal then took up the remainder of the tract addressing how the words of institution should be understood, concluding with citations from Calvin again (his commentary on 1 Corinthians), the *Consensus*, the Genevan Catechism, and lastly Jan Łaski.[25]

Westphal's sequel is his 1552 exegetical work, *Recta fides de coena Domini*, which treated at length (170 pages) Paul's text on the Eucharist in 1 Corinthians 11.[26] Westphal's arguments were careful, but added little to what had been said in the first eucharistic controversy. All the same, his treatment of the sacramentarian gloss on the words "which is given for you" deserves some comment. Westphal indicted his interlocutors as blasphemers for saying

21. Rorem, *Calvin and Bullinger*, 47.

22. *New Schaff-Herzog Encyclopedia of Religious Knowledge*, ed. Samuel Macauley Jackson and George William Gilmore (Grand Rapids: Baker, 1950), 12:328, accessed at http://www.ccel .org/ccel/schaff/encyc12/Page_328.html.

23. Joachim Westphal, *Farrago confusanearum et inter se dissidentium opinionum de coena Domini, ex Sacramentariorum libris congesta* (Magdeburg: Rodius, 1552).

24. Westphal, *Farrago*, fD1a–fD5a.

25. Westphal, *Farrago*, D5b–D6a, D6b–D7a, D7a–D8a, and D8a–E2a.

26. Joachim Westphal, *Recta fides de coena Domini* (Magdeburg: Lottherus, 1553).

that were the Lutherans correct, then Christ's words "quod pro vobis datur" (which is given for you), by dint of the identity obtained under the Lutheran form, would have made bread and wine fixed to the cross for the faithful. Westphal responded that the words actually demand the bracing truth that the sacramentarians sought to deny—namely, that the body on the cross, now resurrected, is what is given in the Eucharist—negating the spiritual phantasm imagined by the Zwinglians. The bread broken as the Communion of the body of Christ is not an analogy and symbol of the passion but is the very fellowship in it. To Westphal—and this became a point when his contest with Calvin unfolded—there was no Christ apart from his flesh and blood, and no benefits apart from his life-giving *corpus*. But this was to be a point only later, for at the moment Westphal seemed little interested in Calvin as a target. The real aim of the tract was Westphal's defense of the Lutheran doctrine as a liturgical matter; he maintained that in the Eucharist is confected salvation itself, a salvation that is bound with the words of institution, words wholly eviscerated by the Reformed in their forms of service. For Zwingli in Zurich, the words of institution, which of course effect nothing, were treated in two parts: "Take, eat!" was treated as a command, while "This is my body" became the substance of that which is remembered, and not a commentary on the elements as received or taken. In Strasbourg and Geneva, there were no prayers of consecration but merely the rehearsing of the account of Paul, which left ambiguous in the text itself whether the species had been affected.[27] Later on in the text, it was obvious, because it was baldly stated, that the bread and the wine remained just that and that faith should not rest on them, for they still remained but bread and wine even though now consecrated to another purpose.[28] This section of his work Westphal had anticipated from the very beginning of his treatise when he commented on Paul's words "I received from the Lord, *et cetera*," which cast the whole treatise as not a justification of the Lutheran eucharistic doctrine per se, some defense of consubstantiation or

27. CO 6:193–200. See Bard Thompson, *Liturgies of the Western Church* (Philadelphia: Fortress, 1961), 197–208.

28. Kilian McDonnell, *Calvin, the Church, and the Eucharist* (Princeton: Princeton University Press, 2015), 235–38. See CO 6:200: "And let us not amuse ourselves with these earthly and corruptible elements, which we see with the eye, and touch with the hand and merely find Christ here, as if fastened to bread or wine. For we should now be disposed to be nourished and vivified by his (Christ's) substance, when the elements are so raised above all earthly things that they may attain to the heavens and enter into the kingdom of God, where He dwells." (Et ne nous amusons point à ces elemens terriens et corruptibles, que nous voyons à l'oeil, et touchons à la main pour le chercher là, comme s'il estoit encloz au pain ou au vin. Car lors noz ames seront disposées à estre nourries et vivifiées de sa substance, quand elles seront ainsi eslevées par dessus toutes choses terrestres pour attaindre iusque au Ciel et entrer au Royaulme de Dieu, où il habite.)

ubiquitarianism (words he neither used nor would own), but an apologia of the central Christian act in the Mass.[29]

Later in 1553 Westphal produced his *Collectanea sententiarum Divi Aurelii Augustini*,[30] a florilegium drawn almost exclusively from Augustine, though with two citations from Cyril of Alexandria at the very end. The whole text runs 125 pages, and most of the citations are little more than paragraphs, though some run for a few pages. Westphal followed a polemical commonplace in using the fathers, frequently citing them as though their words spoke for themselves (e.g., Bishop John Jewel and Thomas Harding arguing over Jewel's Challenge Sermon and the *Apologia Ecclesiae Anglicanae*). All the same, given Westphal's putative audience, the Lutheran faithful, the passages come across in a great torrent, presenting the Lutheran doctrine (in contrast to the confusion of the Reformed) as that which was consonant with the church catholic and, in particular, the epitome of catholicism to the Lutherans, Augustine himself.

Westphal's appeal to the fathers was hardly something new in the Reformation era, and indeed the Reformed and Lutheran alike made use of the fathers with varying degrees of ardor and with various polemical ends. Obviously, for all Protestants Holy Scripture was the final and complete authority within the church and sufficient for life and godliness. The Reformers did vary in their relative assessment of Scripture's perspicuity or clarity, and Luther himself was very wary of the unlearned and uninformed reading of the Scriptures by the laity. But whatever its opacity, Scripture for Protestants was the final court of appeal, even over the fathers. All the same, that it could be shown that the fathers did not stand with the Catholics was an asset in arguing that Protestantism faithfully followed, for example, Augustine, whereas Rome did not.[31] Although the use of the fathers among the Protestants did not follow exactly this arc, it still fulfilled the basic need to point out and criticize innovation, and this is what Westphal sought to do with his citations of Augustine and Cyril. Indeed, Cyril proved himself far more useful to Westphal's ends than Augustine, for ultimately the substance of the divisions between Lutheran and Reformed kept coming

29. Westphal, *Recta Fides*, f. 6a–f. 8b. (A6a–A8b); see also his explanation of the words of institution as the consecration and blessing, f. 16–17a (B8a–B8b).

30. Joachim Westphal, *Collectanea sententiarum Divi Aurelii Augustini Episcopi Hipponensis de Coena Domini: addita est confutatio vindicans à corruptelis plerosque locos, quos pro se ex Augustino falso citant Sacramentarii per Joachimum Westphalum* (Regensberg: ex officio Ioannis Carbonis, 1555).

31. See especially Pierre Fraenkel, *Testimonia Patrum: The Function of the Patristic Argument in the Theology of Philip Melanchthon* (Geneva: Librairie Droz, 1961); and for both Calvin and Westphal, Esther Chung-Kim, *Inventing Authority: The Use of the Church Fathers in the Reformation Debates over the Eucharist* (Waco: Baylor University Press, 2011), which strongly emphasizes the second eucharistic conflict, with three of six chapters touching it directly.

back to the question of Christology: the Lutherans accusing the Reformed of
Nestorianism, the Reformed citing the Lutherans for Monophysitism or Eutychianism (though these terms are not synonymous, the Reformed brandished
them equally), and both sides claiming to adhere to Chalcedon in its purity.[32]

Westphal, though clearly having touched on Calvin's thought, was not aiming at Calvin per se, but Calvin took up the challenge to answer the Hamburg
minister, the whole matter brought to his attention by the Polish Reformer
Jan Łaski.[33] At first Calvin seems not to have wanted to enter the lists, even
thinking that Westphal was so inconsequential an intellect that he could let
one of his lieutenants (i.e., Pierre Viret) handle it. In truth, Westphal's tracts
came out at a most inopportune time for Calvin, when both the Servetus affair and the final confrontation with the Genevan patriots were afoot. Yet
respond Calvin did in 1555 with his *Defensio sanae et orthodoxae doctrinae
de sacramentis*,[34] a short treatise of some fifty pages written as a response on
behalf of all the Swiss. He sought more than just Swiss approbation, however,
as he sent it as well to Melanchthon, whom he wanted desperately not only
to approve it but ultimately to turn his back on Luther's doctrine and declare
himself, if not Calvin's disciple, at least his fellow traveler. Melanchthon answered with silence.[35] That same year Westphal responded with his *Defensio
Iusta*,[36] his longest tract so far, some 150 pages in which he took on Calvin
in particular, drawing on Calvin's own words to pit him against the rest of
the Swiss church. Calvin's response, his *Second Defense*,[37] largely lost him
the battle: his tone was intense and vitriolic, but also incredibly tone-deaf.

---

32. On the Lutheran side, see John R. Stephenson, *The Lord's Supper*, vol. 12, *Confessional
Lutheran Dogmatics* (St. Louis: Luther Academy, 2003), which aside from making the Lutheran
case, in many ways better than Sasse, has a subchapter devoted to Calvin's "receptionism," and
also one titled "Reformed Denial of the Real Presence Proceeds from Reformed Christology,"
56–58.

33. Bruce Gordon, *Calvin* (New Haven: Yale University Press, 2009), 240.

34. John Calvin, *Defensio sanae et orthodoxae doctrinae de sacramentis* (Geneva: Robert
Etienne, 1555).

35. Following the Schmalkaldic League's defeat in 1547, Melanchthon as de facto head of
the Lutherans accepted Charles V's interim religious settlements that allowed the Lutherans
to retain their articles on justification but required acceptance of Catholic teaching on other
matters. This did not sit well with many Lutherans. Once Charles V had been defeated by the
Germans at Innsbruck in 1552, and following the Peace of Augsburg in 1555, Melanchthon
still played coy on a number of issues, feeling the invectives of a number of "true" or Gnesio-
Lutherans, including Westphal.

36. Joachim Westphal, *Adversus cuiusdam Sacramentarii Falsam Criminationem, Iusta
Defensio* (Frankfort: Petrus Brubacius, 1555). Though the words are inverted in the title, on
the pages of the book they read *Defensio Iusta*.

37. John Calvin, *Secunda defensio piae et orthodoxae de sacramentis fidei, contra Joachimi
Westphali calumnias* (Geneva: Jean Crispin, 1556).

He targeted as his audience the churches in Saxony, which he thought largely sided with Melanchthon as regards the Eucharist, the so-called Philipists as opposed to the Gnesio-, or true, Lutherans. Calvin had badly misread the situation. Numerous Lutheran ministers and theologians responded, sending Westphal detailed confessions, including the church of Magdeburg of Matthias Flacius Illyricus. Not only was Westphal given ammunition but numerous other Lutherans joined him in penning responses.[38] The Reformed were not lacking in champions either, as both Bullinger[39] and Bernardino Ochino responded.[40] Yet having entered the lists, Bullinger still wrote Calvin telling him he had failed in his assessment of the situation and that all of Germany was now arrayed against the Swiss: "You esteemed them few who follow that crass opinion of the corporeal presence. You wish that the tolerable sense of the *Augustana* returned. . . . Now all their squadrons sally forth, all bearing their weapons, all rising against us, all fighting on behalf of Westphalism!"[41]

Bruce Gordon depicts a Calvin who now buckles under the onslaught, not only from the weight of Westphal and the Lutheran response, but as well from his growing unease about France and the winds of war. By the summer of 1557 Calvin thought the situation called for a united Protestant front, and he began to press Melanchthon on the matter, even to the point of curtness: "If a means of pacification is sought for, our only hope lies in a conference which I doubt not that you desire, but I wish that you called for more courageously."[42] This probably made it all the easier for Melanchthon, at a colloquy in Worms in the

---

38. Westphal countered with his *Confessio fidei de Eucharistiae Sarcamento, in quo Ministri Ecclesiarum Saxonia solidis Argumentis sacrarum Literarum astruunt Corporis et Sanguinis Dominm Nostri Iesu Christi et cetera* (Magdeburg: Ambrosium Kirchner, 1557).

39. Heinrich Bullinger, *Apologetica expositio, qua ostenditur Tigurinae ecclesiae ministros nullum sequi dogma haereticum in coena domini, libellis quorundam acerbis opposita, & ad omnes synceram veritatem & sanctam pacem amantes Christifideles placide scripta* (Zurich: Gesnerum, 1556).

40. Bernardino Ochino, *Syncerae et verae doctrinae de coena domini defensio per Bernardinum Ochinum Locarnensium ecclesiae pastorem, contra libros tres Ioachimi Westphali, Hamburgensis Ecclesiae praedicatoris* (Zurich: Gesner, 1556). Ochino entered the fray in 1556. He had just finished writing on purgatory when from his perch in Zurich he went after Westphal. In truth, Ochino saw that it was not only Westphal he was confronting but Luther himself, and thus sought to dispatch the troubling question of how it was that God had given Luther such clarity on the gospel, but not at all on this other matter. For Ochino, the thoughts of youth, especially those on religion, are hard to shake, and Luther had shown himself unwilling to reform in so many areas, such as the keeping of the hours.

41. *CO* 16:483–84. "Existimabas tu pauculos esse qui crassam illam corporeae praesentiae opinionem sequerentur. Volebas sensum tolerabilem reddere confessionis Augustanae. Ac in hac causa sequutus est te et *Lascanus* noster. Suasimus nos ne huic pelago vos crederetis ete. Nunc turmatim excurrunt omnes, arma ferunt, omnes in nos insurgunt, omnes Westphalismum propugnant."

42. Gordon, *Calvin*, 248.

fall of the year, to denounce the Swiss openly, leading Bullinger to denounce Melanchthon as no different from Luther. Calvin wrote Bullinger and tried to cover for his friend by saying that these were the words of a tired old man.[43] Calvin responded also once more, and for the last time, to Westphal with *The Last Admonition of John Calvin to Joachim Westphal*,[44] to which Westphal responded with two more works, *Apologia* and *Confutatio*.[45]

Lamentably, there was a paucity of writings covering the second eucharistic controversy, especially given its breadth. When the dust had settled, it had pulled most of the main Reformers into its whirlwind, and it can easily be read as extending into the next decade. And though various monographs and a host of articles have touched on various aspects of the question, Wim Janse laments that its history has not yet been written.[46] He also points out that what has been done is almost always confessionally tainted, authors betraying their assumptions by the order of the protagonists' names. But the matter itself was a confessional battle. Westphal's initial foray sprang from his reading of the Zurich *Consensus*, and he tacitly asserted in his initial writings that in subscribing to the *Consensus* Calvin had left his first confession—namely, the *Augustana*. Peter Martyr Vermigli in a letter to Calvin lamented: "There are many who would like to stop this dispute for the sake of peace; but since it has broken out again without our fault, we may not leave the truth without defense. As long as it is not firmly established, in regard to the doctrine of the Lord's Supper, there is an important doctrine wanting in the Church, and peace cannot be hoped for."[47] Yet peace is what Calvin actually wanted, and like Bucer before him, he quickly found himself in a no-man's-land between Zurich and Wittenberg, and he essentially had to eat his Zurich crow, despite

---

43. Gordon, *Calvin*, 249.

44. John Calvin, *Ultima admonitio Joannis Calvini ad Joachimum Westphalum* (Geneva: Jean Crispin, 1557).

45. Joachim Westphal, *Apologia Confessionis De Coena Domini, Contra Corruptelas et calumnias Ioannis Calvini* (Ursellis: Nicholas Henricus, 1558); *Confutatio aliquot enormium mendaciorum Ioannis Calvini, securae Apologia adversus eius furores praemissa* (Ursellis: Nicholas Henricus, 1558).

46. Wim Janse, "The Controversy between Westphal and Calvin on Infant Baptism, 1555–1556," *Perichoresis* 6, no. 1 (2008): 3–43. See also Joseph Tylenda, "The Calvin-Westphal Exchange: The Genesis of Calvin's Treatises against Westphal," *Calvin Theological Journal* 9 (1974): 182–209; and Tylenda, "Calvin and Westphal: Two Eucharistic Theologies in Conflict," in *Calvin's Books: Festschrift Dedicated to Peter De Klerk on the Occasion of His Seventieth Birthday*, ed. Joseph Tylenda (Heerenveen: J. J. Groen & Zoon, 1997), 9–21. In *Inventing Authority*, Esther Jung-Kim, while covering the controversy, is essentially concerned with Calvin's and Westphal's uses of the church fathers.

47. Vermigli to Calvin, quoted in Karl Benrath, *Bernardino Ochino, of Siena: A Contribution towards the History of the Reformation*, trans. Helen Simmern (London: James Nisbet, 1876), 233–34.

his initial treatise being so close to the Lutherans on such key points as the Eucharist as a means of grace. Gordon notes that Calvin

> had lost the battle with Westphal, whom he had so badly underrated. A large part of Westphal's success was to do not so much with his own theological acumen, though that was considerable, but with the manner in which he had effectively used Calvin's own words to demonstrate the shifting and perhaps even contradictory character of the Genevan's teaching. . . . In so doing he had managed to tear the tissue of alliance between Geneva and Zurich. . . . Calvin generally mauled his opponents, but not this time.[48]

In a sequel to the whole affair, the one theologian who gave a great deal of attention to Calvin's exchange with Westphal, the nineteenth-century German Reformed theologian John Nevin, from his seat at Mercersburg Seminary entered into a long debate with the Princeton theologian Charles Hodge over the nature of the Eucharist. Hodge asserted that the high point, the summa of Reformed orthodox thought on the Eucharist, was reached in the *Consensus Tigurinus*.[49] Nevin responded in his work *Mystical Presence* and in a long article in *The Mercersburg Review*.[50] His bracing arguments pointed out that Hodge stood guilty of the very charge Westphal had sought to make against the Reformed, that of advocating empty symbols, destitute of the grace of God; therefore, Hodge had shown himself to be no heir of Calvin.

As regards Calvin, the whole affair with Westphal demonstrated, as with Caroli and the antitrinitarians, that Calvin often stood isolated on a theological island of his own making. He certainly had allies in Bucer and Melanthon, among others, in regard to his eucharistic doctrines, but both of them were little more than broken reeds as far as Calvin would have been concerned when the *Consensus* appeared, for Bucer would die the next year, and Melanchthon had shot his bolt on the issue in controversy over the Augsburg Interim and proved no help to Calvin at all. Indeed, Calvin himself, in a move that seems a betrayal of his life in so many other areas, conceded essential points of his eucharistic theology to Bullinger in an attempt to find a united front. Ultimately his quest for unity only brought greater division, and this while his native France stood on the brink of the war that would spill so much blood over that syllable, *hoc*.

---

48. Gordon, *Calvin*, 249.

49. "No document, therefore, can have a higher claim to represent the true doctrine of the Reformed Church than this 'Consensus'" (Charles Hodge, *Systematic Theology* [New York: Charles Scribner, 1873], 3:631–32).

50. John W. Nevin, *The Mystical Presence, a Vindication of the Reformed or Calvinist Doctrine of the Eucharist* (Philadelphia: J. B. Lippincott, 1846); Nevin, "Doctrine of the Reformed Church on the Lord's Supper," *The Mercersburg Review* 2 (1850): 421–548.

10

The Radicals

Italia *as More Trouble Than* Iberia

In 1559, while packing his effects to return to his native Poland, the Tübingen student and noble Michael Zaleski was attacked and murdered. The Polish students clamored for an investigation, which turned up more than they might have wished, for among Zaleski's remains was a manuscript of a work, *Declaratio Iesu Christi filii Dei*, by one Alphonsus Lyncurius Tarraconensis, a pseudonym, though unknown at the time, of the jurist Matteo Gribaldi.[1] The work is part of a chain linking the antitrinitarian theology of the Italian radicals and the future unitarian church of Poland. While words such as "Unitarianism" or "Socinianism" still have some intellectual cachet, the Reformation iterations of these died out in the seventeenth century, and little trace of them survives in the two lands where once they thrived—namely, Poland and Hungarian Transylvania. People came afterward to take up their mantle and carry on their legacy, beginning with the Deists in England, and then they were given some due in the Enlightenment, but lived on only in the United States.[2] And it is to Deism that one must look for the intellectual roots of modern atheism,[3] for having separated God from history, separating him

1. George Hunston Williams, *The Radical Reformation* (Kirksville, MO: Sixteenth Century Essays and Studies, 2000), 1229–30.
2. See Earl Morse Wilbur, *A History of Unitarianism: In Transylvania, England, and America* (Boston: Beacon, 1969).
3. Michael J. Buckley, *At the Origins of Modern Atheism* (New Haven: Yale University Press, 1980).

from the universe, from both its cosmogonies and cosmologies, was but the next necessary and logical step, one that the *philosophes* of the eighteenth century were ready to take. Denis Diderot asked the question in the Enlightenment, can an unnecessary God exist? The obvious answer is no, as Diderot set out in his fascinating dialogue *D'Alembert's Dream*, and thus cutting the last shreds of the tattered knots of Aristotelian teleology, already shredded by the Deists. But the characters to be covered in this chapter were not Deists, and while they might in some minds provide an "apostolic succession" going back to Arius (and many of them did look to Arius as their father), their real value was that they made it necessary for Calvin and other Reformers to cast their theology in sharper and clearer terms. George H. Williams cites the early Reformation as largely ambivalent about the question of the nature of the Trinity and the incarnation. Only when Michael Servetus reemerged in the 1550s, followed by the rise of the antitrinitarians, did the Reformers become sufficiently alarmed to start addressing the matter in earnest. Indeed, for Williams, the radical Reformers drove "the magisterial reformers to gain fluency in patristic syntax."[4] This description undersells what the Reformers were doing, however, by missing that they had built their entire initial understanding of the sinner's reconciliation with God on the theology that was given its full explication by Anselm in *Cur Deus Homo*. If justification were the point on which the Reformation rose or fell, than the prior question of *Cur Deus homo* had to be answered as Anselm had answered it. Thus the controversies that surrounded the radicals touched the Trinity necessarily, but they also touched the very question of Christ the mediator. This, too, the radicals knew.

To varying degrees the radicals of the later sixteenth century looked back to Servetus, but there is no clear and direct line from the Spaniard to them, though some lines there were. Instead, later antitrinitarianism owed its inspiration to two men—namely, Matteo Gribaldi and Giorgio Biandrata. Gribaldi was Servetus's champion after his execution, but he did not fully follow or comprehend his theology, and this is why a direct line from apostle to student fails. Yet it may have been enough that the student was like his master, for there was a distinct line in the mind of the sixteenth-century theologians, a discernable succession of the antitrinitarianism: "Girolamo Varro testified that at Geneva it was said that the Devil had begotten Servetus, and Servetus Farges (Gribaldi), and Farges Giorgio (Biandrata), and Giorgio Paul (Alciati), and Paul several more."[5] Servetus, however spectacular his mind, life,

---

4. Williams, *Radical Reformation*, 460.
5. Quoted in Wilbur, *Unitarianism*, 214.

and death, had seemingly little impact on the Italian community in Geneva. Indeed, Calvin saw the source of all the problems in the Italian congregation that touched the question of the Trinity as arising from Gribaldi, as he wrote to Peter Martyr Vermigli: "These days in the Italian Church are ones of trouble. Gribaldi spreads the peculiar seed of his errors, the greatest of which he here gives: that God is One, who is the Father of Christ, that the monarchy is fully the Father alone. Christ truly is secondary, even as the firstborn among many gods."[6]

Matteo Gribaldi: The Origin of Later Radicalism

Gribaldi, even during the trial of Servetus, played his cards to the authorities of the Genevans apparently with little thought to the danger that beset him. He let it be known that he never thought someone should be executed for mere opinion, and asserted that he found nothing particularly odious about Servetus's views, for he had himself held such views since childhood. These sentiments brought Gribaldi into conflict with Calvin. But Calvin's refusal to have an open discussion about the question with Gribaldi (Earl Morse Wilbur says Calvin "haughtily refused"[7]) led Gribaldi to leave Geneva, complaining about his treatment from Calvin in a letter to the congregation at Vicenza, later reprinted by Castellio.[8]

Gribaldi, born in Turin in 1505, studied law in Padua and, having excelled in his studies, became one of the better-known jurists of his day, teaching law at multiple universities across Europe, including Padua and Grenoble.[9] He made his first home in northern Italy, teaching law at the University of Padua. Because of a marriage into wealth, he was the owner of an estate in Farges in Bernese territory, some twenty miles west of Geneva. He went to Farges every summer, frequently passing through Geneva, and thus knew Calvin, and apparently was well respected in the Italian congregation. The congregation itself had originally

6. CO 17:176: "His diebus in ecclesia Italica aliquid fuit turbarum. Gribaldus semina quaedam suorum errorum sparserat, quorum summa huc redit: unicum Deum esse, qui pater est Christi: ut monarchia sit penes solum patrem. Christus vero secundarius et quasi primogenitus inter multos deos."

7. Wilbur, *Unitarianism*, 216.

8. Sebastian Castellio, *Contra libellum Calvini in quo ostendere conatur haereticos jure gladij coercendos esse* (Amsterdam: n.p., 1612).

9. Gribaldi entered into the controversies over the methods of studying law in the sixteenth century, siding with the "Bartolists" against the philological methodology championed by Valla, Bude, and Baudouin. See Donald R. Kelley, *Foundations of Modern Historical Scholarship: Language, Law and History in the French Renaissance* (New York: Columbia University Press, 1970), 92.

been under Bernardino Ochino, from 1542 till 1545, but it had become inactive in the years up to 1552—that is, just prior to Servetus's arrival. The Italian community clearly welcomed Gribaldi at his summer visits, and his more humanist sympathies probably found a ready outlet among them. Back in Padua, however, his views were increasingly coming under suspicion. The university was home to thousands of Lutheran students who had formed their own republic within the university, established to guard their liberties. Gribaldi became associated with them and was reputed to have written a treatise on Francesco Spiera, a Protestant lawyer who recanted his faith under duress from the Inquisition and died in the throes of self-recriminations and doubt.[10] Spiera became a Protestant commonplace of the tortured and compromised conscience. Gribaldi became a watched man and had to flee Italy in 1555. He first headed to Zurich, where the former Italian bishop Pietro Paolo Vergerio resided. Gribaldi had known Vergerio, and Vergerio had been attending Spiera at his death and doubtless was a source for Gribaldi's tract, if indeed Gribaldi himself was not a witness to the event.[11] When Vergerio had first quit Italy, Gribaldi had written a letter of introduction for him to the church in Zurich, but both Zurich and Vergerio suspected Gribaldi of having taken a more radical turn, especially after he flaunted a copy of Servetus's *De Trinitatis erroribus*, acquired as a gift in 1554.[12] Initially, Vergerio believed Gribaldi to have gone completely over to Servetus's way of thinking, complaining to Bullinger that Gribaldi had become an evangelist for Servetus. In September of 1554 Gribaldi had sent a letter to the Italian congregation espousing his views, which eschewed the patristic language on the Trinity; he failed to speak of Christ as one essence with the Father.[13] All the same, Bullinger having obtained from Gribaldi an acceptable confession of his orthodoxy, Vergerio seems to have changed his position and warmly recommended his old friend for a position at the University of Tübingen, then under the patronage of Duke Christopher of Württemberg.[14] Gribaldi, prior to going to Tübingen in 1555, stopped in Geneva, where Calvin initiated a confrontation by, according to Gribaldi, refusing to shake his extended hand. Gribaldi left in a fury and, when passing through Zurich, complained of this treatment to Bullinger. Bullinger warned Gribaldi about the danger he had just escaped, which elicited from Gribaldi a denunciation of Servetus and a full-throated expression of the Nicene faith.[15] With his

    10. Cf. M. A. Overell, "The Exploitation of Francesco Spiera," *Sixteenth Century Journal* 26, no. 3 (Autumn 1995): 619–37.
    11. Williams, *Radical Reformation*, 950.
    12. Wilbur, *Unitarianism*, 216; Williams, *Radical Reformation*, 951.
    13. CO 15:246–48.
    14. CO 15:767.
    15. Wilbur, *Unitarianism*, 217.

trinitarian bona fides again intact, Gribaldi proceeded to Tübingen, where he not only filled a university post but also became a councillor to the duke. With Gribaldi had come two students from Padua, both originally from Poland, Peter Gonesius, who would play no small part in the future of Polish antitrinitarianism, and the above-mentioned tragic young nobleman Michael Zaleski.[16] That Gribaldi's two wards clearly had radical sympathies speaks to the disposition of Gribaldi at this juncture. But while Vergerio backed his old compatriot, in Geneva Calvin's colleague Beza took to the offensive, playing the complete skeptic about Gribaldi and his orthodoxy, and writing Vergerio, scolding him for his sympathies.[17] Calvin wrote to Melchior Wolmar, his old professor from Paris, now teaching at Tübingen, complaining that the vain and boisterous Gribaldi preached polytheism, believing in at least two gods.[18]

In the face of his Genevan detractors, Gribaldi sought to show himself orthodox, and writing to Martinengo, the minster of Geneva's Italian congregation, he gave his declaration of faith in the Nicene definition of the creed. Wilbur wants to gloss this as Gribaldi just being airy or breezy in his assertions, but this interpretation strains the purpose; Gribaldi hoped to skate by the theological scruples of his would-be jailers. In fact, he only made things worse, as the next year the orthodox Italians Vergerio and Peter Martyr Vermigli were both convinced of their countryman's fraud. Vergerio apparently went looking for confirmation of this, for while on a trip to Geneva he came upon information—tracts and books from the pen of Gribaldi himself—that confirmed his heterodoxy.[19] Vergerio wrote to Duke Christopher that he feared Gribaldi had played him false. The duke thereupon summoned Gribaldi to appear before the university senate, which confronted him with the evidence that had been sent; the lawyer's only tactic was to become evasive in the face of questions. He admitted that he had written some unsound things, having no other recourse, since the evidence before him clearly indicted him. All the same, he affirmed the faith of the Nicene and Apostles' creeds, but this tardy and suspect confession would not satisfy his detractors. The senate demanded that he embrace both the Athanasian formula and the parts of the Theodosian Code on the Trinity—that is, those that had been part of the creed in its final form, and as were expanded in the code.[20] Gribaldi quibbled that these were

16. Williams, *Radical Reformation*, 1009–10.

17. *CO* 15:838.

18. *CO* 15:644.

19. Wilbur, *Unitarianism*, 219.

20. Wilbur, *Unitarianism*, 220, intimates that the appeal to the Theodosian Code was linked to the Athanasian Creed, but the code came well before the Athanasian Creed, which was based entirely on Augustinian theology and did not appear until the early sixth century, while the

matters of words and asked for time to write out his thoughts. The university senate gave him three weeks, time that Gribaldi did not need after all, for he immediately fled Tübingen and made for Farges, leaving behind almost all of his possessions. Apparently he went by way of Zurich, for from there he wrote back to the university that he felt this was the best way out for all concerned, meaning himself and the university.[21]

The explanation carried no weight with Duke Christopher. He had Gribaldi's library searched and information forwarded to Berne about "his subject" taken from both the library and from the records of Gribaldi's appearance before the senate. Initially Berne seemed content to let him alone, but from Farges Gribaldi sought to disseminate his ideas, and as the Bernese had ordered him watched, he was arrested and endured nine days of strict theological examination. Some in Berne wanted his death, but others argued for banishment, which in the end was what was enforced. His obligations to Württemberg were taken into account in his sentencing (skipping out on his duties to the university), and his estate at Farges was made the property of Berne but would be returned were he ever to recant in the presence of Duke Christopher and obtain acquittal in Tübingen. Gribaldi begged to submit an orthodox confession to the Bernese ministers. When the time came, he wavered again, and even though he signed the confession, the city council imputed him with bad faith.[22] Though Gribaldi was banished from Bernese territory, his family was allowed to stay, Farges actually being his wife's inheritance.

Upon the death of Gribaldi's wife in 1558, Nikolaus Zurkinden, then secretary to the town council of Berne and a proponent of toleration, interceded on Gribaldi's behalf to the council. Gribaldi had appealed to Berne on the basis of concern for his children, and thus he was allowed to return to care for them.[23] All the same, he was informed that he was to keep his beliefs to himself. Duke Christopher offered him his post at Tübingen were he but to submit a trinitarian confession of faith, which he did, but the university senate overruled the appointment. In 1559, upon invitation, he returned, after a fourteen-year absence, to his old post in Grenoble, but there arguments within the faculty had partisans bring up his doubtful orthodoxy, and the government ordered Grenoble to dismiss him or else face the university being suspended. After this Gribaldi vanished from the historical record. All we know is that

Theodosian Code was early fifth century; cf. J. N. D. Kelly, *The Athanasian Creed* (New York: Harper & Row, 1964), 35–37.
21. Wilbur, *Unitarianism*, 220.
22. Williams, *Radical Reformation*, 977.
23. CO 17:207.

he died of the plague in September 1564, with nothing known of his children "save that fifteen years later one of his sons came to Tübingen to settle some outstanding matters relating to his father's property."[24]

While the tale of Gribaldi ended less horribly and infamously than that of Servetus, in his day his contemporaries saw him as the source of all sorts of evil, although not fully recognizing him for what he was. Calvin, as mentioned, had written Vermigli that Gribaldi, and not Servetus, was the source of theological troubles in the Genevan Italian community, but he mistook what Gribaldi taught for the doctrine of Servetus.[25] Gribaldi essentially taught a form of tritheism, or probably better put, polytheism. The triad of persons were self-subsisting natures or existences, but the Son and the Spirit were not God in the same way that the Father was, but possessed a dignity and power inferior to that of the Father. Ironically, while Calvin thought him the specter of Servetus, Gribaldi really was the source of that very thing that Servetus sought to avoid—namely, a multiplicity of deities. Gribaldi thus through such writers as Valentine Gentili and his student at Padua, Peter Gonesius, would introduce a doctrine of three distinct divine beings to whom worship is owed, all borne out by Gribaldi in both his *Apologia* for Servetus and his *Declaratio Jesu Christi Filii Dei Authore Michaele Serveto*.[26]

The more important of these two is the *Declaratio*. Originally thought by both Stansilas Kot and Roland Bainton to be the work of Servetus, and identified as such even as recently as the 2004 Spanish edition of Servetus's complete works, its English translators, Peter Zerner, Peter Hughes, and Lynn Gordon Hughes, saw it for what it was and were able to identify the text as Gribaldi's.[27] Essentially, Gribaldi wrote the *Declaratio* using Servetus as a pseudonym, but his fealty to Servetus did not keep him faithful to the Spaniard's theology in key respects. The translators saw that the work was written in complete ignorance of Servetus's 1552 *Christianismi restitutio* and thus did not follow

24. Wilbur, *Unitarianism*, 222.

25. Calvin, *Institutes* 1.13.23. Cf. Brannon Ellis, *Calvin, Classical Trinitarianism, and the Aseity of the Son* (Oxford: Oxford University Press, 2012), 54.

26. Matteo Gribaldi, *Declaratio: Michael Servetus's Revelation of Jesus Christ, the Son of God and Other Antitrinitarian Works by Matteo Gribaldi*, trans. Peter Zerner, Peter Hughes, and Lynn Gordon Hughes (Providence: Blackstone Editions, 2010), especially his *De vera Dei et Filii eius cognitione sermo*, 214–27. See also Williams, *Radical Reformation*, 953.

27. See the introduction of Gribaldi, *Declaratio*, xxviii–xxxix. The translators believe the text was written sometime around 1557, as one passage seems clearly to engage Calvin's comments in his 1555 commentary on Luke. The first time that we have a record of the *Declaratio* is among the papers of Michael Zaleski, a Polish student murdered in Tübingen in 1559. Since the tract was part of the investigation into the orthodoxy of the Polish students at the university, it was preserved as evidence. For the full bibliography of the work of Stanislas Kot, see Williams, *Radical Reformation*, 1344.

the trajectory of Servetus's thought.[28] In fact, the author of the *Declaratio* began with *De Trinitatis erroribus*, but then charted his own course in both the *Declaratio* and the shorter *De vera Dei et Filii eius Cognitione Sermo* (another pseudonymous treatise, ostensibly preached by Servetus at the stake), adopting certain Neoplatonic motifs by which the Son is a deity from the Father, but a lesser deity, though divine all the same: "The Son is god from the Father, and as it were constituted by the Father god of all, recognizing in himself the deity and supremacy of the Father, although this distinction of the divine names is not found among the Greeks and Latins, and each [member of the Trinity] is called by the one, common name of 'God.'"[29] Gribaldi did affirm Servetus's notion about the substantial Word changing into a person at the incarnation: "Indeed previously he was an incorporeal, impassible, invisible substance which afterward at a set time was made a visible and passable body in the virgin's womb."[30] Yet unlike Servetus, who could speak of Christ as God only in a derivative sense (in that he was to be honored), Gribaldi gave to "the man Jesus, the Son of God," a natural divinity that other beings (also gods) did not have, which Jesus obviously possessed "through the superabundant grace and munificence by which he was chosen by God above all others, who were chosen by God and divinely illuminated, which the scriptures call gods, because Christ is the son, and through a natural grace, a God unlike others who are earthly men and partial gods."[31]

As mentioned, the *Declaratio* first appeared among the effects of the Pole Michael Zaleski, which speaks to Gribaldi as its author and signals the increasing influence of radical theology in Poland. Already in 1525 Poland had a Lutheran presence, bolstered by the secularization of the Teutonic Knights when their grand master, Albert of Brandenburg, converted to Protestantism and was made the first duke of Prussia by the Polish king the Roman Catholic Sigismund.[32] His duchy was built on the secularized lands of the order. Albert was actually cited by the empire for this act of apostasy, but the political situation was never one that allowed his prosecution. Thus Poland provided

28. Gribaldi, *Declaratio*, xxii–xxiii. Kot had thought it a transitional text between *De Trinitatis erroribus* and *Restitutio*, whereas Bainton and Alacala had taken it as an early draft of *De Trinitatis erroribus*.

29. Gribaldi, *De vera Dei*, 220, in *Declaratio*. I have used my own translation here, as the translators chose to insert the word "made" into the text so that the beginning of the quotation reads "the Son is [made] God by the Father" (221). This hardly seems to be Gribaldi's point, since he would rather not speak of the Son as created.

30. Gribaldi, *Declaratio*, 140.

31. Gribaldi, *Declaratio*, 106.

32. Howard Louthan, "A Model for Christendom? Erasmus, Poland, and the Reformation," *Church History* 83, no. 1 (2014): 18–37.

more than just a refuge for Lutherans, and it was there that the radicals would flourish, and there Gribaldi's tritheism would emerge as well, though not without the unwitting help of Calvin and one of his other tormentors, Francisco Stancaro, and this in what was known as Lesser Poland.[33]

Francisco Stancaro: Turning Calvin into a Tritheist

By the 1540s Poland had turned toward Geneva, led by the Polish noble Jan Łaski, who had come to the Reformation via Erasmus, who left him his library. Łaski ministered in Emden and spent time in England during the reign of Edward VI, returning to his native Poland in 1556 only to witness the Reformed church become embroiled in controversy in 1559 centered on Francisco Stancaro. Stancaro, like Gribaldi, came from Italy, born in Mantua in 1501. The scion of a converted Jewish family, he was gifted in Hebrew and contended with the Jewish communities of his day, arguing for the identity of the son of David and the son of Joseph.[34] Stancaro also possessed, according to his Italian intimates, an overweening sense of his own importance, and was someone who easily made himself unwelcome; one characterized him as "a snail which leaves behind it a trail of slime."[35] He held a university post at Padua from 1540, but fell under suspicion by the Inquisition and was imprisoned in 1543. He quickly made his escape, however, and next turned up and taught briefly in Vienna, but was dismissed by order of Ferdinand in 1546. From there he went in succession to Regensburg, Augsburg, and Basle. In Basle in 1547 he published a Hebrew grammar, along with a treatise on the sacraments.[36] He then went to Transylvania, where he was awarded a doctorate, and then on to Kraków, and from there to Königsberg, the capital of the new Prussian duchy, where he began a dispute with Andreas Osiander over the question of Christ as mediator. Stancaro opposed Osiander's teaching that Christ was mediator in his divine nature, since for Stancaro a mediator is necessarily inferior before the one he mediates, and as Christ is not inferior to the Father, his mediatorship must reside in his human nature. Stancaro soon

33. Lesser Poland is the region of southern Poland that includes modern Kraków and borders the Carpathian Mountains and Transylvania to the south.

34. George H. Williams, "Francis Stancaro's Schismatic Reformed Church, Centered in Dubets'ko in Ruthenia, 1559/61–1570," *Harvard Ukrainian Studies* 3 (1979): 932.

35. Williams, *Radical Reformation*, 854.

36. Francisci Stancari Mantuani, *Ebreae Grammaticae Institutio* (Basle, 1547); Mantuani, *Della Riformatione, si della dottrina Christiana, come della vera intelligentia dei sacramenti, etc.* (Basle, 1547). The treatise on the sacraments was written in Italian, as it was dedicated to the signoria of Venice.

made himself unwelcome and left Königsberg in 1551. From there he went to Frankfurt-am-Oder, where he taught at the Brandenbrug Academy, and the question of Christ's mediatorial role again emerged, this time with another Lutheran theologian, Andreas Musculus. The elector of Brandenburg sought intervention from Melanchthon, who sided with Musculus; the result was Stancaro's departure from Frankfurt and an inveterate disdain for Melanchthon. After years of wandering and traveling through Transylvania again, he settled in Pinczów in Lesser Poland in 1559. When there previously in 1551, he had helped organize the first synod of the Reformed church. Yet according to Beza's disciple Peter (Statorius) de Thionville in a letter to Calvin written that fall, Stancaro was then reviving Nestorianism. De Thionville wished Calvin to answer Stancaro, who had accused the Polish Reformed church of Arianism.[37] Calvin responded, however, by expressing more concern that Giorgio Biandrata was in Pinczów than with what Stancaro was up to, and the sequel proved him justified in his concerns, though Calvin perhaps could have saved the Polish Reformed church a great deal of grief had he addressed their concerns about Stancaro right away. This assumes, however, that an early reply from Calvin would have been sufficient for the matter and not counterproductive, as the case ultimately proved to be.

Stancaro, well read in the church fathers and the medieval doctors, was reportedly possessed of great skills as an orator—when in Basle he had held the chair of rhetoric.[38] Consequently, in debate he proved himself far too formidable for almost everyone, and it was noted by his opponents, including those who sent letters to Calvin, that no one was his match, and thus the appeal to Calvin to act on behalf of the Polish Reformed church. In one confrontation with Jan Łaski, Stancaro got the better of him to such a degree that the aging noble actually hurled a book at him. In almost every dispute Stancaro bested his interlocutors, which explains Łaski's frustrations, and Williams wrote that so gifted was Stancaro that he "could have successfully defended even an absurd cause."[39] Lacking the ability but not the resolve to answer Stancaro as it wished, the Polish church still censured him and sought a dogmatic response. The result was a Polish confession that emphasized Christ's threefold office of prophet, priest, and king; because Calvin saw Christ's keeping of the Mosaic law throughout his life as part of redemption, Williams notes the shift in emphasis for the Poles

37. Pierre de Thionville to Calvin in CO 17:601.
38. Joseph Tylenda, "Christ the Mediator: Calvin versus Stancaro," *Calvin Theological Journal* 8 (1973): 7.
39. Williams, *Radical Reformation*, 1029.

from the Anselmian model of a satisfaction theory of the atonement to a penal substitution model.[40]

Calvin eventually did enter the fray, sending the Poles his response to Stancaro in two short treatises contained within separate letters. The first he sent in the summer of 1560 after yet another Polish minister, John Lusenius, had written relating the seeming triumph of Stancaro because no one could step forward after the death of Łaski to answer him.[41] Calvin's short treatise focused on the specific item of contention: whether Christ's divinity was essential to the office of mediator. He did address what he took to be Stancaro's real reason for objecting to the orthodox doctrine—namely, that he was inflated with contempt for the faith (*fastu turgidus*) and driven by ambition (the mother of heresies) to do harm.[42] On the doctrinal issue, to Stancaro's insistence that the Polish Reformed church (and by implication Geneva and Zurich, at the least) was embracing Arianism by making the Son inferior to the Father by dint of his being mediator in his divine nature, Calvin pointed out that only a divine person could enter into the heavenly sanctuary; however, he confusedly elaborated on the question by positing Christ as mediator in both natures, instead of asserting that he is mediator in his divine person as the Word and Son, mediating between the divine and the human. This comes out in his confusion, voiced in the *Institutes* as well, that Christ appears a composite person: "Indeed it is true to say that all things, by which he accomplished reconciling God to us, were attributed to the whole person, so that they ought not to be separately attributed to one nature only."[43] Calvin does concede that as long as Christ is mediator, he submits himself to the Father, which would seem the very point at issue for Stancaro, but there was no other way, according to Calvin, that Christ could be mediator.

Calvin's second response came, but only following a strategically written letter he received from his agent, Sebastian Pech, in September 1560. Pech, an associate of Łaski and an acquaintance of the Polish prince Radziwill, had been asked to deliver a letter from Calvin to the prince, as well as a copy of Calvin's commentary on the book of Acts dedicated to Radziwill. Pech, writing from the book fair in Frankfurt, asked for a response from Calvin to Stancaro, and seemed to have no knowledge of Calvin's first efforts. Pech

40. Williams, *Radical Reformation*, 1032. Williams gives the text of the confession (*De mediatore*) in note 131, which begins at the bottom of 1030 and takes up the entirety of 1031.

41. Tylenda gives a full translation of the text in "Christ the Mediator," 11–16. The letter is signed by all the pastors of the Genevan church.

42. *CO* 9:337.

43. *CO* 9:340: "Vere etiam dicitur omnes, quibus ad reconciliandum nobis Deum functus est, actiones ad totam personam spectasse, ut non debeant separatim ad unam tantum naturam restringi."

spared no detail in telling Calvin what a cur Stancaro was, and that Stancaro would not scruple, having been censured by the Polish church, to make common cause with the Catholics against the Reformed. To effect this, Stancaro approached the papal nuncio in Kraków, Bernardo Bongiovanni, protesting that his faith was that of the medieval doctors, save on one issue (what that issue was may only be guessed). Pech told Calvin that the nuncio remained unmoved by Stancaro's declarations; he then ended his letter by relating how Stancaro had made an index of the relative corruption of the several churches, drawing the conclusion that the "papists are bad, the Lutherans are worse, the Swiss and the Sabaudians [Waldensians] are the worst of all."[44] Calvin initially balked, but events brought more letters. Following a synod that took up the question of "Stancarism," when missives from Strasbourg, Basle, Geneva, and Zurich had been read, the synod fell into a riot when the noble Jerome Osolinksi asserted that since Stancaro considered the Genevan and Zuricher reports to be forgeries, the whole affair should be tabled, with a gag order imposed on all parties till Calvin, Bullinger, and Vermigli could each address the matter. The din of the reaction shook the church where the synod was held, but nonetheless, Osolinski's recommendation was followed, though hardly to the letter, as both sides flooded the designated arbiters with more letters. Stancaro himself wrote Calvin, slighting the whole conversation about Christ and his mediatorial office per se, but asserting that both Arianism and Eutychianism were now being spread throughout Poland in the name of the Reformers. He pointed out that this Arianism asserted that the Trinity was in fact not one but three gods, with three wills and of three substances: "They are teaching Arianism here, that the Father, Son, and Holy Spirit are not one God, but three gods, thus separated from each other as three men are separated from each other, and these three gods are three substances, three wills, and thre separate operations, as three separate spirits."[45] Stancaro's letter was

44. Quoted in Joseph N. Tylenda, "The Controversy on Christ the Mediator: Calvin's Second Reply to Stancaro," *Calvin Theological Journal* 8 (1973): 133, and CO 18:183.

45. CO 18:260–61: "Docent hic Ariani, patrem filium et spiritum sanctum non unum esse deum sed tres deos, ita a se invicem separatos ut tres homines a se invicem separati sunt, et hos tres deos tres esse substantias, tres voluntates, et tres operationes separatas, ut tres spiritus separatos." As to the charge of Eutychianism, it arises from Stancaro's assertion that these heretics teach that Christ's humanity holds eternally within his divinity (such as it was) the office of mediator: "In addition the Son of God, our Lord Jesus Christ, is less than the Father in his divine nature or according to his divinity, and yet according to the same was without origin, that is, from eternity, and is also to exist in the future, that is, without end, chief priest and mediator, according to his humanity, truly victim and priest." (Filium praeterea Dei, Dominum nostrum Iesum Christum, minorem esse patre in divina natura vel secundum divinitatem et secundum eandem fuisse sine principio, id est ab aeterno, et esse et futurum esse i.e. sine fine, sacerdotem pontificem et mediatorem, secundum humanitatem vero victimam et sacrificium.) (CO 18:261)

followed by yet more from both his allies and foes, and in such numbers that both Bullinger and Calvin were nettled, Bullinger finding it tiresome that the Poles should need him to answer such trivial matters. Calvin's exasperation came also from his belief that the Poles had suppressed his initial response to them.[46] But now, prodded by what he would consider a false dilemma, and also more alarmed by other concerns for the Poles, Calvin issued his second tract on Stancaro.

Calvin's *Responiso ad Nobiles Polonos* was about twice as long as his first, but still not a substantial treatise.[47] Tylenda notes that it has all the appearance of haste, as Calvin slips back and forth between first-person singular and plural. There is also the repetition of much information from the first, though the second included patristic citations. Calvin's response did little to alter matters, and indeed in the end the two responses together seem to have made the situation in Poland only worse, though not as regards the matter of Stancaro. Calvin asserted in both treatises that it is proper to speak of Christ as inferior to the Father as regards economy and dispensation: "If it will be asked about his essence, we know that in God nothing is lesser or greater. But since, on account of the capacity or our infirmities, the eternal Son of God, that he might mediate between us and God, in his very person and office of mediator he is fittingly called inferior to the Father according to the rule of piety."[48] This would seem to play directly into Stancaro's argument that the Reformers had embraced a species of Arianism. Calvin was, of course, saying nothing new, and indeed he was guarded in not even going as far as the fathers, who in speaking of the monarchy of the Father could assert the logical priority of the Father in respect to origin, though not in respect to essence, for the Son and Father were one in essence. Calvin took pains to point out that the simplicity of the divine essence could admit nothing greater or lesser, and thus the essence of Father and Son is identical. Yet as Williams points out, Calvin's Christology had already admitted some difficulties—namely, his assertion that the Son was a being composed (*composita*) within the economy of the two natures (as opposed to the Person of the Son uniting the two natures in himself) and thus inferior to the Father.[49] Consequently, from the vantage of Stancaro's adversaries, Calvin would seem not to have helped at all but only to have made matters worse, for the position that benefited most

46. Tylenda, "Second Reply," 138–39.
47. CO 9:349–58; the first letter ran barely five columns.
48. CO 9:353: "Si quaeratur de essentia, scimus in Deo nihil esse minus et maius. Sed quia, pro infirmitatis nostrae captu, apparuit aeternus Dei filius, ut medius esset inter nos et Deum, in ipsa mediatoris persona et officio apposite ad regulam pietatis dicitur patre inferior."
49. Williams, *Radical Reformation*, 1039. For *composita*, see *Institutes* 2.14.

from the controversy and from Calvin's language was the antitrinitarianism of Giorgio Biandrata.

Giorgio Biandrata: The Tritheist Apostle to the Poles (and Valentine Gentili, His Silas)

In order to answer Stancaro many of the Polish Reformed had followed the lead of Biandrata, who had used both Calvin's and Stancaro's theology as a way to introduce his own brand of tritheism—namely, that for Calvin Christ was indeed divine as mediator, and that for Stancaro, since the Son mediated humanity to the Father, the Son was inferior to the Father qua his mediatorial person—namely, as Son. Biandrata in fighting Stancaro in the name of orthodoxy slipped in his own peculiar tritheistic theology. The arrival of Valentine Gentili, author of a tritheistic tract, who had fled Geneva after public humiliation and subscription under pressure to a trinitarian confession of faith, further aided Biandrata.[50] Biandrata's strategy sought to disarm Stancaro of his skill in theology by asserting the primacy of the Apostles' Creed (irony indeed in light of Calvin's stance with Caroli) as a dogmatic formulation, something that appealed to the humanist Łaski. When called to account for his views, owing to Calvin's denunciations of him, Biandrata argued that the Nicene Creed and Athanasian formula were opposed to the more primitive (or pure) Apostles' Creed. Events validated Calvin's concern about Biandrata's presence, for by 1562 the majority of the Protestants of Poland had either gone over to antitrinitarianism or were willing to countenance it.[51]

The outlines of Biandrata's early life reveal a remarkable and gifted intellect. Born in Piedmont in 1516, he studied at Montpellier, taking a degree in arts and medicine in 1533. Having a particular interest in the study of women's medicine, he became so widely known and highly regarded after composing some works on the subject that in 1540 he was summoned to the court of Sigismund of Poland, where he became for twelve years the physician to the queen, the Milanese-born Bona Sforza, and then to Transylvania, where he attended on Bona Sforza's daughter, Isabella of Hungary. While in Poland he befriended the queen's confessor, Francis Lismanino, who would eventually become one of the leaders of the Reformed church.[52] By 1553 he was back in

---

50. Valentini Gentilis, *Confessio*, in *Antitrinitarische Streitigkeiten: Die Tritheistische Phase (1560–1568)*, ed. Irene Dingel, *Controversia et Confessio* 9 (Göttingen: Vandenhoeck & Ruprecht, 2013), 107–16. See Wilbur, *Unitarianism*, 232–34.

51. James Miller, "The Origins of Polish Arianism," *Sixteenth Century Journal* 16, no. 2 (Summer 1985): 239.

52. Williams, *Radical Reformation*, 935.

northern Italy and by 1556 was in Pavia, where his theological writings came
to the attention of the Inquisition, and so he made his way back to Geneva.
He quickly fell in with the Italian congregation and was elected one of their
four elders in 1556. In November of 1557 he became a citizen of Geneva.
Biandrata's views on the question of the Trinity soon scandalized the Italian minister, Martinengo, to such an extent that even though then in failing
health, he refused to see him as his physician. Biandrata sought audiences
with Calvin, coming to him days on end with numerous questions in various
forms. Biandrata wanted clarification on to whom the name of God applied;
what the terms "person," "essence," and "substance" as found in the creeds
meant; and to whom prayer may be addressed.[53] Calvin eventually wrote out
a protracted response to Biandrata's questions, his *Ad questiones Georgii
Biandratae, responsum D. Ioannis Calvini.*[54] Even with Calvin's efforts, the
situation admitted of no improvement, and the ministers in the Italian congregation were becoming increasingly concerned. The rising level of vexation
can be seen in Calvin's letter to Vermigli, relating how Martinengo, on his
deathbed, begged Calvin and the other ministers to do something about the
plague brought on by Gribaldi.[55] Biandrata and others were summoned before Calvin and told that they would not be punished for what was past, but
that they must desist from teaching heresy. Biandrata quickly took his leave
of Geneva and could only return when his friend Giovanni Paulo Alciati was
able to obtain safe conduct for him.

At this point Calvin composed another confession of faith and presented
it to the Italian congregation on May 18, 1558.[56] All were expected to subscribe, though all could voice their views and opinions without hesitation.
The three-hour discussion turned on the questions already raised in Calvin's
dispute with Caroli, and many within the community voiced apprehension
at the "communitarian" doctrine that Calvin advanced, asserting that this
introduced a quaternity into the Godhead; they cited the dispute concerning
Joachim of Fiore's denunciation of Peter Lombard, addressed by the decree
of the Fourth Lateran Council, *Firmiter*. Alciati, a refugee from Piedmont,
became so adamant that he refused to sign Calvin's confession, and he convinced others to do the same. The confrontation stiffened Calvin's resolve,
and ultimately he did secure the signatures of the Italian congregation, with
the exceptions of Alciati and Biandrata, who promptly fled.[57]

53. Wilbur, *Unitarianism*, 224.
54. CO 9:325–32.
55. CO 17:176.
56. For the confession, CO 9:385–89.
57. Williams, *Radical Reformation*, 975–76.

In an extended letter in June 1558, Nikolaus Zurkinden told Calvin that Biandrata had fled to Farges to see Gribaldi, Zurkinden asserting that he held them both as brothers despite their errors. Zurkinden, one of the epoch's pronounced defenders of religious toleration, had already written Calvin in 1554 following the execution of Servetus. Even though he did not fault Calvin for the execution and had no love for Servetus's errors, he enjoined Calvin to take a more tolerant position toward heretics.[58] From Berne Biandrata went to Zurich, where he tried to convince Vermigli that he was orthodox in his theology, but his fellow Italian would have nothing to do with him. Having been asked to leave Zurich, Biandrata traveled in the Grisons, but he soon went to Poland, where he rejoined the Reformed pastor and correspondent of Calvin Lismanino. Biandrata's arrival had not come unannounced to Lismanino, for Calvin had already sent him an ominous warning: "What kind of monster is Giorgio Biandrata; no rather, how many monsters would he feed; warn the brethren before the pious experience him, so that they might quickly guard themselves!"[59]

When Biandrata arrived in Poland in 1558, Laelius Socinus (Sozzini) accompanied him. Socinus had been to Poland already in 1551, at the time enjoying the favor of Calvin, who had written a letter of recommendation to Prince Radziwill on Socinus's behalf.[60] Biandrata feigned orthodoxy, satisfying Łaski with his confession, and Peter Statorius de Thionville and Lismanino both sought to reconcile Biandrata with Calvin. But Calvin wrote back, accusing the Poles of embracing Biandrata, a barbarian and a beast.[61] This assessment received confirmation when Vermigli wrote Calvin that Lismanino had been completely taken in by Biandrata, for Biandrata had gained his confidence when he had cured Lismanino of a childhood malady; this called for another letter of warning.[62] Calvin's admonitions were too late, for Biandrata had already convinced Prince Radziwill and the synod of the Polish church of his orthodoxy. Calvin, in his new edition of the commentary on Acts, dedicated to Radziwill, attacked Biandrata.[63] But the Polish church believed Calvin had

58. CO 17:204–8; 15:19–22, 115–16.
59. CO 17:378: "Quale monstrum sit Georgius *Biandrata,* imo quot monstra alat, antequam experiantur pii fratres admone ut sibi mature caveant."
60. CO 17:181. Bullinger had also written a recommendation for Socinus to Łaski; see Wilbur, *Unitarianism,* 303.
61. CO 17:677.
62. CO 17:498.
63. CO 18:158: "Behold, from other regions a certain doctor, George Biandrata, worse than Stancaro for infected by a worse error, and nourished in his mind by a secret poison." (Ecce ex altera parte medicus quidam, Georgius Biandrata, Stancaro deterior, quo magis detestabli errore imbutus est, et plus occultae virulentiae in animo alit.)

misjudged Biandrata, and Radziwill wrote to both him and Bullinger, sending one of his own clergy to deliver the letters. Calvin remained unconvinced and responded by attacking Biandrata, though all the while declaring his friendship to Radziwill:

> And since I desire you flourish no less in the illustrious esteem you enjoy before everyone, than in your dignity and power, it is not a little troubling to me that by his crooked arts [Biandrata] has crept into your graces. If it were believable to me, that this man, whose impiety was known to me, was in your company only, certainly I would have been content with a private admonition, and I would have taken account of your dignity. But I thought it better that he ought to be unmasked by a public show to others, so that everyone might guard themselves from so harmful a disease. Therefore the particular reason of indignation vanished: since it was it was not in the least my purpose to slight your reputation, since I consider that the message I sent concerned a man unknown to you, or who at least became your familiar through a position of necessity, and never through friendship.[64]

Events unfolded in the following months along the lines that Calvin had warned. Specifically, Valentine Gentili (more below) had arrived from Switzerland and published his tract that taught pure tritheism. Lismanino, who waged polemical war with Stancaro by assailing the assertion of Stancaro that his opponents would fall into Arianism, ironically appeared to vindicate both Calvin and Stancaro. Lismanino, even though he adamantly maintained his orthodox confession, was damned by association with Biandrata and Gentili, as an anonymous tract appeared accusing him of tampering with the Trinity.[65]

The years 1562 to 1564 saw the formal organization of the Polish antitrinitarian church, aided by the Italian radicals, including in no small measure Giovanni Valentine Gentili. Gentili was born in Cosensza in Calabria in 1520, and we first learn of him as a teacher of grammar (*grammatica*) at Naples. The south of Italy, and especially Naples, was a place of flourishing religious ferment along humanist lines under the aegis of Juan de Vives. Among those who had gone to Naples to learn at Vives's feet was the Florentine Augustinian

---

64. *CO* 19:44: "Et quoniam vos non minus praeclara apud omnes existimatione quam dignitate et potentia florere cupio, mihi non parum dolet obliquis suis artibus ita eum obrepsisse in vestram gratiam. Si mihi credibile fuisset, hominem, cuius mihi comperta erat impietas, vobis esse familiarem, certe privata admonitione fuissem contentus, idque nomini vestro dedissem. Sed aliorum potius causa publice traducendum esse censui, ut sibi omnes a peste tam noxia caverent. Ergo praecipua indignationis causa evanuit: quia mihi nihil minus fuit propositum, quam famam vestram oblique laedere, quum verba me facere putarem de homine vobis incognito, vel saltem qui nullo amicitiae vel necessitudinis gradu vos attingeret."

65. Wilbur, *Unitarianism*, 305.

friar, and friend of Calvin, Peter Martyr Vermigli. Gentili's conversion occurred later than Vermigli's (Vermigli fled Italy in 1542), but Gentili seemed
animated by the same spirit. He came to Geneva in 1556, attracted by Calvin,
and became involved with the Italian congregation. On the night of the May
18 meeting, Gentili claimed illness, and he refused to subscribe to Calvin's
confession, until persuaded after a conference with Calvin himself. Nonetheless, he continuously queried Calvin on the matter and began expressing his
views privately. Someone informed Calvin about his unorthodox opinions;
he was arrested and cited before the Consistory on July 11, 1558.[66] The first
examination sought to determine whether Gentili was guilty of perjury, sedition, and mutiny. He protested that he had never dissented from what he had
confessed and did not dissent at all from Calvin. At the next interrogation,
his accusers came forth, and Gentili flatly contradicted them. Calvin also
showed up, trying to show that Gentili was in error for saying that in the Old
Testament the name of God is only applied to the Father. This failed as well.
Gentili composed a treatise confessing what seems an orthodox confession,
that the Father is the monarch and source of divinity of the Son and Spirit,
who are eternal and equal in glory and power with the Father. But he then
slipped into an almost homoiousian (of like substance) statement that the Son,
though of the same substance as the Father, is still as to his eternal existence
inferior to the Father.[67] His confession, following lines laid down already by
his fellow Italians at the May meeting, accused Calvin of professing a quaternity and not a Trinity, and he cited the fathers against Calvin. Calvin drew
up a substantial, bitter invective.[68] At the third exam, again asked whether he
agreed with what he had signed, Gentili said no, as that now appeared to him
to teach a quaternity, whereas he confessed the Trinity. He asked for counsel,
and when this was denied, he realized his peril.

At the next exam he was obsequious, groveling. But then the council brought
in people to assail his character. The lawyers to whom the council had turned
over everything "pronounced him worthy of death for his perjury and heresies,
ignored his recantation as feigned, declared him unworthy to be pardoned,
and called attention to the mischief he might do if set at liberty."[69] While his
crimes called for the stake, it was deemed that a sword would do, especially
given his contrition. He was to be executed the next day, but when the next day
came, the judgment was suspended till more could be ascertained about his
guilt. At some point during the trial, a letter came from an Italian businessman

66. CO 21:698–703.
67. Williams, *Radical Reformation*, 977.
68. CO 9:399–410.
69. Wilbur, *Unitarianism*, 232.

in Lyons asking for clemency, suggesting that Gentili's views should be laid at the feet of Biandrata and that Gentili could prove a powerful ally. Another confession was taken from Gentili, and this time the council agreed to commute the death sentence, as long as he performed an *amende honorable*.[70] The next day in front of the Hôtel de Ville, dressed only in his shirt, without hat and shoes, he confessed his crime and burned his writings. He was then paraded around town, accompanied by a trumpet. He was forbidden to leave the city, but that ban ended in two weeks. Once he had made his way outside the city, he never returned, but fled immediately to Gribaldi's estate in Farges, joining Alciati and Biandrata, and there he formally renounced his renunciation. The constable of Gex, however, demanded of him a fresh orthodox confession of faith, to which Gentili responded with a short commentary on the *Quicunque vult*, the Athanasian formula, which would later be published in Poland.[71] From there Gentili fled to Lyons, where he composed a book titled *Antidota*. The book, dedicated to the Polish king, answered Calvin's 1559 *Institutes*, which at two places took on Gentili (1.13.23 and 2.6.4).[72] From Lyons he traveled to Grenoble, where Gribaldi had resumed life. He went there ostensibly for his health. He came under suspicion by the Catholics, but his profession of faith, wholly anti-Protestant and particularly anti-Calvin, won him time; he left, returning to Farges, where the local governor at Gex arrested him, having learned of his trial in Geneva. Giving assurances of intending no trouble, Gentili won his release and traveled to Lyons, where he published yet another treatise. Though claiming the treatise was not intended for publication, he ended up in prison nonetheless, though he was soon released. Realizing he would not be safe in Lyons, he accepted an invitation from Biandrata to come to Poland with Alciati in the summer of 1562. There they openly taught tritheism and were able, despite the best efforts of those loyal to the Swiss Reformers, to bring division within the Polish Protestant ranks. Since Biandrata appeared to many as the best one to answer Stancaro and to resolve the crisis, antitrinitarianism became a seeming champion against Stancaro. Stanislas Paklepka, a past student of Vermigli, wrote Vermigli, imploring his teacher for aid, insisting that if he would not pen an orthodox rebuttal to Stancaro then the very stones would cry out.[73] In the summer of 1562 the Reformed church in Poland

70. CO 9:415–18.

71. Dingel, *Antitrinitarische Streitigkeiten*, 107–16.

72. No manuscript has ever been found, though Benedict Aretius's *Vita* of Gentili reproduced the work, *Valentini Gentilis iusto capitis supplicio Bernae affecti breuis historia et contra eiusdem blasphemias orthodoxa defensio articoli de sancta Trinitate* (Geneva: Franciscus Perrini, 1567). This was translated into English in 1696 as *A Short History of Valentinus Gentilis the Tritheist* (London: E. Whitlock).

73. Williams, *Radical Reformation*, 1044.

formally split, with the major church affirming, the minor church denying, the orthodox formulations of Geneva and Zurich. The radicals and tritheists asserted that the eternal Son was mediator from eternity and from eternity divine, but not in the same way as the Father. To the radicals, the economic functions of God in redemption became definitive in speaking about the eternal existence of God.[74] Gentili, along with Alciati, continued in Poland until finally a royal diet at Parczów in August 1564 expelled them. At first Gentili went to the Anabaptists in Moravia, and from there back to Savoy hoping to find Gribaldi; after learning of Gribaldi's death from the plague, he returned to Farges. He was promptly arrested by the same constable who had confronted him previously. Gentili asked for a disputation on the Trinity. Beza wrote to Haller in Berne, asking him not to let Gentili get away, as he had almost ruined the Reformation in Poland. He was transferred to Berne, where after two weeks his trial commenced and where he openly confessed all that was imputed to him. He was sentenced to death by the sword and was beheaded the next day, September 10, 1566. Beza visited Gentili while he was imprisoned in Berne, but he maintained his tritheist profession of faith all the way to the block.

As for Biandrata, the synod in March 1562 had exonerated him when it found his simple but precise confession of faith, the one for which the Polish Reformed church upbraided Calvin, to be blameless. Further, the synod wrote Calvin insisting that Calvin speak only of the one God and not of three distinct divine persons, whereas Biandrata confessed that "Christ is the Son of God most high and eternal," but, it should be noted, not that Christ is the most high and eternal Son of God. The synod marked a decisive turn for the Polish Reformed church, as Biandrata, in an effort to curtail Stancaro's seeming rhetorical and doctrinal advantage, convinced the Polish ministers to desist from philosophical terms regarding the Trinity—terms such as "essence" and "generation," which appeared foreign to the life of the biblical God—a move that paved the way for the radicals' declension from orthodoxy to spread more widely.[75] Biandrata, though not a gifted theologian by any means, had nonetheless shown himself to be a masterful orchestrator of affairs by manipulating synods into antitrinitarian courses in the name of answering Stancaro. Calvin, Bullinger, and Vermigli clearly never fully understood the game that was afoot in Poland (Vermigli died that year), or they might well have handled Stancaro differently, and Calvin might have taken greater pains to set out more precisely his doctrine of Christ's mediatorship and what the Word's relation to the Father entailed.

74. Williams, *Radical Reformation*, 1045.
75. Wilbur, *Unitarianism*, 310.

Though Biandrata was formally banned from Poland in 1564, he had already spent time from late 1562 onward in Transylvania, attending on the queen, Isabella. He thus had a ready place of retreat once the edict of 1564 barred his return to Poland. Wilbur and Williams detail how his career there followed with great effect some of the same patterns as in Poland.[76] Having been the physician to Isabella of Hungary, Biandrata returned to Transylvania in 1563 to assume this office for her son, John Sigismund, who then lay near death. Upon recovering, the prince found in Biandrata someone who stood above the ever-growing rift within the Protestant church of Hungary and Transylvania. Initially the Hungarian church had been Lutheran, and the Calvinists, dubbed sacramentarians, were considered schismatics. Originally John Sigismund had been a devout Lutheran and wanted his kingdom to remain such, fostering mutual tolerance between Roman Catholics and Lutherans by a decree of 1557. But by 1562 the sacramentarians or Reformed had become so prominent that the nobility were seeking for the king to impose a solution. With the conversion to the Reformed faith of one of the Lutheran leaders, Francis Dávid, and with the aid of Biandrata, matters soon turned to heresy. First trained in Wittenberg and gifted as an orator and rhetorician in German, Hungarian, and Latin, Dávid, even as a Lutheran in 1560, had voiced suspicion about the Trinity. Dávid had probably read Servetus among others; the Calvinists, ill organized and lacking any creed, became for Dávid the targets of the same tactics that Biandrata had used in Poland.

Dávid as superintendent of the Reformed churches enjoyed an advantageous perch from which to reform doctrine. First, the Calvinists had no creed, but had rejected both Catholicism and Lutheranism, and by 1565 Biandrata had persuaded the king to dismiss his court preacher, one Alesius, and in his stead appoint Dávid. Resistance to Biandrata's and Dávid's program came from the Calvinists, and in particular Peter Melius, who was in correspondence with the Swiss. A series of synods ensued in the spring of 1566, which resulted in a consensus, but this only superficially preserved unity. Biandrata in his replies to the orthodox Calvinists largely spoke not on the Trinity but against the use of scholastic distinctions, a proposal that met with no dissent.[77] With this decision in hand, Biandrata and Dávid openly embraced the Apostles' Creed (as Biandrata had previously done with Łaski) and denounced any talk of substance or essence as regards the Trinity. With this action the lines suddenly hardened, and the antitrinitarians found themselves in the ascendant in Transylvania, owing foremost to the favor of the king (who gave Biandrata

76. Wilbur, *Unitarianism*, 29–35; Williams, *Radical Reformation*, 1109–19.
77. Williams, *Radical Reformation*, 1111; Wilbur, *Unitarianism*, 32–33.

and Dávid a printing press) but also to the 1557 edict of toleration that gave
them carte blanche to teach as they wished. Melius countered with his own
invectives, summoning a synod to Debrecen, whence the Reformed pastors
hurled anathemas, even suggesting that Dávid should be stoned.

In response Biandrata and Dávid produced their first book, *De falsa et vera
unius Dei Patris, Filii et Spiritus Sancti congnitione.*[78] The book is a pastiche of
a number of works, with only the first part containing the titled sections. A
curious element of the book was eight images, purportedly of the Trinity, in
a chapter titled "De horrendis simulachris Deum Trinum et Unum adumbran-
tibus." These eight pictures, drawn ostensibly from Catholic sources, proved
scandalous to such as Melius, and he accused the authors of blasphemy and
"mockery of the Christian religion."[79] The images had indeed come from
trinitarian churches and left the trinitarian party red-faced at the revelation.
One showed a crude, three-faced image on an altar, with Biandrata's commentary underneath: "The pope expelled Bifrons [twin-faced] Janus from the
city, so that Trifrons might rule the world."[80] In the main, the book directly
assaults the doctrines of the Trinity and incarnation. Beyond the embarrass-
ment of the woodcuts from ostensibly trinitarian churches, the book's effect
is hard to measure. What is known is that the antitrinitarians were in the
ascendant and probably formed the majority in Transylvania, despite the best
efforts of Melius, who was not resident there. At one point he tried to entice
Biandrata and Dávid out of Transylvania, but as they had no guarantees of
safety, they refused. A grand but inconclusive disputation was held in Alba
Iulia in 1568, where five disputants from each side accomplished little except
the exasperation of the trinitarians. Some wanted to end the dispute after nine
days, to which the king responded that this would be an admission of defeat.
They stayed, but the king soon realized that nothing new was being said and
so the next day dismissed the affair. Two items did emerge: Biandrata was
shown as no match for Melius and his followers, so he retired from the lists;
and Melius made grand use of the language the Reformers had once slighted
(Trinity, consubstantial, etc.), whereas in the course of the debates Dávid
never appealed to anything other than the Bible.[81] On the radicals' side, with
Biandrata humbled, Dávid now emerged as the new leader of the party and

78. Giorgio Biandrata and Francis Dávid, *De falsa et vera unius Dei Patris, Filii et Spiritus
Sancti congnitione, libri duo* (Albae Juliae: Authoribus ministris Ecclesiarum consentientium
in Sarmatia et Transylvania, 1567).

79. Wilbur, *Unitarianism,* 35.

80. Biandrata and Dávid, *De falsa et vera,* 23b. Wilbur, *Unitarianism,* 35n22, gives a précis
of all the pictures, which were based on images in either Italy or Poland.

81. Williams, *Radical Reformation,* 1114.

the champion of the antitrinitarians. After the disputation, John Sigismund reissued the decree of toleration, which all but legalized the antitrinitarian party as its own church, and the next year a disputation held in Várad using the Hungarian language (hitherto all disputations had been done in Latin) ensured the triumph of the antitrinitarians. John Sigismund now formally identified with them, and in tow came all the leading Magyar families.

In 1569 Biandrata, who possessed a copy of Servetus's *Christianismi restitutio*, used this as the basis for a book, a dual work titled *De regno Christi* and *De regno antichristi*.[82] Dedicated to John Sigismund, it used Servetus without attribution and marked the high point of the collaboration of Dávid and Biandrata, but even within this volume the beginnings of a fissure may be discerned, for Biandrata did not oppose paedobaptism, whereas Dávid did and included his thoughts on it in the volume (which thoughts he probably took from Servetus). In 1578 a divide opened between Dávid and Biandrata when, at a meeting in Kolozsvár, Dávid taught items that did not sit well with Biandrata: that Christ could not be addressed in prayer, that since he was never called God by the apostles he could not in any way be thought of as a god, and that Jesus could have been Christ the redeemer even if he had not died. While Biandrata got Dávid to refrain from speaking openly about these matters at first, this restraint did not last. Biandrata suspected (and accused) Dávid of slipping into Judaism, and at this point he persuaded Faustus Socinus to come to Transylvania to take up matters with Dávid. Faustus had followed his uncle Laelius's footsteps to Poland, and now this uncle and nephew, tormentors of both Calvin and his heirs, must be treated before returning to Biandrata.

Laelius and Faustus Soccinii: Calvin's Thought Fermenting

Born in Siena on March 25, 1525, Lelio Sozzini—he later Latinized his name to Laelius Socinus—pursued his father's vocation, the study of law.[83] His father had won acclaim as a jurist, teaching law in Pisa, Siena, Padua, and Bologna, and the young Socinus took up his studies in Padua. Like many in his day, he turned the new tools of humanism, especially philology, to the study of law; convinced that all law found its source in God, he began studying Scripture,

82. Wilbur, *Unitarianism*, 41–42.
83. For the sources on Laelius Socinus, and his nephew Faustus, see Friedrich Trechsel, *Die protestantischen Antitrinitarier vor Faustus Socin*, 2 vols. (Heidelberg: Carl Winter, 1939–44). The literature on these two, especially Faustus, is large, and Faustus himself left an immense oeuvre, much of which can be accessed at the Post-Reformation Digital Library, http://www.prdl.org/index.php.

seeking law's origin.[84] He would later relate to Melanchthon that his desire to find the *fontes iuris*, the source of law, led him to the study of Hebrew and then to the further study of the Bible, which would lead him to reject the popish antichrist.[85] This accorded with his humanistic faith in the competence of reason, and thus he came to disdain dogmatic traditions in theology of any kind. In 1546 Socinus left Padua for Venice, where the Inquisition had been kept at arm's length, and took up with the radical circle of intellectuals at Vicenza in 1547. This date would have significance in later Socinianism, cast as the beginning of the reformation of the Reformation, for in this year also he left Italy for the Grisons, and there began to travel among the Reformed cities.[86] He went first to Geneva, and from there to Basle, and then to the court of the Huguenot queen Marguerite of Navarre, and by early 1548 he was in England.[87] Whom he saw in England is not known, though Ochino, an Italian and former head of the Capuchins, was the minister in the London Stranger church, and the expatriate Florentine Peter Martyr Vermigli was in Oxford and also often in London. By the end of the year Socinus was back on the Continent, returning to Geneva. In May of 1549 he began a ten-year correspondence with Calvin that touched on a number of issues. His deference was palpable, alluding to Calvin in prophetic terms and seemingly leaning on his obsequiousness to press Calvin on pointed issues, such as if the church truly exists within the home of a Reformed Christian, why cannot a child be baptized there, as opposed to submitting the child to the superstitious rites of the popish antichrist (which very thing Calvin had counseled, though with the caveat that the family was to ignore the superstitions of the papist temples).[88] Eventually Calvin grew, if not tired, at least exasperated with the exchange, for he thought he was making no discernible headway with Socinus,[89] though the correspondence would prove an important element in Calvin's thought as regards the questions of merit and the atonement.

In 1555 Socinus took up the question of merit in the Christian and in Christ, especially in light of Calvin's treatment of the question. As was touched on

84. Wilbur, *Unitarianism*, 239.

85. Williams, *Radical Reformation*, 878.

86. Williams, *Radical Reformation*, 878n100 (which takes up the whole of page 879) gives the genealogy of the importance of the date, which was doubted by later historians, including Wilbur (*Unitarianism*, 80–84).

87. No records in England testify to Socinus's stay there, but a 1559 letter to Socinus from Łaski's confidant Utenhove, who had been in England with Łaski, alludes to their meeting there; and further, Łaski greets him, which "suggests a longer acquaintance going back to Łaski's superintendency in London" (Williams, *Radical Reformation*, 880n102).

88. *CO* 13:272–74.

89. *CO* 13:307, 464, 517.

briefly in the chapter on Bolsec, Calvin held the merits of Christ as an aspect of predestination and grace (*Institutes* 2.17.1), and this position arose from the questions put to him by Socinus, questions that would bear fruit in the thought of his gifted nephew, Faustus. Socinus saw a contradiction in the formulation of merit: How could grace be completely free and gratuitous yet at the same time depend on the merits of Christ, merits obtained by what would be termed the active obedience of Christ whereby he kept the law, fulfilling as second Adam what the first had failed to do?[90] In Socinus's mind, God the Father accepted the merit of Christ, making grace actually a quid pro quo accomplished by someone other than the recipient and thus not purely gratuitous at all. Calvin responded that the Father did not accept the obedience of Christ based on any merit found in Christ's righteousness, for nothing created could obligate God. Therefore, God accepts Christ's righteousness purely by an act of choice, based on nothing foreseen in Christ; as such, Christ's acts are by the predestination of God, making the incarnation the great example of predestination.[91] Calvin's replies to Faustus, the substance of the letters of 1555, he collected and published that year in *Responsio ad Aliquot Laelii Socini Senensis Quaestiones*.[92]

From Basle Socinus traveled to Zurich, where he worked on his Hebrew with Konrad Pellikan. There he befriended Bullinger, with whom he began conversations about his doubts. "Wherever he went, Socinus inevitably won friends by his courtly manners, his breadth and depth of culture, his frank and attractive character, crowned by irreproachable morals and a deep and sincere piety."[93] In the fall of 1550 he entered the University of Wittenberg, lived for a time as Melanchthon's guest, and continued his inquiries, but all with a seeming coolness that never betrayed his real doubts or perhaps even his real thoughts. Socinus never seemingly expressed doubts, but simply offered a string of difficult questions and played the assiduous student. To later writers, such as Beza in his life of Calvin, this simply confirmed that Socinus was a

90. John Murray, *Redemption Accomplished and Applied* (Grand Rapids: Eerdmans, 1955), 20–22; and Murray, *Select Lectures in Systematic Theology*, in *The Collected Writings of John Murray* (Edinburgh: Banner of Truth Trust, 1977), 2:151–57.

91. Calvin, CO 2:386–92, *Institutes* 2.17.1: "Therefore when we treat of the merit of Christ, we do not place the beginning in him, but we ascend to the ordination of God as the primary cause, because of his mere good pleasure he appointed a Mediator to purchase salvation for us. Hence the merit of Christ is inconsiderately opposed to the mercy of God."

92. In *Dogmatica et Polemica*, 160–65, in *Consilia*, CO 10:153–78. See Wulfert de Greef, *The Writings of John Calvin*, trans. Lyle D. Bierma, expanded ed. (Louisville: Westminster John Knox, 2008), 199–200. The text is translated in Mary Beaty and Benjamin W. Farley, *Calvin's Ecclesiastical Advice* (Louisville: Westminster John Knox, 1991), 25–32.

93. Wilbur, *Unitarianism*, 241.

dangerous hypocrite.[94] His persona as a trusted Protestant can be seen in his
1551 trip to Poland (he had met Polish students at Wittenberg). Armed with
letters of introduction from Melanchthon, he headed via Breslau and Prague to
Kraków. Melanchthon described him as "his intimate friend, learned, honest,
discreet, a lover of public peace, faithful and upright in every respect."[95] In
Kraków he fell in quickly with the Italians of the city, in particular Lismanino,
the confessor of Queen Isabella. But he soon left Poland, and traveling by way
of Moravia he came through Zurich and at last to Geneva at the end of 1551.
It was here that Calvin's exasperation with Socinus came openly to the fore,
for Socinus had arrived in the midst of the Bolsec controversy. Socinus urged
Calvin to take a milder approach in his dealings with dissent, and Calvin
responded, in so many words, that Socinus asked too many questions; while
having called Socinus "my Laelius" and "my most dear brother," Calvin also
noted that Socinus was beset by the "sweet enticements of curiosity [*dulcibus
curiositatis illecebris*]."[96] When Socinus wrote Bullinger asking him about the
questions revolving around the Bolsec affair and the matter of predestination,
Bullinger replied at some length, urging him not to persist in indulging his
curiosity.[97] Despite Bullinger's admonitions, Socinus continued his questions.

In the spring of 1552 he returned to northern Italy to visit his father in
Bologna. He missed a letter from his father telling him to avoid Italy, as the
Inquisition was asking about him. Unable to stay in Bologna, Socinus spent
the summer and fall of 1552 in Siena, and wintered in Padua. In the fall of
1553 he returned to Padua and there stayed with Gribaldi for a few months.
Doubtless he was residing with Gribaldi when news of Servetus's execution
came, and thus with Gribaldi Socinus now entered into the Servetus affair. He
framed his letters in cautious terms: Servetus was a heretic and wrong, but he
did not deserve death for what he believed. Socinus went to Basle and there
lodged with Castellio, who already was bristling at Geneva. When word that
Socinus had taken up with Castellio reached Beza, he concluded that Socinus,
like Servetus, was a dangerous heretic. Beza jumped to the conclusion that it
was Socinus who wrote Castellio's *De haereticis, an sint persequendi*,[98] though
Calvin seems not to have thought so, for he continued his correspondence
with him. But Vergerio and Martinengo from Geneva each wrote to Bullinger
now complaining of Socinus's trinitarian heresies. Eventually Bullinger wrote
Socinus, telling him of people's fears. Socinus responded, taking offense and

94. CO 21:142, 149.
95. In Wilbur, *Unitarianism*, 242.
96. CO 14:229; and Williams, *Radical Reformation*, 882.
97. Trechsel, *Antitrinitarier*, 2:447–52; and Wilbur, *Unitarianism*, 243.
98. CO 15:166.

asserting that he had no idea why anyone would think him other than orthodox on the Trinity; he maintained that he professed what the Bible and the Apostles' Creed taught on the question. Bullinger eventually claimed himself satisfied with what Socinus confessed, but in 1554, while Socinus was resident at Zurich, Bullinger demanded from him a written public record of his faith.[99] Bullinger accepted the confession with a large amount of sympathy. Its translator, Edward M. Hulme, thought it something that a casuist could have written with ease,[100] and rightly so. The confession asserted that Socinus had always professed from his youth the Apostles' Creed, but mentioned no others; he then went on with his wondrous nonconfession:

> I have lately read others also, and attribute all the honor I can and ought to the very old creeds of Nicaea and Constantinople. Moreover, though ignorant men obstinately deny it, I recognize that the terms Trinity, persons, hypostasis, consubstantiality, union, distinction and others of the kind are not recent inventions, but have been in use for the last thirteen hundred years, from the time of Justin Martyr, almost throughout the whole Christian world, and that too for the most convincing and cogent reasons.[101]

Socinus realized that his temerity had brought him to a dangerous position and acknowledged the same, asserting: "I have been more curious than certain Pythagorean Zealots could bear, but now our heavenly Father has shown himself so gracious to me that I am quite confident that henceforward I shall behave myself with more discretion in holy concourses of men."[102]

Socinus completed the remainder of his life as part of the Italian congregation in Zurich, most of whose members had come from Locarno in 1555. In 1556, however, upon his father's death, he made an extended stay in Italy in an attempt to acquire his inheritance. The Inquisition, hot on to the whole Sozzini family, had confiscated his share in his father's inheritance, and had branded brothers and nephews as heretics, imprisoning his brother Cornelio in Rome. Socinus conspired to return to Italy as the agent of a foreign principality, which would thus shield him from the Inquisition. Thus it was that Calvin, Bullinger, and Melanchthon wrote to John Łaski, to Maximillian, king of Poland (and future Holy Roman emperor), and to Prince Nicholas Radziwill respectively,

99. The original Latin can be found in John Henry Hottinger, *Historiae Ecclesiasticae Novi Testamenti v. IX* (Zurich: Schaufelbergerian, 1667), 421–27.
100. Edward M. Hulme, "Lelio Sozzini's Confession of Faith," in *Persecution and Liberty: Essays in Honor of George Lincoln Burr*, ed. Jameson J. Franklin (New York: Books for Libraries Press, 1931), 216–19.
101. Hulme, "Confession," 216.
102. Hulme, "Confession," 217.

recommending Socinus to their service. Socinus obtained as well letters from
Ferdinand of Austria. Once in Italy, he secured the aid of both Luigi Priuli,
the doge of Venice, and Cosimo I, the Grand Duke of Tuscany, in hopes of
retrieving his patrimony, but they could do nothing.[103] He returned to Zurich
only in 1559 with a brother and his son. For the remaining years of his life
he largely kept his own theological counsel, though he corresponded broadly,
including with Calvin about the Polish church. He died relatively young at the
age of thirty-seven on May 14, 1562. Upon hearing of his uncle's death, his
nephew Faustus (not the nephew living with him), having fled his native Siena
for Lyons, made the trip to Zurich and collected his uncle's literary remains.
Among them Faustus found his uncle's most radical thoughts, comprehended
in his late work *Brevis explicatio in primum Iohannis caput*. In it the elder
Socinus had extolled a Christology more radical even than Servetus's, which
doubtless pushed his nephew into new thought regarding the nature of the
Godhead. For Laelius, Christ as the Word of God was only so from the beginning of the proclamation of the gospel after his baptism. He reinterpreted
John 1, arguing that "*in principio*" had no eternal or cosmological reference
and that Christ "in the world which he made" meant nothing other than
Christ's proclaiming the light to show the world its darkness and creating
the new world by healing the sick, proclaiming the gospel, and so on.[104] The
text circulated in manuscript, chiefly among the Poles and the Hungarians of
Transylvania, and only appears in print in excerpted form in later Socinian
writings that came from Biandrata's press in Alba Iulia, first with Faustus's
1562 *Explicatio primae partis primi capitis Johannis*, but then more fully in
Biandrata's *De vera et falsa . . . cognitione* of 1568.

Laelius Socinus's clandestine faith, while certainly present in his lifetime,
especially when viewed in retrospect, remained carefully concealed from his
supposed coreligionists both in Geneva and Zurich. Its fullness only shone
forth once in the hands of his capable and brilliant nephew Faustus, who had
fled Italy in 1560 to take up residence in Lyons. His father, Laelius's brother,
had been a lawyer but died in 1541, leaving Faustus (born in 1539) to be reared
by his mother and grandmother. His grandmother left him a quarter of the
family estate, and upon her death he pursued his academic life in earnest. He
had some education from his uncle Celso, a canon lawyer in Bologna, and
probably imbibed radical tendencies from him. Faustus seemingly possessed
them enough that when Laelius left Italy, so did he, though not following his

103. Williams, *Radical Reformation*, 969.
104. Lelio Sozzini, *Brevis explicatio in primum Iohannis caput*, Bivio: Biblioteca Virtuale
Online, 2006, http://bivio.filosofia.sns.it/bvWorkTOC.php?authorSign=SozziniLelio&titleSign=
BrevisExplicatio.

uncle's trail. That Faustus knew much about his uncle's thought and religious views should be seen in the fact that he saw to it to obtain Laelius's literary remains at his death. Returning to Lyons with his uncle's writings, he used Laelius's work on John 1 when he composed his own treatise, *Explicatio primae partis*.[105] In the *Explicatio* Faustus first set forth a doctrine that would be put to crucial use in his later theology—namely, that Christ was divine in his office but not in his nature.

Faustus traveled to Basle and there met Castellio, who may have had some influence on Faustus, but the younger Socinus already was far more radical than the elderly Castellio. At the end of 1563 Faustus returned to Siena and remained in Italy till 1574 in the employ of Isabella de Medici, daughter of the Grand Duke of Tuscany Cosimo I. With Cosimo's death, however, he returned to Switzerland and settled in Basle, where, secured in his station by the rents from his properties in Siena, he took up the study of theology, of both the fathers and the contemporary Reformers. He also entered into a number of theological disputes, the most important being that with the Huguenot minister Jacques Couvet in 1579.[106] Socinus had argued that the benefits of Christ arose from his office, not his divine person or nature, and that his priestly and royal offices were assumed only upon his ascension.

In his treatise responding to Couvet, *De Iesu Christo Servatore*, which Wilbur calls his most important contribution to systematic theology,[107] Socinus set out his own take on the question of salvation within the context of Christology and, as is implicit in the title, made the case that Christ "redeems" humanity not through a propitiatory sacrifice that renders satisfaction to God but through his offices (that is, as *servatore*).[108] In *De Iesu Christo Servatore* Faustus took up anew the questions his uncle had posed to Calvin in 1555, and with Calvin's responses in hand he weighed in on the question of the atonement as a fulfillment of the law by Christ's obedience and as a satisfaction of divine justice through Christ's death.[109] Socinus stated that the problem of merit encumbers all Christian thought, both Catholic and Reformed; he took special aim at Calvin and his discussion of Christ's merit

105. Faustus Socinus, *Explicatio primae partis primi capitis Johannis*, ed. Jerome Moscorvius (Racovia: Sebastian Sternacius, 1618); Williams, *Radical Reformation*, 979; and cf. Williams's discussion of the subsequent confusion of the two works, 972n68.

106. Williams, *Radical Reformation*, 985; and Alan W. Gomes, "Faustus Socinus and John Calvin on the Merits of Christ," *Reformation and Renaissance Review* 12, nos. 2–3 (2010): 189–205.

107. Wilbur, *Unitarianism*, 392.

108. Faustus Socinus, *De Iesu Christo Servatore, Hoc Est, Cur et qua ratione Iesus Christus noster seruator sit* (Racovia: Alexius Rodecius, 1594).

109. Williams, *Radical Reformation*, 986–87.

in the *Institutes* (2.17.1–6). Following Scotus, Calvin had asserted that Christ merits nothing for us apart from God accepting Christ's obedience and death as meritorious based wholly on the divine decree. Socinus sought to show that this cannot work, since were Christ to merit salvation by his obedience, then merit would be not gracious but dependent on works; and were Christ's merit based merely on the decree of God as God's gracious act, then how could Christ alone truly be a mediator and savior, since his salvific work would be merely accidental? Socinus wrote that Calvin had contradicted himself on this, at some points asserting the inherent righteousness of Christ, and at others that it was based on the decree.[110] Socinus hoped to smash the satisfaction theory of the atonement, which had been built on Anselm's *Cur Deus homo* and orthodox Christology.[111] If Anselm's foundation could be destroyed, what need was there for a divine Christ to reconcile us to God?

Faustus Socinus sits somewhat outside the parameters of this study but ultimately and fittingly caps this chapter as someone who stood on the shoulders of Gribaldi, Biandrata, Gentili, and Laelius Socinus to torment Calvin's heirs in Poland and Transylvania. It is not a little ironic that Biandrata called on Socinus, whose theology had completely bypassed that of Servetus, Gribaldi, Gentili, and Biandrata himself. Socinus paved the way for later unitarianism, though unlike later Unitarians and Deists, he accepted the supernatural origins of Christ—that is, the virgin birth—even though he denied him any preexistence apart from a form in the mind of God. To Faustus, Christ was a mere human adopted by God and given divine power after the ascension to govern the world according to his office. Ironically, Faustus built his dogmas of the offices of Christ off the work of Calvin and Osiander.[112]

And this brings the chapter back to Calvin. Calvin's arguments with Stancaro, and with Laelius Socinus before him, created for Calvin the dilemma

---

110. Socinus, *De Iesu Christo Servatore*, 285. Socinus treats the matter in his short section of *De Iesu Christo Servatore* 3.6 (282–87).

111. Gomes, "Faustus," 199–201, asserts that Faustus Socinus had not read Calvin rightly, and that what Calvin really meant was that prior to accepting the merits of Christ, God had decreed that he would accept the merits of the mediator, the incarnate Christ (and Gomes cites Polanus's rather Apollinarian assertion on this, which is wholly beside the point given Calvin's composite christological formulations). Gomes admits that he here contradicts Alister McGrath (see McGrath, *The Intellectual Origins of the European Reformation* [Grand Rapids: Baker, 1995], 103–9; note that Gomes cites another edition of the McGrath book) and takes into account the criticisms of Calvin as an inaccurate theologian, but his reading of Calvin would make Calvin identical in his thought to such late medieval nominalists as Gabriel Biel and Robert Holcot, who held that God graciously accepted the works of the penitent, no matter how meager and lacking in merit, merely by his grace. See also Gomes, "*De Jesu Christo Servatore*: Faustus Socinus on the Satisfaction of Christ," *Westminster Theological Journal* 55 (1993): 209–31.

112. Williams, *Radical Reformation*, 982.

that the mediator who at once reconciled us to God's eternal justice had to do so by an act of divine casuistry. The Father need not have had the incarnation as it was,[113] for the Father's acceptance of the Son's righteousness was based solely on an act of the divine will, and not predicated on the divine righteousness of the Second Person of the Trinity. Thus Calvin, working off a Scotist tenet with all the appearances of being washed through late medieval nominalism, posited a completely arbitrary Christ, and one who was also *composita persona* and not purely the Second Person of the Trinity. For all Calvin's blandishments about the Son as *autothean*, it is not the Second Person of the Trinity who is mediator, but now two tertium quid—namely, the fictive mediator who is less than the Father on some level, and divine justice—that become a mediator via the divine arrangement by which Christ fulfills humanity's covenant obligation in his priestly office. Calvin's second address on the Stancaro controversy, though much to Stancaro's unhappiness, was to the great delight of Biandrata. Biandrata took Calvin's muddled Christology, one that struggled with a composite Christ that had an *autothean* person keeping his divine righteousness at infinite arm's length from the objects of the covenant, and then used this to batter both Stancaro and the orthodox Reformed with a Christ that now emerged in some respects qua person as inferior to the Father. This gave Biandrata the very permission he needed to preach tritheism, doubtless to Calvin's great horror. Calvin did not survive to take up the fight, dying in late May of 1564. Calvin never asserted that justice was other than an eternal attribute of God, for he remained committed to the Augustinian doctrine of the divine simplicity. But despite this being the case, Calvin needed a mediator of a covenant that was purely legal—that is, that was purely impersonal—for it was not reconciliation to the persons of the Trinity that was in view, but reconciliation to divine justice. This is the whole upshot of his exchange with Laelius Socinus reproduced in book 2 of the *Institutes*.

Biandrata's appeal to Faustus Socinus in 1578 marks the public breakdown of antitrinitarian thought. Socinus came as asked and lodged with Dávid at his parsonage in Kolosvár, though at Biandrata's expense. The division between Dávid and Biandrata had broken down to an irreparable breach, since for Biandrata, Dávid's refusal to worship Christ (to Dávid this was a superstitious as worshiping the saints) threatened the antitrinitarian churches who could masquerade before the Catholics and Reformed as at least worshiping Christ.

---

113. Richard Muller, "Scholasticism in Calvin: Relation and Disjunction," in *Calvinus Sincerioris Religionis Vindex / Calvin as Protector of the Purer Religion*, ed. Wilhelm H. Neuser and Brian G. Armstrong (Kirksville, MO: Sixteenth Century Essays and Studies, 1993), 261. Muller is citing *Institutes* 2.12.1.

Dávid refused to bend on the question, and Biandrata, having the king's ear, had Dávid arrested, much to the chagrin of the Transylvanian Unitarians (as they would be called). The Hungarian and Transylvanian Unitarians, resenting Faustus Socinus's part in the whole affair, that he had been solicited to be a foil to Dávid, as a consequence would never label themselves Socinians. But the breakdown revealed something more, namely that having now vitiated their christological doctrines of any link to Reformed Christologies, let alone to any patristic or medieval ones, and in some ways owing to Calvin's own peculiarities of placing redemption and mediation not in the one divine person, but in his offices via the covenant, opened the door for the more detailed unitarianism of Faustus Socinus, the prelude of the Deism that formed the seedbed of Diderot's later thought.[114]

114. This is not to say that modern atheism can find its roots in Calvin's thought, or that how Calvin reacted to the questions of his day flows as a clear and easily marked stream that empties into Enlightenment unbelief—indeed, far from it. Instead I am suggesting that Calvin's thought opened avenues of inquiry that can be seen as venues for later developments and gave certain thinkers, such as Faustus Socinus, a means to break apart the link between Christ's divinity and human salvation. Calvin would have found such thought quite contrary to his own, and indeed odious. Whether it is consistently contrary, however, can be debated.

Conclusion

Dort, wo man Bücher verbrennt, verbrennt man am Ende auch Menschen. (Where they burn books they will ultimately burn a man.)[1]

Richard Muller in a 1997 essay on Calvin and scholasticism noted that Calvin's animus toward the scholastics should be taken as an evolving reality, for he became more and more dependent on the medieval theologians as his scholarship and life as a scholar progressed. For Muller, Calvin's antischolasticism was largely an anti-Sorbonnist attitude, arising out of Calvin's defense of the French Reformed church. Muller's insight brings out again two points that have formed leitmotifs in this work: first, that Calvin did not come to Geneva in 1536 with a fully formed theology that just needed greater explication, and second, perhaps more importantly (which redounds to the first point), Calvin always remained committed to France and to the reform of the church from whence he had come. This second could only be accomplished by a Christian faith that faithfully preached the Word, rightly administered the sacraments, and, above all, guarded the first two by the implementation of discipline; in short, Calvin's three marks of the true church, all lacking to some degree, and generally to a damnable degree, in Rome.

Thus the scholastics he loathed—namely, the doctors and the masters of the Sorbonne—threatened one burgeoning part of his ministry; yet, the medieval scholastics—for example, Aquinas, Scotus, and Lombard—increasingly emerged in his life as a pastor and scholar, especially in his

---

1. Heinrich Heine, "Almansor: Eine Tragödie," first appeared in *Die Gesellschafter* (Berlin: n.p., 1821); expanded in *Tragödien nebst einem lyrischen Intermezzo* (Berlin: Dümmler, 1823).

commentaries, though also in his Christology. In particular Muller (citing
Institutes 2.12.1) notes that Calvin, to avoid binding God by a necessity,
leaned on Scotus to propose that the mediator need not be both God and
human, but was so only by dint of the divine decree.[2] This admission came
on Calvin's part after he was pushed on certain questions about the mediator by Laelius Socinus. Calvin's response was attacked by Faustus Socinus,
though years after Calvin's death. Calvin's making the constitution of the
mediator dependent on the decree, and one bound to offices that Christ
performed within the constraints of the covenant, ultimately made for a
different mediator than the Logos—namely, justice—and thus the justice
of God that justifies a Christian (a created righteousness regardless of
how Calvin could parse it) now stands as a different mediator, one other
than the Divine Logos. None of this would have surprised Calvin, for his
pseudo-Nestorianism, whereby he had a composite Christ (though he did
not use the fictive creature of Nestorius, the *prosopon* of union), fit this
paradigm of created righteousness that fulfills the demands of God, since
God had so ordered the world in the decree. Calvin did not wish to abandon
either what Nicaea or Chalcedon taught, and while he certainly could read
Greek, his access to Greek texts was very limited. Only by reading Cyril
of Alexandria in translation could Calvin ever have come to the assertion
that Cyril taught Calvin's peculiar doctrine of the aseity of the Son. Thus
his formulations in Christology rested more on his own readings of the
scholastics through his Protestant glasses, and his theology emerges as
neither patristic nor medieval.

In short, Calvin was an ad hoc theologian. This accusation may seem unfair,
all the more so when we recall that most theologians actually are ad hoc, in
that they do some of their best work in the midst of controversy, bringing
their intellects and piety to bear on questions not previously considered or
now considered in a new light. One need only think of the works of Augustine
composed in the midst of controversy, and the same holds for the works of
many others, such as those who contended in the trinitarian and christological controversies, or even of Luther. In truth, one may say that all theology is
an answer to one or more of the questions that plague the particular mind of
individual theologians. But when I make the assertion that Calvin is ad hoc,
I do not mean this. Rather, Calvin, unlike Luther or Peter Martyr Vermigli,
was not trained in theology; he had no catechetical school to fall back on, as

2. Richard Muller, "Scholasticism in Calvin: Relation and Disjunction," in *Calvinus Sincerioris Religionis Vindex / Calvin as Protector of the Purer Religion*, ed. Wilhelm H. Neuser
and Brian G. Armstrong (Kirksville, MO: Sixteenth Century Essays and Studies, 1993), 261.

did, for example, Athanasius.[3] If we remember that Athanasius, a product of the renowned catechetical school in Alexandria, was only about twenty when he wrote *On the Incarnation of the Word,* we can see what value his formal education had for him. Calvin did indeed have a formal education, and the skills he acquired in philology and rhetoric were not slight, but these two disciplines, particularly the rhetorical, dominated Calvin's early works. Vermigli could spend a great deal of time telling his readers why they should believe something, and his *Dialogus,* while possessing certain difficulties as regards Christology,[4] nonetheless stands as a starkly different piece of theology from, for example, Calvin's 1541 *Treatise on the Holy Supper.* Calvin still possessed a rare intellect, but one that seemed bent on thinking that, at least initially, the only source material for theology was revelation, as if theology were nothing more than humanistic enterprises in textual analysis. And indeed this is the way, as François Wendel points out, that one should read Calvin's *Institutes*; the *Institutes* serve as prolegomena for reading Holy Scripture, and all is subservient to, or is the fruit of, preaching and commentary.[5] Thus, while Calvin could not escape using language that early in his career he would rather not have employed (e.g., Trinity), he also realized the great benefit that accrued from the use of the church fathers and the medieval scholastics. Calvin's synthesis produced a system with numerous idioms, but the logical rigorism of a Vermigli that influenced the later Protestant scholastics is not Calvin's métier.

But what made Calvin and Calvin's thought was not merely the theological interactions he had with previous theologians, near or remote, but also all those around him who as friends or tormenters pushed him in one direction or another through the several crises that plagued his ministry. A silent subtext, at least in chapter 1, is the formative, austere influence Guillaume Farel had on him. In 1534, and probably in 1536, Calvin had attended Mass, first at Claix and then in Ferrara, and he had called on Nicodemite Jacques Lefèvre d'Étaples in 1534, but by 1537, as Farel's second at Geneva, he was decrying Nicodemism, even as he wrote felicitous letters to Louis du Tillet. By the 1540s François Baudouin, and in the 1550s the Enfants, all came to realize that Calvin's theology had little room for those not given to Calvin's

3. Richard Muller argues a similar point, that Calvin picked up his scholasticism in a mediated way, often in preparation for sermons and commentaries, in "Scholasticism in Calvin: Relation and Disjunction," in Neuser and Armstrong, *Calvinus Sincerioris,* 252, 264.

4. Gary W. Jenkins, "Dinner with Raphael: The Prolegomena of Peter Martyr Vermigli's Eucharistic Intellections," *Zwingliana* 36 (2009): 103–13.

5. François Wendel, *Calvin: Origins and Development of His Religious Thought,* trans. Philip Mairet (New York: Harper & Row, 1963), 146.

rigorism—or as Ronald Knox would call it, enthusiasm[6]—an element that
for Calvin was necessary to protect the purity of the church and that Calvin
believed the church needed in order to both survive and thrive. This same
exacting and rigorous disposition ruled Calvin as regards the treatment of
heretics. Calvin certainly seemed of two minds in his dealings with Servetus
and Gribaldi, though he certainly did not have the patience of Nikolaus
Zurkinden. In the case of Servetus, Calvin could have turned him over to the
authorities in Vienne at any time, for he knew who he was and where he lived,
but he never bothered till put on the spot about his correspondence with Servetus. Valentine Gentili would certainly have faced the fate of Servetus had he
the courage of his conviction that the Spaniard possessed. But it was not just
wayward heretics who caused Calvin precisian headaches, for he suffered these
as well from the *moyenneur* Baudouin, who perhaps tortured him even to a
greater degree than did the antitrinitarians; for Baudouin, the shape-shifting
werewolf, deceitful in his embrace of Protestantism, did not preach a false
doctrine as easy for the faithful to discern as had the flamboyant Servetus.

The Eucharistic controversy that sprung from his jousts with the Gnesio-
Lutheran, Joachim Westphal, whose theological and tactical mind he greatly
underestimated, presents the precise Calvin in a different key, one theological,
but one that has always in view the French Reformed church. One could
argue that Calvin's eucharistic theology took him closer to Wittenberg than
to Zurich, but on the matter of the real presence Calvin was adamant (and
in this he was of a piece with all sides in these controversies). When Westphal
attacked the "sacramentarians" Calvin could not resist the challenge, one that
Bullinger regretted that his colleague had taken up. Calvin always seemed at
the ready for controversy. His old mentor Bucer, however, never seemed to have
such problems. Vermigli could certainly enter the lists to joust with such as
Johannes Brenz on the question of the Eucharist, but he seems far less in the
eye of the storm than Calvin. Ultimately, the difference between Calvin and
his fellow Reformed seems to go back to two previously mentioned points.

First, Calvin was French, and he never forgot his *patria*. This explains why
Baudouin sat so heavy in his stomach, as undigested meat, for Baudouin with
his championing of the *Augustana*, ironically a document that Calvin once
at least formally seems to have embraced, seemed to Calvin to threaten the
purity and coherence of the French Reformed church. Baudouin wanted more
than Castellio's tolerance; he hoped for rapprochement, for union. In Calvin's
mind this was a road back to spiritual harlotry and idolatry, a way that would

---

6. Ronald Knox, *Enthusiasm: A Chapter in the History of Religion* (Oxford: Oxford University Press, 1950).

compromise the purer religion of the French Reformed church. This love of France can be seen in the Westphal controversy as well. Westphal first used Calvin as a club to demonstrate that the Reformed had no clear doctrine of the Eucharist and that no one should take the Zurich Consensus seriously. Calvin had to respond, for he hoped for a wide support for the church in France, and he feared a French civil war, a war in which the Huguenots could benefit no end from German aid. Calvin was under the false assumption that Melanchthon would rally to him on the question of the Eucharist. In the end, Calvin only stirred up the ire, much to Bullinger's chagrin, of the whole of Saxony. Again, the point comes back to Calvin as French.

The second matter concerns the year 1541. By this time Calvin had firmly established in his mind the distinctions between Rome and the pure faith, but prior to this his dealings had been marked by what could be interpreted as a measured restraint, even with Catholics. This can be seen in the reply to Sadoleto. Calvin certainly did not back down from the cardinal bishop over the question of justification by faith alone, and while he also littered his letter with barbs, this sanitized letter reads completely amicably when compared with his later writings. However he deferred to Sadoleto, his nearly contemporaneous correspondence with du Tillet transcended deference. Friendship certainly bridled his pen, and one needs to remember that Calvin had already published his treatise on Nicodemism, in which he essentially had accused those who attended Roman temples of taking part in idolatry and communicating with demons. Calvin's stance against Nicodemism went from strength to strength, and whatever half measures may have characterized his attitudes in the 1530s, they would not be the standard.[7] But with 1541 and the collapse of the efforts of the Erasmian party attendant on the failure of Regensberg, Calvin, who had attended the colloquy there, could see only a hardening of the respective confessions. The emperor certainly had come to this conclusion. Doubtless Caroli's triumph at Metz also brought out a more militant Calvin. Calvin thus became far more vehement about the purity of faith, as can be seen in his brooking no dissent, even on minor points, which can be easily observed in the case of Castellio when he was ejected from Geneva.

This disposition, however, is brought into even greater clarity when considering the case of the Genevan minister Henri de la Mare. De la Mare, an émigré from Rouen, had been one of the ministers in Geneva during Calvin's first years there from 1536–38. He remained after Calvin and Farel had been

7. David F. Wright, "Why Was Calvin So Severe a Critic of Nicodemism?," in *Calvinus Evangelii Propugnator: Calvin Champion of the Gospel; Papers Presented at the International Congress on Calvin Research, Seoul, 1998*, ed. David F. Wright, A. N. S. Lane, and Jon Balserak (Grand Rapids: CRC Product Services, 2006), 66–90.

expelled, and he subsequently associated with the Articulants while Calvin was in Strasbourg. Despite his political leanings, it was Henri de la Mare, along with Jacques Bernard, who penned the formal letter to Calvin in Strasbourg asking for him to return. Yet by 1546 de la Mare was expelled from Geneva, and the years between 1541 and 1546 depict a grim picture of the wretched existence of de la Mare.[8] Soon after Calvin's return, de la Mare was transferred to the outlying village parish of Foncenex, whose châtelain, Pierre Somareta, proved an ardent but corrupt ally of Calvin. The parish church was in disrepair—no windows, no pulpit, etc.—and monies sent for its maintenance were pilfered by Somareta. The parsonage, with a collapsed wall, may well have been worse off than the parish building. Despite repeated pleas, de la Mare was left in penury, his mostly peasant flock left abandoned.

Naphy paints a sobering and shocking picture of a minister virtually harassed. De la Mare stood opposite Calvin on the Bolsec affair, and he also was a personal friend to two men completely at odds with Calvin: Pierre Ameaux and Jean Troillet.[9] Ameaux was a Genevan cardmaker, whose livelihood was circumscribed by law. Complaining about his situation, he was put in charge of Geneva's gunpowder supply. One night at a dinner he viciously attacked Calvin as a despot, and word leaked out. He was publicly humiliated, having to march through the streets in just his shirt while begging forgiveness from Calvin. Troillet was a Burgundian monk whom Calvin refused to allow to become a minister, so he took up a life as a notary. He would be censured for siding with Bolsec.

Thus de la Mare fell afoul of Calvin by his associations, but Calvin's animus actually goes back to his refusal to follow Calvin into exile. Calvin's letters betray his disdain for de la Mare even before 1546.[10] The neglect that de la Mare suffered at the hands of Calvin and his associates can only be seen as pure spite. Somareta, more than confederate in this abuse, not only did not pay any recorded price for his corruption but thrived under Calvin. Naphy notes that it is difficult to see how this could be anything other than "a concerted attempt to make his life miserable."[11] de la Mare was jailed in March 1546 for his vocal support of his friend Ameaux, and Calvin and the company of pastors refused to seek reconciliation. Thus, when the call came from Calvin and the company of pastors to sack de la Mare, the magistrates approved it.

8. William G. Naphy, in his *Calvin and the Consolidation of the Genevan Reformation* (Manchester: Manchester University Press, 1994), 59–68, gives the whole sorry story of Henri de la Mare in detail.
9. Naphy, *Consolidation*, 66–67.
10. Naphy, *Consolidation*, 60.
11. Naphy, *Consolidation*, 67.

The magistrates did give de la Mare a letter of attestation, which allowed him to take a parish in Gex in Bernese territory, and they also reimbursed him for repairs to his parish that he had paid for himself.

De la Mare and Castellio illustrate the narrowness that arose from the certainty that was both Calvin's sense of calling and his vision of what a pure church, a pure godly commonwealth, should be. Perhaps his view of himself as a prophet clouded his judgments about the state of other people's motives; for after all, if they withstood the prophet, what did this say about the state of their souls? Clearly Calvin considered neither de la Mare, nor Castellio, nor the Enfants, as ones who sought to further the cause of Christ's church, truly and purely reformed, and as such they were a threat to the godly order. Calvin's despairing impatience in the case of du Tillet had become an oppressive fanaticism in the years following his return to Geneva, a preciseness that tolerated little in way of any deviation, and certainly any deviation as regards Geneva.

But on two counts Calvin seemingly did hold some things as negotiable. For all his vaunted desire to have Communion celebrated weekly in Geneva, in the end it was never fully implemented, for the frequency of the sacrament seemed but an ancillary concern in the face of the need for the book of discipline. Calvin was not ready to go to the wall for weekly Communion but certainly was over discipline. Calvin's desire for the frequent celebration of the Eucharist thus seems to have been only something attached to the question of discipline and not something he thought as important as guarding the morals of his congregation. A more telling instance of Calvin yielding on a matter is in his dialogue with Bullinger over the Zurich Consensus, but this seems to have brought his hardened disposition up against his love of the French church.

Calvin's sense of his calling, directly from God, set him in a position, if he acted on his convictions, of being the defender of the purer faith. "Purity" was a watchword for Calvin. Without discipline how could the church not slip back into idolatry and superstition, given the depravity of the human heart? Perhaps as prophet he could see more clearly the depravity of Baudouin and Bolsec, the arrogance of Caroli and Westphal. Perhaps it was as a prophet that he still held out hope, at least in the 1530s, for du Tillet. Thus the two points cited above, rigorous discipline leading to purity and an evolving doctrine that defined what this was (and always in line with it), go a long way to explaining how Calvin could address himself differently to seeming similar questions (why burn Servetus but not Gribaldi?). Perhaps the precise Calvin, driven by his own expectations of what he believed God's call demanded of him, was himself his own greatest tormentor. Though someone so constituted could not help but have multiple tormentors.

Bibliography

As the bibliography for this subject follows closely the history of the Reformation in Switzerland, France, the Rhineland, and the Low Countries during the life of Calvin, a comprehensive bibliography is impractical. I have therefore included only modern monographs.

Backus, Irena. *Historical Method and Confessional Identity in the Era of the Reformation: 1378–1615*. Studies in Medieval and Reformation Traditions. Leiden: Brill, 2003.

———. *Life Writing in Reformation Europe: Lives of Reformers by Friends, Disciples and Foes*. Aldershot, UK: Ashgate, 2008.

Bainton, Roland. *Hunted Heretic: The Life and Death of Michael Servetus, 1511–1553*. Gloucester, MA: Peter Smith, 1978.

———. *The Travail of Religious Liberty*. New York: Harper, 1951.

Balserak, Jon. *John Calvin as Sixteenth-Century Prophet*. Oxford: Oxford University Press, 2014.

Beaty, Mary, and Benjamin W. Farley. *Calvin's Ecclesiastical Advice*. Louisville: Westminster John Knox, 1991.

Bietenholz, P. G., and Thomas B. Deutscher, eds. *Contemporaries of Erasmus: A Biographical Register of the Renaissance and Reformation*. Toronto: University of Toronto Press, 2003.

Brown, Elizabeth A. R., ed. *Jean du Tillet and the French Wars of Religion: Five Tracts, 1562–1569*. Medieval and Renaissance Texts and Studies 108. Binghamton, NY: Center for Medieval and Early Renaissance Studies, 1994.

Burnett, Amy Nelson, ed. and trans. *The Eucharistic Pamphlets of Andreas Bodenstein von Karlstadt*. Early Modern Studies 6. Kirksville, MO: Truman State University Press, 2011.

Chung-Kim, Esther. *Inventing Authority: The Use of the Church Fathers in the Reformation Debates over the Eucharist*. Waco: Baylor University Press, 2011.

Comerford, Kathleen R., Gary W. Jenkins, and W. J. Torrance Kirby, eds. *From Rome to Zurich, between Ignatius and Vermigli: Essays in Honor of John Patrick Donnelly, SJ*. Leiden: Brill, 2017.

Cottret, Bernard. *Calvin: A Biography*. Translated by M. Wallace McDonald. Grand Rapids: Eerdmans, 2000.

Crottet, Alexandre. *Chronique protestante de France, ou documents historiques sur les églises réformées de ce royaume*. Paris: n.p., 1846.

———. *Correspondance française de Calvin avec Louis du Tillet, chanione d'Angoulême et curè de Claix sur les questions de l'Église et du ministère évangélique*. Genève: Cherbuliez, 1850.

D'Amico, John F. *Renaissance Humanism in Papal Rome*. Baltimore: Johns Hopkins University Press, 1983.

Davis, Thomas J. *The Clearest Promises of God: The Development of Calvin's Eucharistic Teaching*. New York: AMS Press, 1995.

———. *This Is My Body: The Presence of Christ in Reformation Thought*. Grand Rapids: Baker Academic, 2008.

Douglas, Richard M. *Jacopo Sadoleto, 1477–1547: Humanist and Reformer*. Cambridge, MA: Harvard University Press, 1959.

Ellis, Brannon. *Calvin, Classical Trinitarianism, and the Aseity of the Son*. Oxford: Oxford University Press, 2012.

Erbe, Michael. *François Bauduin (1520–1573): Biographie eines Humanisten*. Gütersloh: Mohn, 1978.

Evennett, H. O. *Cardinal of Lorraine and the Council of Trent*. Cambridge: Cambridge University Press, 1930.

Farge, James K. *Biographical Register of Paris Doctors of Theology, 1500–1536*. Toronto: Pontifical Institute of Medieval Studies, 1980.

Ganoczy, Alexandre. *The Young Calvin*. Translated by David Foxgrover and Wade Provo. Edinburgh: T&T Clark, 1988.

Gerrish, B. A. *Grace and Gratitude: The Eucharistic Theology of John Calvin*. Eugene, OR: Wipf and Stock, 2002.

Gordon, Bruce. *Calvin*. New Haven: Yale University Press, 2009.

Gouwens, Kenneth. *Remembering the Renaissance: Humanist Narratives of the Sack of Rome*. Leiden: Brill, 1998.

Greef, Wulfert de. *The Writings of John Calvin*. Expanded ed. Translated by Lyle D. Bierma. Louisville: Westminster John Knox, 2008.

Guggisberg, Hans. *Sebastian Castellio, 1515–1563: Humanist and Defender of Toleration in a Confessional Age*. Translated by Bruce Gordon. Aldershot, UK: Ashgate, 2002.

Hinigman, Francis M. *La Diffusion de la Réforme en France: 1520–1565*. Geneva: Labor et Fides, 1992.

Holtrop, Philip C. *The Bolsec Controversy on Predestination, from 1551 to 1555: The Statements of Jerome Bolsec, and the Responses of John Calvin, Theodore Beza, and Other Theologians*. 2 vols. Lewiston, NY: Edwin Mellen, 1993.

Kelley, Donald R. *Foundations of Modern Historical Scholarship: Language, Law and History in the French Renaissance*. New York: Columbia University Press, 1970.

———. *François Hotman: A Revolutionary's Ordeal*. Princeton: Princeton University Press, 1973.

Kilroy, Gerard. *Edmund Campion: A Scholarly Life*. Farnham, UK: Ashgate, 2015.

Manetsch, Scott M. *Calvin's Company of Pastors: Pastoral Care and the Emerging Reformed Church, 1536–1609*. Oxford Studies in Historical Theology. New York: Oxford University Press, 2013.

McNeill, John T. *The History and Character of Calvinism*. Oxford: Oxford University Press, 1954.

Muller, Richard A. *Calvin and the Reformed Tradition: On the Work of Christ and the Order of Salvation*. Grand Rapids: Baker Academic, 2012.

———. *Christ and the Decree: Christology and Predestination in Reformed Theology from Calvin to Perkins*. Grand Rapids: Baker Academic, 2008.

———. "Scholasticism in Calvin: Relation and Disjunction." In *Calvinus Sincerioris Religionis Vindex / Calvin as Protector of the Purer Religion*, edited by Wilhelm H. Neuser and Brian G. Armstrong, 247–65. Kirksville, MO: Sixteenth Century Essays and Studies, 1993.

Naphy, William G. *Calvin and the Consolidation of the Genevan Reformation*. Manchester: Manchester University Press, 1994.

Pernot, Jean-François, ed. *Jacques Lefèvre d'Etaples (1450?–1536), Actes du colloque d'Etaples les 7 et 8 novembre 1992*. Paris: Honoré Champion Éditeur, 1995.

Piaget, Arthur. *Les Actes de la Dispute de Lausanne, 1536: publiés intégralement d'après le manuscript de Berne*. Neuchâtel: Secrétariat de l'Université, 1928.

Reid, Jonathan A. *King's Sister—Queen of Dissent: Marguerite of Navarre (1492–1549) and Her Evangelical Network*. 2 vols. Leiden: Brill, 2009.

Sasse, Hermann. *This Is My Body: Luther's Contention for the Real Presence in the Sacrament of the Altar*. Minneapolis: Augsburg, 1959.

Stephenson, John R. *The Lord's Supper*. Vol. 12 of *Confessional Lutheran Dogmatics*. St. Louis: Luther Academy, 2003.

Trueman, Carl R., and R. S. Clark, eds. *Protestant Scholasticism: Essays in Reassessment*. Carlisle, UK: Paternoster, 1999.

Turchetti, Mario. *Concordia o tolleranza? François Bauduin (1520–1573) e i "Moyenneurs."* Geneva: Librairie Droz, 1984.

Walsh, Michael J. *The Cardinals: Thirteen Centuries of the Men behind the Papal Throne*. Grand Rapids: Eerdmans, 2011.

Wandel, Lee Palmer, ed. *A Companion to the Eucharist in the Reformation*. Leiden: Brill, 2014.

———. *The Eucharist in the Reformation: Incarnation and Liturgy*. Cambridge: Cambridge University Press, 2005.

Wendel, François. *Calvin: Origins and Development of His Religious Thought*. Translated by Philip Mairet. New York: Harper & Row, 1963.

Wilbur, Earl Morse. *A History of Unitarianism: In Transylvania, England, and America*. Boston: Beacon, 1969.

———. *A History of Unitarianism: Socinianism and Its Antecedents*. Boston: Beacon, 1972.

———, trans. *Two Treatises of Servetus on the Trinity*. Cambridge, MA: Harvard University Press, 1921.

Williams, George Hunston. *The Radical Reformation*. Kirksville, MO: Sixteenth Century Essays and Studies, 2000.

Zachman, Randall C., ed. *Calvin and Roman Catholicism: Critique and Engagement, Then and Now*. Grand Rapids: Baker Academic, 2008.

———. *Calvin as Teacher, Pastor, Theologian: The Shape of His Writings and Thought*. Grand Rapids: Baker Academic, 2006.

Zuidema, Jason, and Theodore Van Raalte. *Early French Reform: The Theology and Spirituality of Guillaume Farel*. Farnham, UK: Ashgate, 2011.

Author Index

Subject Index